Most ^{UN}Likely to Succeed

Most ^{un}Likely to Succeed

The Trials, Travels, and Ultimate
Triumphs of a "Throwaway Kid"

A memoir by

Nelson Lauver

Five City Media
New York, NY

Most Unlikely to Succeed

The Trials, Travels, and Ultimate Triumphs of a "Throwaway Kid"

Published by Five City Media, New York, NY

Quantity discounts are available for companies, organizations and educational institutions. For more information please contact the publisher, Five City Media at info@fivecitymedia.com, or contact the author's representative at info@theamericanstoryteller.com.

Book cover and interior design:
Peri Poloni-Gabriel, Knockout Design, www.knockoutbooks.com

Publisher's Cataloging-in-Publication

Lauver, Nelson C.
    Most unlikely to succeed : the trials, travels, and
ultimate triumphs of a "throwaway kid" : a memoir / by
Nelson Lauver.
    p. cm.
    LCCN 2010939634
    ISBN-13: 978-0-9830403-0-9
    ISBN-10: 0-9830403-0-3

    1. Lauver, Nelson C. 2. Dyslexics--United States--
Biography. 3. Illiterate persons--United States--
Biography. 4. Radio personalities--United States--
Biography. 5. Dyslexia. I. Title.

RC394.W6L39 2011   362.196'8553'0092
                 QBI10-600216

Printed and bound in the United States of America

This book is dedicated to my mom and dad.

While June and Ward Cleaver were inside the TV set

with a slew of writers and directors,

Clair and Thelma Lauver were winging it

in real-time, unscripted.

Table of Contents

Author's Note

GROWING UP, I THOUGHT I was the only kid like me in the world. I thought I was all alone. Many years later, as my life changed for the better, I slowly came to understand that my story was, and is, the story of millions of Americans who struggle with literacy.

I can't tell you how many times someone has approached me as I've walked off stage and said, "Nelson, you just told my story — we share the same story!"

After one speaking engagement in York, PA, an elderly man *ran* from the back of the theater to the front and enthusiastically exclaimed, "Nelson, I can't read!" He, of course, wasn't excited about the fact that he couldn't read, but by the fact that after almost three quarters of a century he finally realized that he was not alone.

Moreover, my story is everybody's story in that we all have something, some obstacle with which we've had to wrestle, or with which we still wrestle. What I finally figured out was that I was the only person who could do anything about what was holding me back. That simple realization moved my life forward in a quantum leap. Sure I had help, but I had to be willing to reach out for that help. I feel that giving voice to my story gives voice to others who have yet to find their voice

— those who have yet to reach out for help, or those who are still, out of fear and shame, struggling needlessly with difficulties in their lives.

I should mention that a number of names have been changed in the telling of this story. I should also mention that while I pride myself in having a very good memory, I may not recall verbatim the dialogue of every conversation I detail in this book. Others may recall things slightly differently. I did my very best to tell this story accurately, based on my memories.

Chapter 1

An Unapologetic Slap

EARLY 1960s: McALISTERVILLE, PENNSYLVANIA, population eight hundred, was a bustling little Rockwellian village one hour northwest of the state capital city of Harrisburg. Our self-sufficient little hamlet was just one of dozens along Pennsylvania Route 35, a two-lane blacktop country road paralleling the seventy-plus mile range of the Shade Mountain. Route 35 doubled as Main Street as it passed through McAlisterville on its way to other small towns that were exactly like ours, yet totally different.

Main Street was lined with old log houses that had been built by the pioneers in the late 1700s. The logs had been covered over with brilliant white clapboard siding, long before I was born. A few stone and brick houses found their way into the mix and were prized by their occupants.

Three churches, Farmer's National Bank, Kipp's Market, Leister Bros. Hardware, Seller's General Store, Shirley's Restaurant, Dr. Yoder's office, and a small Ford dealership all called Main Street home. School Street was the only significant street that intersected with Main Street, crossing at the village center known as the Town Square. Besides more houses, School Street was home to the Post Office, the Clair C. Stuck Funeral Home, Mrs. Page's brick apartment building, the McAlister-ville Volunteer Fire Company, a community building, the Shellenberger

Shirt Factory, Mr. Goodling's Shoe Store and, of course, the McAlisterville Elementary School. The homes on School Street, just like on Main Street, were all in good repair, with manicured lawns, pretty flower beds and spacious front porches where residents whiled away warm summer evenings, drinking iced tea on their porch swings as horses pulling Amish buggies clippity-clopped on by.

Most McAlistervillians had a job right there in town, or not too far away. Farmers, including the Amish, lived and worked in the surrounding valleys and ridges and came to town regularly on business. A few people, including my dad, commuted as far as Harrisburg to work.

Dad had a full-time job as a brake inspector with the Pennsylvania Railroad. It was his responsibility to make sure every passenger train that arrived from New York, Philadelphia, Baltimore, and Washington, left the Harrisburg Station with good brakes. And they would certainly need them as they headed west, following the Susquehanna and Juniata Rivers through the Appalachian mountain passes, then braving Altoona's famous Horseshoe Curve before stopping briefly in Pittsburgh. The trains would continue on through the night, chugging westward, eager to make Chicago by morning.

Dad was a gentle soul with wavy brown hair and a ruddy complexion. He had kind brown eyes and an honest, yet devilish, smile. His build was broad and muscular. He possessed boundless energy and ambition and was irresistibly outgoing; striking up a conversation with strangers was second nature to him. No matter where he ventured, he was eager to swap a story and share a laugh. His dream was a life filled with all the trappings of success and wealth. Growing up on a farm made him physically tough and gave him the strength and fortitude to breeze through basic training during World War II. Dad came home from the Army brimming with confidence. He was convinced he could do anything he set his mind to.

When dressed for work, Dad meant business. His black steel-toed work shoes were well-polished and his blue cotton work clothes were always freshly laundered and pressed. He wore his sleeves rolled up one click and was ready to do what had to be done. On his left hand was a plain gold wedding band, which was bent to the formation of his finger from years of heavy lifting. On his right ring finger he wore a gold and ruby ring with the symbol of the Masonic brotherhood embedded in the stone. While working, he'd sometimes take it off and put it in his pocket to protect it — but his wedding band never left his finger.

Besides his job on the railroad, Dad had two sideline businesses. He owned a small heating oil delivery service and also had a contract for hauling gravel to maintain the township roads. Several times a week Dad entered the local quarry and picked up a load of stones to apply to the roads wherever township supervisors deemed necessary.

The quarry was on a ridge overlooking town. All of McAlisterville shook as the men in the quarry called, "FIRE IN THE HOLE!" With each blast of dynamite, limestone boulders fell to the quarry floor. By the end of the day the boulders were no more. They'd been pulverized into millions of peanut-sized stones and were now ready to play their part in the infrastructure of our modest corner of America.

Years of blasting and digging had created an awe-inspiring gray-and-white canyon of limestone and quartz. Millions of years earlier, massive glaciers had passed through, compressing the stone deep in the earth. Now men in hard hats and heavy equipment chipped away daily at what the ice age left behind and loaded it into my father's dump truck.

Careless quarry workers constantly banged the loader bucket into the sides of Dad's truck as they filled it. He found it infuriating but accepted the dents and scratches as part of the cost of doing business.

One man in the quarry was unlike the rest. He was meticulous, courteous, and respectful. He took great care when loading trucks, and because of this, Dad held Nelson Charles in high regard. He was the only loader operator who never damaged his truck. Dad knew Nelson Charles only from their mutual work at the quarry, but he identified strongly with him. Being kind and respectful to others was the mark of a true gentleman, and Nelson Charles exuded these qualities.

When I was born in the summer of 1963, Dad already had a name picked out for me: Nelson Charles Lauver.

Several days after Mom and I came home from the hospital, Dad stopped downtown at Dr. Yoder's office to square-up for the delivery. Doc's nurse wrote up the bill — thirty-five dollars — which included the additional delicate procedure that most baby boys of the era received to ensure their male anatomy adhered to the norms of the day.

Doc Yoder was one of Dad's best friends. They had met when Doc and his wife moved to town some years earlier and took the apartment just below Mom and Dad. On the day they moved in, Dad went down to shake his hand.

"Hello. You must be the new doctor in town, Dr. Yoder? I'm Clair Lauver."

"It's nice to meet you, Mr. Lauver."

It was apparent from the get-go that the formality of Mr. and Dr. was awkward for two young guys in their thirties, so Dad offered a solution: "How about you just call me Clair, and I'll call you Doc?"

They became instant pals. Doc was stocky with a round face and a gravelly voice. He sported a crew cut and, even as a young man, had salt-and-pepper hair. He looked and sounded the part of a wise doctor, and his dry sense of humor made him popular with everyone in town.

Although I don't remember it, Doc Yoder was the first person I ever met. He welcomed me into the world with a firm grip on my ankles and an unapologetic slap to my delicate backside.

Right before my birth, Mom, Dad, my brother Carl (age three), and my sister Susan (age eleven) moved out of the apartment building they shared with the doctor and his wife. Dad, with the help of the GI Bill, bought a stone house four doors down the street, and the Yoders soon built a house close by on Town Hill.

In spite of Dad's close friendship with Doc, my mom was seldom in agreement with any diagnosis Dr. Yoder made, and she often referred to him as "that goddamn pill pusher!"

My mother never served in the Navy yet possessed the linguistic prowess of a salty sailor. Her mastery of swear words and their appropriate use, considering the situation at hand, was impressive. It was an art form passed down from her mother, who likewise had never served in any naval capacity. The ladies on Mom's side of the family simply came by the gift of language naturally.

Mom was a guy's girl. She was pretty, street-smart, and tough. She took bull from no one. Dad's drinking buddies, even Doc, appreciated her direct style, albeit brutal at times.

Besides Doc, my dad's other pals were Peanut, the reluctant World War II hero, and George the Banker.

Peanut was a dead ringer for Ernest Borgnine. He, like most of the guys in McAlisterville, had fought in the "Big One." But what no one knew, and what Peanut didn't share, was his distinction as a bona fide, certified American hero. Peanut's medals for bravery were kept in a secret place at home. He didn't talk about the war, and he used humor to mask the painful memories.

Peanut was a comedic genius and a master of witty banter. Not even professional comedians of the time, or any time since for that matter, could hold a candle to the innate talents of Eugene "Peanut" Landis.

Peanut could say anything and make it funny. It was the twinkle in his eye, his body language, the laugh lines on his weathered face, and his deep voice that could be thrown to any part of the room. Peanut could get away with saying what others couldn't. He could swear or tell off-color stories, even in polite company, and everyone laughed. Peanut was the funniest man in McAlisterville. The sheer mention of his name caused people to break out in laughter. Everyone loved Peanut.

George the Banker was Peanut's straight man. He was distinguished and handsome with a thick head of meticulously combed, snow-white hair. He wore fine suits and only the best-quality shoes. He was the chairman of the Juniata County Republican Party.

If Peanut was the funniest man in town, George was surely the savviest man in town. His every thought, word, and movement was as calculated as the money in his bank. He had sound habits and was highly disciplined. Dad always said, "Get a few drinks in George and he loosens up just fine." It was true. Peanut took great delight in mussing up the banker's perfectly groomed hair, and after a few drinks George didn't bother to fix it. He became carefree and fun-loving. He told stories, stomped his feet, laughed, and puffed on nickel cigars.

The names "Peanut, Doc, Clair, and George" collectively rolled off the tongues of townspeople almost as a singular phrase. They were the McAlisterville "Rat Pack."

My earliest recollection of life in McAlisterville is getting into the family Ford. I was about three-and-a-half years old at the time. I remember Mom opening the passenger door and me hopping up on the front seat. The red vinyl dash was the color of licorice and looked invitingly tasty. As Mom closed the door and walked around to the driver's side, I inched up on the seat and put my mouth on the dash, sucking with all I had to see if I could get the taste of licorice out of it.

Mom opened the driver's door, got in, positioned her dress, adjusted the rearview mirror to check her lipstick with an approving lip smack, readjusted the mirror for driving, put the car in reverse, slapped me a good one on the back of the head as she barked, "What the hell are you doing?" and backed out of the driveway.

I matter-of-factly sat back in the seat. Getting a "what the hell are you doing" coupled with a slap upside the head was obviously nothing new from the woman who refused to suffer fools gladly.

We were off to Grandma and Grandpa Lauver's house. They often babysat me while Mom did her errands. My older siblings, Carl (now six) and Susan (fourteen) spent their days in school.

From as early as I can remember, Carl was pegged as a devil child. During my first few years on earth, Mom did her best never to allow us to be alone together for the honest-to-God fear that Carl could kill me. From the time he was a little boy, he had a sadistic streak and delighted in the pain of others.

Susan, on the other hand, was a kind, pretty blonde and one of the most popular girls in town. Practically a teenager by the time I was born, she was often out with her girlfriends.

Both Susan and Carl put in their time being babysat by Grandma and Grandpa. Now it was my turn.

Grandpa was a farmer and a preacher at the highly-conservative Cedar Grove Brethren in Christ Church. Mom wasn't one of them. She grew up in the city — Harrisburg. Much to the chagrin of many in my grandpa's church, Mom wore jewelry, lipstick, cat-eye glasses, sleeveless dresses, and high-heeled shoes that were probably cobbled by the devil himself. She visited the beauty salon once a week to have her hair done, and when the time was appropriate received a permanent wave and color to maintain her stylish blonde up-do. We didn't attend Grandpa's church on Sundays. Instead, on special occasions or when my parents were feeling guilty about our heathenism, we found ourselves sitting in the pews of the local Lutheran Church.

Grandpa and Mom tolerated one another for the sake of good family relations. But there is no doubt that had Grandpa been the decider regarding whom his eldest son would marry, it certainly wouldn't have been Thelma, the city girl. Grandpa would have preferred a country girl from the Brethren in Christ Church, someone who was raised to understand her station in life as a dutiful wife serving her husband. She would have worn a prayer covering at all times, except when letting her hair down to entertain her husband at night. And the thought of a wife taking a job outside of the home would have been greatly frowned upon.

On the other hand, if Mom had the luxury of picking a father-in-law, it probably would not have been the Rev. Harvey S. Lauver, especially after the crack he made about FDR. Once when Mom was explaining at a family gathering that her own father was forever grateful to Franklin Delano Roosevelt for creating the New Deal, Grandpa Lauver asked incredulously, "Oh, is Mr. Roosevelt your father's God?"

That was the moment that the country preacher crossed the girl from the city. Things would never be quite the same again. Grandpa Lauver had not only called into question the integrity of FDR; Mom felt he had, at the same time, belittled the values of her father. Mom's father had worked hardscrabble his whole life, struggling to keep his family fed and under roof. The comment by Grandpa Lauver was considered an insult and one that stayed permanently stuck in my mother's craw.

In spite of the cool feelings between Mom and Grandpa, I spent a great deal of time with my grandparents during my early childhood. Mom worked rotating shifts at the American Viscose Plant up the road in Lewistown. Her job as a beaming operator was a well-paid, highly coveted position in the plant. The rayon fiber she wove on her beaming machine was used in the manufacturing of belted automobile tires. If Mom was working, running errands, or trying to catch up on sleep, I was often with my dad on his oil delivery truck or with Grandma and Grandpa when they had the time to watch me.

My grandpa looked different from all the other grandfathers. He wore a big, black, wide-brimmed hat in the winter and a straw hat in the summer. His clothes were very plain, handmade by Grandma, and suspenders held up his pants. He had a long flowing beard, a symbol of marriage customary in his church. Most of the other kids thought Grandpa was Amish. He dressed like the Amish, and his church was similar to the Amish, just a bit more modern. Not a whole lot, but a bit. He fell into the same category though: the Pennsylvania Dutch Plain People.

Grandma and Grandpa were devout Christians. When I was small, I just thought all old people were extremely religious. I assumed they knew they weren't going to live much longer and wanted to make sure they got to Heaven. I always figured that I, too, would have to get a "dose of religion" when I got old, thinking in my little boy mind that it came automatically with age and the fear of impending death.

My grandparents had thirteen children: nine sons and four daughters.

As they grew into adulthood, they all successfully went their own ways. Only two stayed in McAlisterville: my uncle Rufus, the baby of the family, and my father, the eldest son.

It was Grandpa's desire that my dad would follow in the family tradition and join the ministry, whether he felt the calling or not. World War II was Dad's ticket out. He loved his parents and didn't want to disappoint them, but he had no interest in the pulpit. My grandfather was well-known in the area, and members of the draft board were quick to excuse Dad from military service due to his family's religious beliefs concerning non-violence. Dad quickly disabused the draft board of that notion. Shortly thereafter he was a soldier in the United States Army.

Grandpa reluctantly accepted his son's choice to join the military, and the two exchanged letters regularly while Dad was overseas.

Grandpa had a sober personality. When he smiled, it was often because he was feeling uncomfortable or awkward. The Rev. Harvey S. Lauver struggled with the role that laughter played, if any, in a pious life.

As a minister, he saw himself not only as a preacher of the Gospel but also as a teacher of life's lessons.

I remember the day Grandpa introduced me to the old man who lived on the adjacent ridge. Grandpa held my little hand as we walked to the hen house. His hands were big, callused, bent, and crooked. He told me about the "lonely old man over there."

"You aren't able to see his house because the leaves are on the trees, but he's up there sitting on his porch, waiting for somebody, anybody, to holler 'hello' to him so he can holler 'hello' back."

Grandpa hollered over to the old man, and off in the distance you could hear the old man holler back.

I often ran out and stood on the steps of the henhouse and hollered over to the old man to make sure he was okay and not so lonely. He always made it a point to holler back. "Hello, hello, hello." For months Grandpa watched my concern for the lonely old man on the ridge. I was disappointed and felt like I had lost a friend when Grandpa finally completed the lesson by explaining the concept of an echo to me.

If Grandpa wasn't busy at home with farm chores, he was busy with church work, and if my grandparents were babysitting me, I often went along for Grandpa's preaching duties. Part of tending to the spiritual needs of his flock was the responsibility of guiding the dearly departed out of this world and into the next via The Valley of the Shadow of Death.

With great concern for detail, Grandpa hand-dug graves for parting members of his flock. He carried a wooden, folding carpenters' rule that, when extended to its fullest, was exactly six feet in length. Later that day, or the next, he donned his preaching clothes for the final send-off. My grandmother dressed me in garb she had sewn for just such an occasion. I wore black trousers, a white shirt buttoned to the top with no collar, a black vest, and a black wide-brimmed hat. I looked like an Amish kid and fit in much better than if I had worn the modern polyester clothes my mother bought me at Dank's Department Store in Lewistown. I told myself, "These ain't Amish clothes, they're cowboy clothes! This is probably what Little Joe, Hoss, and Ben Cartwright would wear to a funeral — yeeehaaw!"

Grandpa assured all in attendance of the eternal salvation guaranteed the sinner whose cast-off, lifeless body was properly displayed in the casket near the pulpit. He gave first-hand testimony on the fine character of this servant of God, who would now receive a just reward, after a long life of being tempted by wicked and worldly pleasures.

Grandpa was not the fiery minister that his father, the late great Rev. Solomon "Hellfire and Brimstone" Lauver, was purported to have been earlier in the century. In spite of that, the faithful in the pews still cried out with that old-time religion — Hallelujah! YIP! YIP! AMEN! YIP! Hallelujah! AAAAAAMEN! YIP! YIP!

I sometimes wondered, should I give out a YIP? I wasn't sure. Grandma never yipped. And what if everyone turned around and looked at me?

I always sat with my grandmother in the back of the church. She would nod off for brief moments during the service but quickly caught herself and snapped to attention. She was a petite woman, only five feet tall, whose only relief from the toil as a farm wife came when she could sit in a hard wooden church pew. She was the epitome of the dutiful helpmate whose work was never done.

When the assuring, shouting, and crying were over, the congregation filed out of the pews for one last pass to view the earthly remains of a fellow Christian, who like all Christians, Grandpa constantly reminded, fell short of the glory of God and, yet, was being spirited to Heaven on a promise.

The casket was closed for the final time, and the floorboards of the old church creaked under the weight of the pallbearers as they walked back up the aisle leading to the doors and the cemetery, just outside.

At the gravesite the casket was lowered as loved ones dressed in mourning black gently swayed to and fro, singing, "Going … going … going down the valley. Going … going … going down the valley…."

After everyone went home, Grandpa wrangled back into his overalls and shoveled the grave closed. Pennsylvania law mandated all graves be covered by sunset, and Grandpa strictly adhered to the law. 🌿

Chapter 2

The Boy of Steel

TELEVISION DRAMAS IN THE 1960s depicted the constant struggle between good guys and bad guys. As a four-year-old kid, I loved TV, and the more I watched, the more I came to believe there were two types of people in the world: good people and bad people. To me the line was clear; you were either one or the other.

I didn't like bad guys, and it seemed most people had a hard time standing up to them. Well, everyone except Superman. If you were found out by Superman, you paid. He righted wrongs. Just like the announcer on the TV show said: "Truth, Justice, and the American Way." I was Superman's number one fan.

It was three weeks before Christmas in 1967 when I sat on Santa's lap at the McAlisterville Volunteer Fire House and placed a very special order. As Superman's biggest fan, I needed something to show for it.

That year, Santa came through. On Christmas morning I unwrapped my all-time favorite gift — a Superman suit — identical to the real thing. No more substituting a bath towel (fastened around my neck with a clothespin) for a cape.

Just like Superman, I now had a big plastic "S" on my chest. The big plastic S smelled like a new car and gave me a headache, but I didn't care — I wore the suit anyway. I wore it all the time. I even slept in it. I was obsessed. While wearing it, I watched black-and-white episodes of Superman every day on television and ate my lunch of choice, SpaghettiOs.

I knew the score: the Flash could run fast, but couldn't fly; Batman couldn't fly either; and Robin was just a dork. I liked Popeye because he had big "musckles," but he wasn't as cool as Superman. The Man of Steel was "faster than a speeding bullet; more powerful than a locomotive; able to leap tall buildings at a single bound!" I was always looking "up in the sky," hoping beyond hope that I would see my hero, Superman.

My Superman suit was soon covered with SpaghettiO stains. My mom wanted to wash it, but I wouldn't part with it long enough. There had been talk of holding me down and forcibly removing it, but I knew better. There was no way they could; I was too strong. While wearing my Superman suit, I was the Boy of Steel.

I eventually reached an agreement to let my mother wash the suit from time to time, and when I blew out the candles on my fifth birthday cake in June of 1968, I was wearing my Superman suit.

One Saturday morning in early July, we piled into our black Ford sedan for a trip to Grandma and Grandpa's. Mom was behind the wheel and my sister Susan, was in the front passenger seat, while my brother Carl and I were in the back. There were no laws on the books, yet, requiring kids to ride in carseats or wear seatbelts, so when we went for drives, I often stood and held on to the passenger seat in front of me. This day was no exception, and, of course, I was wearing my Superman suit.

As we drove along the country roads, I watched the world zoom past, but soon my X-ray vision turned to the shiny chrome handle next to me on the back passenger door. I began to concoct a plan.

I waited for just the right moment. I knew it would be the talk of McAlisterville, how Nelson Lauver, the Boy of Steel, opened the door on a moving car and flew out, high into the sky. I was confident I could do it. After all, I had the Superman suit on.

With a burst of excitement and pride, I pulled the door handle and opened the door. But, I didn't have time to even think about putting out my arms to fly. My moment had come at the exact instant Mom rounded a corner, and centrifugal force sucked me from the car and flung me to the pavement.

I rolled eight or ten times, finally landing hard on the shoulder of the road, right beside Mrs. Shillingsford's stately, white two-story home.

I was knocked silly, but not so silly that I lacked the presence of mind to pick up a handful of gravel and throw it in utter disgust that my plan had been foiled.

It took Mom one hundred feet or so to realize what had happened. She slammed on the brakes, threw the car into reverse, and stomped on the gas.

The always lovely and refined sixty-something Mrs. Shillingsford ran from her house classically outfitted in her form-fitting June Cleaver-style dress with an ever-present double strand of snow-white pearls adorning her neck. She was running toward me, armed with a warm, wet washcloth. It happened every damn time. I could probably have every bone in my body broken and suddenly, out of nowhere, an old lady would appear with a warm, wet washcloth to scrub my face.

Mom's customary tone and salty vernacular were somewhat

subdued; first, by the presence of the highly cultured Mrs. Shillingsford, and second, by the relief that I was still alive — in that order, I'm sure.

Mrs. Shillingsford practically rubbed my face off, and all I could think about was my humiliation and that surely, no old lady had ever scrubbed road dust off of Superman's face with a warm, wet washcloth.

I got back in the car with nothing more than a bruised ego and a few new holes in my Superman suit. As we drove away, I could tell that the smile on my dear sister's face was born of the relief that I had survived the episode. Carl, on the other hand, said I was a dumb shit for thinking the Superman suit gave me special powers.

I tried to ignore his ignorance, but he persisted by inventing a little ditty to honor my attempt to fly. He sang, "Dumb shit, dumb shit, Nelson is a dumb shit." He jabbed me hard in the back of the head with his index finger, in tempo, as he continued to sing, "Dumb shit, dumb shit, Nelson is a dumb shit." I was angry, humiliated, and embarrassed; I just wanted my brother to shut up. I kept my back to him, pretending to ignore his stupid song as I secretly curled up my little fist. "Dumb shit, dumb shit" — WHAM, right in the kisser. That stopped the song, but started an all-out war in the backseat of the family Ford with fists, knuckles, blood, tears, snot, screaming, kicking, and hair pulling — there was always hair pulling.

Mom stopped the car, threw it in park, and flung her body around to reach into the back seat and grab hold of us, pull us apart, and throw us into our separate corners. Through clenched teeth, Mom growled, "I swear with God as my witness, if you little sons-a-bitches don't stop it right now, I'll fan your asses till you won't be able to sit for a week!"

For my well-natured sister Susan, whose temperament was more akin to my dad's, this scene was an everyday occurrence in which she chose simply to not get involved.

We continued on our way to Grandma and Grandpa's house.

By August the Superman suit was nothing more than tattered rags and I returned to using a bath towel as a cape.

Carl and I were quite a handful for Mom. Managing our mischievous behavior was beyond the scope of the motherly experience she garnered in raising our well-behaved older sister. It was nearly impossible to find a baby-sitter to watch us — and most who did show up once never showed up again. One of us alone wasn't so bad, but the two of us together proved almost impossible.

Unless Mom could send us off on the heating oil delivery truck with Dad, convince Grandma and Grandpa to watch us, or find a baby-sitter who had never heard of the Lauver boys, she had to take us along to her part-time job, cleaning the local bank.

It wasn't difficult to find a suitable time to clean Farmer's National Bank in McAlisterville. Like most small-town banks, it had banker's hours. Ten to two, Monday, Tuesday and Wednesday; Thursday, ten to twelve; Friday, ten to eight; Saturday, ten to noon; closed Sunday.

Nobody ever stood in line or took a number to see a teller at Farmer's National Bank. Customers sat on long, high-back, mission-style walnut benches polished to an almost gilded sheen.

The customers themselves kept track of who was next to see the teller. There could be as many as twenty-five people in the bank lobby on a Friday evening, and everyone always knew who was "Next!"

Although we never had much trouble with crime in McAlisterville, loaded revolvers stood at the ready underneath each teller's window, prepared to defend the deposits of hardworking locals.

Dad's pal George, the well-dressed, distinguished white-haired bank manager had a World War I era high-powered rifle hidden, loaded, and ready within arm's reach of his desk, just in case. I can still imagine what it would have looked like to see George chomping on a cigar, fearlessly standing on the street, taking aim, and blowing out the back window of a would-be getaway car. But, unfortunately, no such excitement ever visited McAlisterville.

Mom found cleaning the tile floor of the bank lobby a difficult chore. Being the only bank in town, Farmer's National had constant foot traffic. Rock salt that was used to melt snow and ice on the village sidewalks, coupled with the cinders spread to ensure proper traction on the streets, came into the bank on farmers' boots, shopkeepers' shoes, and old men's galoshes. The muck and grit ground itself into the lobby floor as if it had been applied by a sandblaster.

Mom used full-strength Mr. Clean, pouring it straight onto the lobby floor, then agitating the bejesus out of it with an automatic scrubber machine until the grime loosened. The whir of the electric floor scrubber echoed through the closed-for-business bank and covered the giggles of my brother and me, who sat at George's big banker's desk, snooping through the drawers.

In his middle drawer was a rare treat for two young boys, a Floaty Pen! When it was held right-side-up, a beautiful buxom woman wearing a bustier adorned the side of the pen. But when turned upside down, her bustier magically fell away revealing what her bustier had been boosting.

Carl and I usually had fun together outside of the house, especially when we were out with Mom, wreaking havoc in public places. But at home, Carl was often a bully who took great delight in towering over me as well as our little dachshund, Brindle. When bored, he looked for someone to pick on and could be a nasty devil. He taunted me relentlessly, punched me, hit me, and kicked me. He was older and bigger, and at times, out of control.

I would typically put up with his bullying for only so long. Then, I'd wait till the moment was just right, and when he wasn't expecting it, I'd curl up my little fist and sucker-punch him with all I had. The blood would gush from his nose and mouth, and I'd run and hide behind my mom, assuring her, "Carl started it!"

Mom typically expressed her frustration to any who would listen, saying, "Jesus Christ, I need eyes in the back of my head! I can't turn my back for a second before those boys are up to something!" As time went on, Mom slowly developed ingenious skills to aid her in keeping a reasonable handle on our behavior. Mom found her invention of the "Little Man" highly useful. The "Little Man," she said, was microscopic and lived in her ear. Typically it went something like this....

"All right, I'm going next door to Nancy's for a cup of coffee. I'll be gone for one half hour — and I better not hear tell that there was any fighting or misbehaving while I'm gone."

"And just to be sure," she'd say, "Little Man, I'm taking you out of my ear and putting you way up high on this bookshelf for you to keep a lookout and tell me what happens while I'm gone."

When she returned home she'd call out "Little Man" and pretend to take him down from the bookshelf and place him back in her ear. She'd say, "So tell me, Little Man, what happened while I was away?"

She'd listen intently to "the story" while punctuating with comments like: "Oh really?"… "Who started it?"… "Uh huh."

Carl and I, completely gullible at this age, would panic and immediately spill our guts trying to blame each other for everything that had happened while she was gone.

That little man stood watch over us anytime Mom couldn't. He tattled on us for everything we did. He was a blabbermouth and responsible for Carl and me receiving more lickin's with the belt than I can count.

The worst lickin' I ever got from my parents was when Carl set the living room sofa on fire. He was playing with a stick and poking it in the fireplace. When he thought he heard someone coming into the room, he panicked and shoved the stick down between the cushions of the sofa. Black smoke soon billowed from the cushions, and he knew he was in big trouble. He ran to my parents in the kitchen, on the other side of the house screaming, "Nelson caught the sofa on fire!" Mom and Dad came sprinting into the living room and fought the fire gallantly. After winning the battle, they promptly beat the daylights out of me.

Once I regained my composure and caught my breath, I explained that I was not the firebug, Carl was. My parents were wracked with guilt. I was sure they would collectively beat the shit out of him next, but I guess they were too worn out from fighting the fire and whooping me to find the energy to afford Carl the abuse he deserved.

So, I figured it was up to me. I waited until later that night. I curled up my little fist, and when Carl least expected it, I drew back and released the flying knuckle sandwich. I ran like hell, hid behind Mom, and assured her that Carl had started it.

At home, even with the help of the Little Man, Mom frequently became completely exasperated by the end of the day. When Dad came home for supper, she often demanded he take time out before reading the newspaper to give Carl and me a proper lickin' with the belt.

He always argued against it by saying, "Thelma, it's been a long day. The last thing I want to do is give the boys a lickin'." But she would insist.

Dad would then lower his voice two octaves and say, "Come on boys, up to your room." We'd go along willingly and happily — we knew the drill. Dad would shut the door, take off his belt, and repeatedly hit the bed with it. Carl and I would scream like banshees, as if our hides were being peeled away by eagle talons. We'd rub our faces to make them red and splash a bit of water on them from the sink in the upstairs bathroom. Then we'd return downstairs, where our mother would seem quite satisfied that our father had just beaten the shit out of us.

For as poor as our behavior was at home, it was twice as bad in public places such as grocery and department stores.

Mom dreaded taking us out in public. Sometimes, at the Five & Dime Store in Lewistown, she'd buy us each a plastic whistle, turn us loose, and pretend she didn't know who we were. After checking out, she would easily find us simply by listening for the never-ending whistles. Then, she would gather us up and high-tail it out of the store.

Local merchants soon got wise to the whistle trick, and Mom needed a new strategy. She finally found one that worked: the hat pin.

She carried it in her purse. It was about three inches long. A big shiny fake pearl on one end ensured a solid grip. The other end — the business end — put the fear of God in us. It was sleek, silver, and sharp.

She would pull it out of her purse upon entering a store and, in a low voice, issue the following edict through clenched teeth: "Now look here, you little sons-a-bitches, I swear with God as my witness, if you act up I'm going to stick you right in the ASS with this hat pin!"

Her tone was believable, and we knew she meant business. Our behavior improved dramatically. The hat pin was saved exclusively for public places. She never actually stuck us with it. Just the threat was enough to ensure our good behavior.

Carl's bullying got worse as time went on. If I was spared, it was often our dog, Brindle, who received his teasing and taunting. I'd quietly tell Brindle, "Don't worry girl. I'll get him."

And later, when Carl least expected it, I would curl up my little fist and sucker-punch him, making the blood gush out of his nose like a spigot. Then, I would run like hell, hide behind my mother and assure her Carl had started it. Brindle would wag her tail in delight as Dad sat quietly behind his newspaper, grinning. He understood the settling of a score.

The fall of 1968 was a glorious time in my mother's life. It meant I, too, would be out of the house if only for half a day, and I was eager! I WAS GOING TO KINDERGARTEN!

Finally, the first day of Mrs. Logan's kindergarten had arrived.

It was a warm morning, yet Mom made me put on a cardigan sweater. And although it was only a ten-minute walk to the McAlisterville Elementary School, on this special day, Mom drove. We got out of the car and walked up to the front doors. Mrs. Logan was outside waiting to greet her new students. She was a pretty blonde lady with an encouraging smile; she had dimples. Neatly laid out on a table next to her were red, apple-shaped nametags for every child. Mom found mine and pinned it to my polyester shirt from Dank's Department Store, purchased especially for this monumental occasion. I had taken off the cardigan and left it in the car, and Mom didn't seem to notice.

I looked around and watched all the other kids who were crying their eyes out.

For the life of me, I just couldn't understand why they were crying. I thought, *This is the first day of kindergarten, for heaven's sake! This is what we have been waiting for with great anticipation! Today is the greatest day of our lives! We are no longer babies! We're big kids now!*

Mothers tried to calm their children by telling them, "Everything will be all right," except for my mom. I turned around and suddenly realized she was gone. It was no big deal. I stood there with my hands in my pockets and waited for further instructions from the pretty kindergarten teacher.

We all went inside the classroom, and eventually the mass wailing and gnashing of teeth quelled to a soft whimper.

We were each assigned a seat at a rectangular table for six. One kid on each end, two kids on each side. A pretty, brown-haired girl named Ellie Ramsey, whom I had never met before in my life, sat straight across from me at the table.

When she got up to join all the other girls lined up for the gender-segregated restroom break, she scrunched up her face, pointed her finger at me, and warned, "Don't you dare touch my colored pencils!"

I was surprised and offended by Ellie's unwarranted hostility toward me. As far as I was concerned, I had done nothing to invoke her wrath. In keeping with the longstanding family tradition of diplomacy passed down from my mother's side, I told Ellie, "Don't point your finger at me, and you can stick your pencils for all I care."

Her pencils were all perfectly sharpened and stored neatly in a tall baby food jar with a screw cap. I had no interest in them. But just to make sure she knew I wasn't afraid of her, I unscrewed the lid and dumped the pencils out on the table while she was gone.

When Ellie returned, she took one look at the pencils scattered across the table, then turned on her heels, running straight for the teacher. Not only did Ellie tattle on me for dumping her pencils, she also informed Mrs. Logan that I told her to "stick 'em." Mrs. Logan scolded me, saying, "If I ever hear such language out of you, Nelson, I'll wash your mouth out with soap." I promptly apologized.

After the Ellie Ramsey event, I was moved to a different table where our competing personalities were no longer a factor.

A few months of kindergarten had passed uneventfully. The presidential election of November 1968 was one week away, and the political machine in McAlisterville was buzzing at a fevered pitch.

Each day we had five minutes of free time to talk amongst ourselves before our parents collected us after school.

I told fellow kindergartners at my table that I was sure of two things: First, "Nixon is going to win the election by kicking Hubert Humphrey's ass," and second, "All of our troubles will be over." I was sure Nixon would fix everything that was broken, especially Vietnam. I had heard him say so on the TV.

We might have been only five, but we were painfully aware of the war in Vietnam. Fathers, uncles, brothers, and cousins went. Almost all of us knew of someone who didn't come back alive or came back all messed up — either shot up or emotionally damaged. We were little sponges and soaked in everything that frightened us, and nothing frightened us more than someone we loved being shot and killed in Vietnam.

Kindergarten was only a half-day and ended around lunchtime. If Mom wasn't at work or sleeping after working the night shift at her factory job, she would sometimes pick me up after school and take me along on errands. Once a month, those errands included a haircut for me.

I loved getting a haircut at Jack's barbershop on Main Street. Jack and his wife, Pat, lived two doors away from us on School Street, and their daughter, Michele, sometimes walked to school with me. Jack and his wife had been high school sweethearts who, at sixteen, "had to" get married because they got "in trouble," as the locals would say. Hence, my friend Michele. Jack and Pat were cool, young parents. My parents seemed old in comparison.

When Mom took me to Jack's barbershop, I would wait just inside the front door until he gave me the word. Jack, in his high-collared, robin's-egg blue barber shirt and polyester pants, would stand beside the empty red barber's chair and call out like the starter at a race, "On your mark, get set ... GO!"

I would make a running dash for the chair, jump into it, and applying Newton's first law of motion, spin it around as I yelled, "GIVE ME A FLAT TOP, JACK!"

The amount of spinning I got out of Jack's barber chair was determined by how fast I ran, how far I jumped, and how hard I hit the chair. It was a true science, and according to Jack, I was the best chair spinner in town.

Jack's was an honest-to-goodness, authentic barbershop with the scents of Clubman Talc, bay rum, and shaving cream wafting through the air.

BUZZ, BUZZ, BUZZ. In no time, I had the perfect cut and a lollipop — and Jack had another dollar to ring his cash register.

When Mom worked the night shift, Grandpa often picked me up after kindergarten. Maybe we'd spend the afternoon sending someone to Heaven via a six-foot-deep hole in the ground or tend to the chickens and gather eggs.

If Grandpa didn't come get me, Dad would show up, and I'd get to ride 'til suppertime in the big oil delivery truck.

Dad's oil business had grown. By now, he had left his job as a railroader and had given up hauling stones for the township, too. He purchased an old building out at the other end of town and converted it into an office and warehouse.

The loud PSHHHH sound of the air brakes on Dad's oil truck announced his arrival to everyone as he pulled up in front of my school. All the kids watched as I ran to the passenger's side and climbed up onto the running board, gripping the door handle with both hands to release it. As I opened the door and jumped into my seat, I held out my left hand for Dad to grab hold and anchor me, then I leaned way out of the truck to grab the inside door handle. I became a human tether as Dad pulled my arm, and together we closed the door. Dad cranked the mammoth engine and released the air brakes. He gave a blast on the air horn as we pulled away, and I waved to all my cheering classmates.

I felt powerful sitting up so high and gazing down at the world all around me. The big motor vibrated through every bone in my little body. As I clicked that seatbelt fast, I always had the same question: "Dad, are we going to Callie's today?"

When my dad said, "Yup!" that was a great day!

Callie Arnold's country store was a fifteen-mile ride from McAlisterville. It was "down the country," as the locals say. There were gas pumps out front, and Dad kept the underground tanks filled with gasoline.

Callie was fun to be around, and I wasn't the only kid who felt that way. Much of Callie's success came from the fact that his place was magical. It wasn't the goods on the shelves or the merchandise on the racks. It was old Callie himself, a seasoned storyteller.

My favorite thing about going to Callie's was sitting down to eat. The Arnolds lived in the back of the store. Dad and I would walk in and go behind the counter and through an archway to their family kitchen. We'd sit at their kitchen table and place our order. Mrs. Arnold always had a smile on her face and a kettle of soup on the stove. She'd make us any kind of sandwich we asked for.

After we ate our meal, Mrs. Arnold sent us to Callie to talk about the bill. There was no menu and no set prices.

My dad said, "Callie, that really hit the spot. What do I owe ya?"

"Clair, I don't want your money, just get on out of here!"

"Now Callie, here's two dollars."

Incredulous, as if my dad was somehow accusing him of being a profiteer, Callie bristled and said, "Two dollars! God will send me to the devil for stealing. It was just soup and sandwiches, and the boy hardly ate much at all. Thirty-five cents would be more like it."

Dad laid a dollar bill down on the counter and threatened to walk out if Callie refused to pick it up.

"Clair, if you walk out, I'll just throw that dollar bill in the fire. Give me fifty cents, and let's stop this craziness."

Callie argued with folks all day long about price that way. I don't know how he made any money, but he did okay.

Dad and Callie would finally arrive at a price, and we'd head off to our next stop.

I knew every little old lady, saw-miller, feed-miller, storekeeper, and farmer on my dad's routes.

I knew the details of their lives, like who fought in World War I, World War II, and Korea. I knew who had a son serving in Vietnam. I knew where people bought their shoes, cars, and groceries. I knew how old they were, when their ancestors came to America, where they went to church, who was related to whom, and what cemetery contained their family plot. I knew whether they were Republican or Democrat and who their dentist was, if they had one. I knew how many cows each farmer was milking, and the list went on and on.

I effortlessly soaked in the details that swirled around each individual I met. I listened intently to the fascinating small talk of adults at barbershops, country stores, and lunch counters. My curiosity was insatiable.

Riding with my dad on the oil truck, I witnessed ordinary people living their everyday, ordinary lives. And yet, somehow, even as a small boy, I was given the gift of seeing what was extraordinary about them. Riding in my dad's oil truck was priceless and can be counted among the greatest experiences of my life.

One Saturday morning, Dad was off working just like every other day, and Mom was home with Carl and me. She had come off the night shift at the plant and was stretched out on the living room sofa, trying to get some desperately needed shut-eye and hoping we boys would quietly watch our Saturday morning cartoons.

We had only three channels in 1968, maybe a fuzzy fourth if the wind wasn't blowing, the stars were aligned, and the antenna on our roof was catching the signal from Harrisburg just right. I was still in my PJs, snuggled up on the floor with a pillow, a blanket, and our dog, Brindle — engrossed in one of my favorite cartoons, "Sinbad the Sailor

Man." Carl was in the kitchen fixing himself a bowl of Cap'n Crunch to eat while watching cartoons. Carl entered the living room, cereal bowl in hand, and walked right over to the TV, changing the channel from Sinbad to Batman and that dorky Robin. I hopped up from my cozy nest and immediately switched the channel back to Sinbad.

"I was here first!" I screamed. Carl just glared at me and switched the channel again. I ran over and pushed him. He shoved me back, and in no time Brindle was eating Cap'n Crunch off the floor. Our shoving match escalated into an all-out fistfight.

What poor Mom wanted and needed more than anything else during that time in her life was sleep — glorious, glorious sleep. It was quickly becoming obvious that she'd need to get us out of the house that morning in order to get it.

She picked up the phone and dialed. I heard Dad's bookkeeper answer the phone, "Hello, JV Oil Company."

As I stood close to Mom, I heard the bookkeeper say, "Oh, hello, Thelma. Yes, yes, he's here. I'll put him on the line."

Dad picked up the phone from his desk, and I could hear him lean back in his squeaky office chair.

Mom, in a tired and exasperated voice, gave Dad the morning rundown: cereal all over the floor, two bloody noses, her frazzled nerves — quickly followed by the demand, "Come get these little sons-a-bitches out of my sight, or I swear with God as my witness, I'm going to skin them alive!"

I heard him try to reassure her with something like, "Well, boys will be boys."

But she was having none of it and reaffirmed her position that we, "the little sons-a-bitches," were in imminent danger should he not do the right thing and come get us immediately.

Of course, we loved riding on the oil truck with Dad and were delighted when we heard the air brakes out in front of the house.

"Come on, boys, come with me," he said in a tone that clearly led us to believe that our mother was overreacting, and that we had really done nothing wrong other than being born with a Y chromosome.

We climbed up into Dad's truck, and off we went.

The roads in Juniata County were windy and twisty, rough and bumpy. Few were blacktopped, and most were merely gravel at best. Dad had a special air-glide seat with marshmallow-like shock absorbers to minimize the jarring and make long days in the truck more comfortable.

Carl and I shared the passenger's seat, which had no shock absorbers and bounced us around with a quality that only boys our age could appreciate.

We stopped to service a chicken farmer, an old widow, and a fruit grower before making the big fill-up of the run at the Monroe Township Building.

The township had a large tank for supplying its trucks and equipment with diesel fuel. As Dad filled the tank, Carl and I quickly wandered out of his parental view. Way on the other side of the big, white, concrete-block township building was a small abandoned house sitting on the hill overlooking the gravel parking area. Half the windows on the ramshackle house had been smashed out, and Carl was determined to finish the job.

He picked up a rock the size of his fist, and with all the accuracy and speed of an eight-year-old first-string Little League pitcher, sailed the rock up the hill — against gravity, mind you — and through a window pane. It made the most wonderful *kersmashing* noise.

I picked up a rock and gave it the clumsy lob of a five-year-old. My rock fell short of its mark. Carl grinned and called me a sissy.

He sent another projectile with deadly aim, successfully meeting its intended target.

Again I threw a pitiful attempt, prompting my brother to laugh and call me a pussy. The audacity! I was no pussy, and damn it, I'd show him.

I clearly understood his advantage, being three years older than I, and it only served to bolster my determination. Carl was having the time of his life breaking glass, and I wasn't about to be left out of the fun.

This time I picked up *two* rocks. Instead of wasting them on the out-of-reach windows of the abandoned house, I went looking for a closer target.

I went around the corner of the township building in search of anything made of glass to introduce to my rocks, and there they were: sitting right in front of the building, staring at me, begging to be smashed.

I took careful aim from five feet away. *KERSMASH!* A dead-on hit. I lined up for the second assault … *KERSMASH!* … another dead-on hit. I felt vindicated. I wasn't a sissy or a pussy. I was a successful kersmasher!

When Dad came back to the truck, towing the big fill hose over his shoulder, he stopped dead in his tracks, his jaw agape. He blinked his eyes several times so as to be sure he was seeing what he thought he was seeing. Dad dropped the hose to the ground, and Carl quickly blurted, "Nelson is the one who smashed out your headlights!"

The look on Dad's face was unfamiliar to me as he started to take off his belt. It was anger. I knew what anger looked like on Mom's face but not Dad's — at least not until this moment.

As quickly as Dad started to take his belt off, he put it back on again. In an instant, his expression of anger turned to wonderment. I stood there, still not understanding why I was in trouble for making things go kersmash.

Obviously, Dad had reached far back into his memory and related to the ignorance and innocence of a five-year-old boy.

Monday morning, over breakfast in Shirley's Restaurant at the town square, Dad and his Rat Pack buddies — Peanut, Doc and George — all laughed hysterically as he told the story. He was proud of me in a way, I suppose. But, moreover, he delighted in his son having given him more fodder to blast from the storytelling cannon that made life so interesting in the village of McAlisterville. 🌿

Chapter 3

The Starting Point

IDON'T THINK ANY KID in the history of the world ever loved the first grade more than I did.

Mrs. Parsons was the sort of first-grade teacher that all first-grade teachers should be modeled after. Just as neat as a pin, she was a petite lady in her early forties with a kind, pleasant smile and a passionate dedication to each student's personal achievement.

I never mouthed off to her or gave her a bad time. I was the perfect little gentleman in her presence. She cared about me. She cared about all of us, and I appreciated her for it.

On gray, dreary days, she often called me to the front of the classroom and said, "Nelson, how about perking things up? Sing a song or tell us a story."

"Sure, Mrs. Parsons!" I said as I brimmed with enthusiasm to entertain the class. Not only did it give me the opportunity to stay on her good side, it afforded me a chance to impress Debbie.

I had met Debbie on the first day of school that year. It was love at first sight.

I was standing on the playground inspecting my new shoes from Mr. Goodling's Shoe Store. I looked up, and there she was, twenty-five feet away, talking to another girl. She looked like a movie star! She had a pretty, white smile, beautiful, brown hair, and warm, caring, brown eyes. I had never been so affected by another human being. I felt as if I had been punched in the stomach — in a good way.

I had seen people on television kiss, but to me it had always seemed icky. At the very first moment I saw Debbie, suddenly what had always seemed so icky made perfect sense.

During class, I often found myself staring at her, daydreaming about carrying her lunch tray or defending her honor on the playground. I closed my eyes and thought about what it would feel like to kiss her and hold her hand.

I even told Dad, Doc, George, and Peanut that I thought Debbie was real pretty and that I might even marry her when I grew up. I admitted that I was a bit too shy to come right out and tell her that I loved her. In fact, I had hardly spoken to her at all except maybe to say, "Hello" or "Have a nice day." Every time I got close to her, my heart thumped in my chest, and I could feel my face getting red. I could say anything to anybody, but when it came to Debbie, I was completely tongue-tied.

Doc said, "Congratulations, Nelson. Those are the symptoms of true love."

Peanut thought I should ask her to marry me right away.

"Why wait till you grow up? Hell, if she's that pretty, you'd better make your move now before someone else does!" I knew Peanut was just yanking my chain and that six-year-olds couldn't get married. But, at the same time, I knew he was right about one thing: If I didn't make my move and at least ask her to be my girlfriend, someone else would.

For a week, I stood in front of my bedroom mirror and practiced my words over and over. In rehearsal, I was bold, dashing, and self-assured. Finally, I felt I was ready to come right out and ask her. I decided that I would just walk right up to her and say, "Debbie, I love you. And if you love me, will you be my girlfriend?"

The night before, I took a bath, scrubbed extra hard with a bar of Lifebuoy, and even used my sister's shampoo. I got out of bed extra early in the morning. This was the big day! I put on my favorite shirt and pants and shined my shoes. I tried to make my hair lie down to one side using water and a comb, but there was no use, it did its own thing. I dabbed on Dad's Mennen Skin Bracer aftershave just under each ear.

I waited until recess, opted out of the boys' kickball game, and took up position on the small side porch of the school near the flagpole. I could see Debbie across the playground jumping rope with her friends. She had on a white satin jacket that contrasted beautifully with her dark hair. She looked more gorgeous than ever.

My heart pounded a mile a minute, butterflies filled my stomach, my palms sweated, and my mouth was dry. All the self-assured boldness from rehearsal was gone.

What if she says no? Surely she is going to say yes, because no one could ever love her the way I do, right? I started my approach several times but lost my nerve and retreated back to the porch. I was procrastinating and talking to myself, trying my best to muster the courage to do what had to be done.

"Nelson," I said to myself, "there are only five minutes of recess left. You have to ask! This is your last chance. If you don't ask now, it will probably take weeks to work up your courage again."

Finally, with mere minutes remaining, I asked my buddy, Curtis Seiber, to go ask her if she would be my girlfriend.

"Sure, I'll ask her for ya!" Curt said. Curtis Seiber was a loyal friend and could be counted on at all times. He ran across the playground to where she was jumping rope with her girlfriends. Curtis got Debbie's attention, and the two little girls at the ends stopped swinging the rope and began listening intently to the conversation between Debbie and Curtis.

Debbie's back was to me, but I could see Curtis' face. He was a natural born salesman, and I was sure he was doing his best to present the idea of a Nelson and Debbie romance. He was making a good argument. I could tell by his gestures and body language. But why was this taking so long? It should have been a ten-second question and a three-second answer. She must have had concerns that needed to be addressed before signing on the dotted line. And then I saw her shake her head no. Curt continued to talk for a bit longer, obviously trying to overcome her objections, but finally I saw him nod as he accepted the rejection on my behalf.

Curt came back to the side porch and reported, "Sorry Nelson, I tried, but she said she can't be your girlfriend because she's in love with Troy Sellers."

Of course she was in love with Troy. He was a big, strong jock and had just won the Pee-Wee division punt, pass, and kick contest sponsored by the local Ford dealership. All the girls were in love with Troy Sellers.

I was upset with myself for chickening out and not being man enough to ask her myself, but I did send the best salesman in the first grade. I couldn't be upset with Curt. I appreciated his good effort. He did right by me. Curtis was a good guy with a sense of fair play and always did right by everybody.

I held out hope that Debbie would get sick of Troy and fall in love with me instead. After all, I was a good catch. I was scrappy and could sing. I had a Frank Sinatra thing going for me. Regardless of the letdown, I left school each afternoon with a spring in my step and a song in my heart.

First grade was going well, and under Mrs. Parsons' tutelage, I was beginning to read one-syllable words. *See Spot run. Go, Dick, go. Look, Jane, look!*

Mrs. Parsons made me feel like I was her favorite pupil. She even sent a note home to Mom explaining what an excellent student I was. I beamed with excitement, enthusiasm, and pride as my mother read the note aloud to my dad.

I laid my school clothes out every night and jumped out of bed every morning with the anticipation of another glorious day of learning. I looked out my bedroom window to see if it was raining. Rainy days were the best because Mrs. Parsons might ask me to sing or tell a story to the class.

Mrs. Parsons pulled me aside one day as I was coming in from recess.

"Nelson, where does your mother take you for speaking and voice lessons?" she inquired. I didn't know there were such things. I told her I didn't understand the question. "Oh," she said and seemed surprised, realizing whatever it was she saw in me somehow came naturally.

It was through the guidance and encouragement of Mrs. Parsons that I made up my mind about a future career. Every person in Juniata County listened to WJUN 1220 AM. Ralph Parker, the station owner, had a wonderful voice on the radio. Mrs. Parsons would compare my voice to his and say, "Oh, Nelson, with that voice of yours, I can just hear you on WJUN when you grow up. Don't you think so, Class?" she said, nodding. "Uh-huh," they all responded in unison.

Mrs. Parsons always boosted up all the kids in class, but I felt that she and I had a special relationship. One day, she commented on my apparent comfort with telling a story in front of the whole class.

"You know Nelson, McAlisterville doesn't have a lawyer, and I bet you'd make a good one. People listen to you," she said. "You have a strong voice, and I think you could make a very good argument in the courtroom."

So, it was set. I happily decided, based on Mrs. Parsons' suggestions, that I was going to be either a lawyer or a broadcaster.

I figured if I wanted to go into broadcasting, all I'd have to do is get a microphone and stick an antenna on the top of the Shade Mountain and start my very own radio station. How hard could that be? Everyone in town would be able to listen to me on their radios.

Mrs. Parsons was right. McAlisterville had a doctor, an undertaker, a barber, a shoemaker, numerous shopkeepers, a small-engine repairman, a banker, an oilman, and a car dealer, but no lawyers. If folks needed legal counsel they had to drive the whole way to Mifflintown to see Mr. Brown Fry, Esquire, or Mr. John Welsh, Esquire.

Dad's pal Peanut said attorneys Fry and Welsh were a couple of "crooked bastards." I figured it was no big deal that there were already two of them in the field because I was just a school kid and surely, these two elderly lawyers would be dead, retired, or no competition at all by the time I was old enough to be a crooked bastard too.

I knew it wasn't a good thing to be called a crooked bastard. But I also knew from watching black-and-white episodes of "Ironside" that courtroom attorneys were all about winning cases even if it meant making people angry once in a while. I also liked the fact that the attorneys on the Ironside TV series wore nice clothing like George the Banker. But beyond all of that, I was inspired by the dramatic closing arguments the lawyers made.

I was confident that I could stand in front of a jury in a packed courtroom, make a big speech, tell a few stories, and add another helping of justice to the world. And of course, I could do it better than Troy Sellers ever could! Surely Debbie would be unable to resist me then. We'd get married and have two perfect children, a blond little boy and a dark-haired little girl, who would go to school and get straight A's in Mrs. Parsons' first grade class.

Mrs. Parsons lined us up for dismissal each afternoon. She divided us into three groups: kids who walked home, kids who got picked up by their parents, and kids who rode the bus home. Every day, as I stood in the dismissal line, I stared at Mrs. Parsons, waiting to catch her eye so I could give her a thumbs-up, indicating another great day of school! She'd flash back an agreeing smile. Mrs. Parsons and I were a team!

Dad was now dropping me off in the big oil truck in the morning and picking me up after school at least three days a week. I loved going along with Dad in the truck especially because we'd leave extra early in the morning to have breakfast at Shirley's Restaurant, where we always met up with Doc, George, and Peanut.

My brother, Carl, didn't much care to join in on these mornings. For him, it was boring. For me it was magical — I felt like I became one of the guys. I loved to hear them talk like adults, swapping stories and gossiping like a bunch of old ladies. I would sit quietly and listen. The trick was to make them forget I was there. Then the big talk — the unedited, colorful stuff — came out. As I absorbed the words and the seemingly perfect flow of the interaction between the men, I would zone in on their mannerisms — how their bodies shook when they laughed, how they sipped their coffee. I'd try to pick up my coffee mug — filled with age-appropriate hot chocolate and a dollop of marshmallow — in the same way and practice taking a sip just like they did. They were master storytellers, and I was just an enthusiastic rookie-in-training.

I loved everything about getting together with Dad and his friends for breakfast except for one thing: Doc's new nickname for me. Every morning when we walked through the door of Shirley's, Doc announced to the entire restaurant, "Ladies and Gentlemen, Sir Nellie Boy has arrived." Suddenly, I was no longer a fly on the wall. I became the center of attention for the entire restaurant. I had been one of the guys, but now I was Nellie! A girl's name! I was emasculated and afraid that people would think I was girly. George and Peanut could see that I didn't like it, but Doc enjoyed needling me. The more he realized I didn't like it, the more he would say it. And the name got around. As soon as Carl learned how much it bothered me, it became his nickname for me too.

One morning after our breakfast stop, Dad could see there was something bothering me.

"What's wrong, Nelson? Did Ducky's daughter turn down your marriage proposal?" Ducky was Debbie's father's nickname.

"I didn't ask her to marry me! Curtis Seiber asked her to be my girlfriend, but she said no because she's in love with Troy Sellers. But that's not the problem anyhow!"

"Well, spit it out. What's the problem?"

"It's Doc Yoder, Dad. That's what's wrong! Every morning when we walk through the door of the restaurant for breakfast, Doc announces to everyone that 'Sir Nellie Boy' has arrived. I don't like him calling me Nellie, and I don't like everybody laughing at me!"

"Well, I didn't know it bothered ya that much," Dad said with a devilish look on his face.

"Dad! Nellie is a girl's name! I can't go through life as a lawyer or a broadcaster being called Sir Nellie Boy!"

"Yeah, I guess I can see where that might cause a problem," Dad said. I steamed as we sat there in the oil truck discussing the Sir Nellie Boy situation.

"Well, maybe we need to come up with a plan to turn the tables on old Doc?" Dad said with a chuckle in his voice.

"Really? Like what, Dad?"

"Well, here's what we'll do. We'll get to the restaurant bright and early tomorrow morning before Dr. Yoder. When he comes through the door, you announce to everyone that 'Dr. Shitface has arrived' ..."

"But, Dad, I'm only six years old. I'm not allowed to say shit!"

"I'll overlook it this one time," Dad said.

We went to breakfast extra early the next morning. I stood inside the big front window of the restaurant, watching and waiting for Doc to come out of his office across the street.

It was an exciting morning. I was ready to give Doc a taste of his own bitter medicine, and I couldn't wait!

Finally, the well-dressed country doctor appeared. He walked across Main Street with his usual air of dignity.

I ran from the big front window over to where Dad was sitting with George and Peanut. On Dad's cue, I stood up on a bar stool and tapped a spoon against a coffee mug: clink, clink, clink, clink. The patrons grew quiet, the front door of the restaurant opened, and I announced, "Ladies and gentlemen, Dr. Shitface has entered the building!"

The restaurant, filled with regulars, erupted in laughter far more intense than it ever had when Doc announced the arrival of "Sir Nellie Boy." The building shook from applause and foot stomping. Silverware, plates, and saucers bounced as patrons slapped the counter in hysterical support of an evened score. Tiny Benner, the town plumber, had taken a big gulp of coffee just as I made my announcement. He tried — he really tried — to make it go down, but it was too late. As Tiny found out, it's impossible to explode with side-splitting laughter and swallow coffee at the same time.

As the crowd returned to a low roar, Doc worked his way through the cigar smoke, over to where Dad and I were sitting with George and Peanut. Doc was embarrassed, and his face was red, but he clearly understood that he had set himself up for this. His upset was made even greater by the smiles on the faces of his fellow Rat Packers, who had joyfully participated in taking up the cause of a six-year-old boy and keeping one of their own honest and humble.

"Ah, hey, Nelson," Doc said. "You know, a name like Dr. Shitface … ah … could really stick with a fellow."

"Yeah, yeah, I know, Doc. Sort of like Sir Nellie Boy."

"Well, hey, if that's what this is about, I'll stop calling you that."

"Yeah, that's good for starters."

"What else ya want?" he asked.

"Well, buy breakfast for me and Dad."

He pulled out his money clip. "Hey, not a problem, got ya covered."

"For a week, I meant."

"Yeah, no problem," he said with a tone as if I had his arm twisted behind his back.

I continued just as we had rehearsed while Dad, George, and Peanut struggled to contain themselves.

"And I'd like ya to take me fishing on the Juniata River, Doc."

"Sure, as soon as we get a day when no one is sick, we're headed for the river, Nelson."

"And I really should have a pony."

"Yes, yes, Nelson. Every child should have a pony."

"Ahh, heck, Doc. I'll tell ya what, from here on out, I'll just call you Doc, and you call me Mr. Lauver. We'll be even-steven."

The deal was sealed with a handshake, and I felt very satisfied with the outcome.

Of course, having a moniker like Nellie Boy is enough to bend anyone out of shape. But I guess what really made me most angry was the betrayal I felt. Doc was more than just my friend, I saw him as the protector of the center of the world, a.k.a. McAlisterville, Pennsylvania.

I look back and laugh about it today, but when I was six, I somehow developed the notion that McAlisterville was the starting point for seeing the world. I heard people talk about "traveling cross-country" or "abroad." They were people who had a desire to "see the world." I thought to "see the world," one had to start off from McAlisterville, Pennsylvania. I thought seeing the world was a car ride, and all a person had to do was get on Route 35 going out of town. If they drove long enough they would see the whole world and then come back into McAlisterville from the other side of town.

I figured that no matter where someone lived, if they wanted to see the world, they needed to come to McAlisterville first because that's where the world started.

I didn't quite understand why anyone would want to embark on such a journey. Any person with half a brain knew there were guys from our tiny village who went out into the world and came back in caskets. Somewhere out there was that dreadful Vietnam. It just made no sense at all that anyone would take the chance of getting tangled up in that mess.

I figured those fellows in Vietnam died because Doc Yoder wasn't there.

I thought if a person were sick or hurt, Doc could give them medicine to make them well again. And if someone died, I figured it was because either they didn't know Doc Yoder, or maybe Doc was just too busy giving someone else medicine and didn't have enough time to get to them.

In my mind, McAlisterville was a safe bubble. You could go beyond the bubble if you chose, but it was risky because the farther you went, the farther you were from Doc.

Unfortunately, my notion that McAlisterville was a safe haven, a place where nothing ever went seriously wrong, was about to be tested. My bubble was about to burst. 🌿

Chapter 4

Nelson, Why Can't You Read?

WHEN I ENTERED MRS. WILLIAMS' SECOND GRADE, I was still beaming with the success I enjoyed in Mrs. Parsons' first grade.

Mrs. Williams was a nice lady, and all the older kids I knew who had her said that she was a friendly teacher. They were right. Mrs. Williams didn't have a mean bone in her whole body. She looked like Mary Tyler Moore and was quiet and reserved.

Soon after the year began, I realized something was wrong. All the other kids seemed to be doing fine, but I was struggling.

The words were harder to read, longer, and had multiple syllables. Trying to put them all together in a sentence was difficult. And what was even more difficult than this new second-grade reading was second-grade writing. *I just need to practice more*, I thought. I took my books and papers home each night and hid in my room as I tried to make sense of it all. But even in the quiet confines of my room, there was no progress being made.

One day in class, probably to Mrs. Williams' horror as much as mine, she called on me to read out loud. I stammered and stuttered and mispronounced almost every word.

The other kids were reading well, but I couldn't get through a sentence. A few kids snickered, and soon most of the class was laughing. I stopped reading, but the kids continued laughing.

Mrs. Williams quieted the class and called on someone else to read out loud.

I was so humiliated, I wanted to cry. But crying was not an option. I had a hard-and-fast rule about crying — it was okay when I was alone and nobody was looking or listening, but NEVER cry in front of others because people might think you're a sissy.

That same day at recess, a well-meaning little girl named Peggy asked with great concern in her voice, "Nelson, why can't you read?"

"I don't know, Peggy," I said. I was scared. Troy could read, and so could Curt and Danny and the other boys in the class. I wondered, *Why can't I do this?* I had a terrible feeling of panic in my stomach. I worried that if things didn't soon improve, I would have to give up my dream of becoming an attorney or broadcaster.

After the reading-aloud disaster, I wondered what Debbie must think of me. Surely, she'll never want to be my girlfriend now. I couldn't look at her for weeks for fear of what the expression on her face might say about her thoughts on me and my pitiful inability to read. I made up my mind that never again would I allow anyone to hear me try to read out loud, and luckily, Mrs. Williams never asked me again.

Then report card day arrived. I remember walking home from school and seeing Dad on the front porch. Carl was showing him his report card. Dad smiled and nodded and told him to go in and show Mom. Then Dad saw me, got a big grin on his face, and called out, "Hey, buddy boy, let's see your report card ... and there'd better not be any F's on it!" he joked. I produced my report card, and as Dad studied it, I could see his face drop. His eyes lost their twinkle. It was full of big red F's. He seemed puzzled, disappointed. Obviously, that was the last thing he'd expected after my success in first grade.

He handed the report card back to me and said nothing.

My parents assumed what most parents at the time would have: I needed to pay more attention in class and study more. The constant refrain in my house was, "Did you bring your books home?" "Before you go out and play, I want to see studying." "Did you study your books tonight?"

As the school year marched on, I watched my classmates grow as pupils while I shrank. Some of the class work I understood; most of it I didn't. There was so much confusing information it was overwhelming, and I couldn't take it all in. But I tried and struggled to do my best for Mrs. Williams.

I constantly questioned myself, *Do the other kids think I'm dumb?* Even though I had a hard time in school, I didn't feel dumb. Outside of school everything seemed to make sense, like Dad's oil truck. I knew exactly how the truck worked and the mechanics of how the fuel went through the hose and into the tanks. But I kept questioning. *Nelson, you can't read...why?*

I worried that I would fail second grade. But, somehow, to my great amazement and relief, I passed.

I decided to put the trouble of second grade out of my mind and comforted myself with the thought, *Third grade will be a fresh start and surely things will go better.*

I spent my summer with Dad on the oil truck and swimming at the McAlisterville Public Swimming Pool.

The swimming pool had been built back along the Shade Mountain by the local Lions Club as a community project. A well-to-do man from town donated the land, and the Lions Club spearheaded the fundraising and construction. The McAlisterville swimming pool was an oasis, a wonderful place to spend warm summer afternoons surrounded by friends, evergreens, mountains, and scantily clad, sun-kissed girls.

The water for the pool was supplied by nearby Lost Creek, or, as the locals called it, "Loss Crick." "Loss Crick" started as a spring far up in the Shade Mountain. As it bubbled over the rocks, growing and cascading down out of the mountain, it moved so fast that its pristine waters gained no heat from the sun.

Even during the dog days of summer, the water in the pool supplied by "Loss Crick" was icy cold. But we didn't mind so much. Once past the initial shock of jumping in, you sort of acclimated to the chilly waters.

My family had a lifetime membership because Dad, an active member of the local Lions Club, donated one hundred dollars toward the swimming pool when it was built back in the 1950s. One hundred dollars was a lot of money but paid for itself over and again since we never had to suffer admission charges.

After my poor performance in second grade, I had given up hope that Debbie would want to be my girlfriend. But, Chris Weller, a lifeguard at the swimming pool, became a wonderful distraction and eased my pining for Debbie. While I turned eight years old in the summer of 1971, Chris was well into her teenage years.

Chris was a beguiling beauty in a bikini. A brunette, she had pleasant curves, and her skin was golden brown from hours on the lifeguard chair. She not only looked good, she smelled good too. Her suntan lotion was an alluring blend from the tropics: coconut and pineapple. She made it a point to dive into the pool before taking the chair for her shift. The "wet look" looked good on her. I couldn't help but watch as she ascended her lifesaving throne. I knew it was wrong, but I had to stare. I had a crush.

At the Lutheran church my family occasionally attended, Pastor Kurfman preached on the evils of "eyeing-up women." Obviously, Pastor Kurfman had never seen Chris Weller in a bikini.

I planned on living a very long life and hoped this small indiscretion would be forgotten by the time I was ready to pass through the Pearly Gates. But I was painfully aware that, depending on the soundness of God's memory, I could be banished to the fiery depths of Hell.

I did things on purpose to get in trouble so Chris would blow her whistle at me and sweetly call out my name: "Nelson, you know better than that." I didn't want to get into too much trouble and get thrown off the grounds of the pool but sought just enough so that I would have to "sit out."

Bad boys had to "sit out" at the edge of the pool near the lifeguard's chair for fifteen minutes or more, depending on the severity of their crime. Girls never had to sit out. McAlisterville girls were very well-behaved and minded their manners.

I sheepishly apologized for my poor behavior while doing my time and promised Chris, "I'll never do it again." Of course, she knew better.

At the McAlisterville Fireman's Carnival that summer, I bought a heart-shaped necklace for six dollars and had the carnie jeweler engrave it with "Nelson Loves Chris." Although in the end, I never had the courage to give it to her. 🌿

Chapter 5

The Choice

I ENTERED MRS. CLARK'S THIRD GRADE in the fall of 1971.

Mrs. Clark was a brand new teacher at McAlisterville Elementary, fresh out of college. She was young, maybe all of twenty-three years old, and pretty with long dark hair. Teaching wasn't the only new thing in her life. She and her newlywed husband had a bouncing baby boy.

Mrs. Clark didn't look anything like the other teachers and didn't act like them either. Most teachers at McAlisterville Elementary were much older and dressed very conservatively, but Mrs. Clark wore sleeveless dresses and showed leg. She was funny, entertaining, liked to tell jokes and would say silly things to make us laugh. But, in the blink of an eye, she could shed her good-natured demeanor. What made her laugh, smile, and joke one minute could somehow make her explode in a blind fit of rage the next. Even the smallest things, like forgotten lunch money, tardiness, or a slight indiscretion on the playground might or might not send her into a screaming, face-scrunching tantrum. When she was angered, the tendons tightened in the front of her neck, her face grew red, and she lost all emotional control. Often, at the end of the episode, her anger would turn to sobbing. As a class, we all sat stiff in our chairs like bug-eyed cartoon characters, afraid to make a move.

One day on the playground, a group of us kids were standing around talking about why Mrs. Clark got so angry with us sometimes. One girl said, "Mrs. Clark has the same thing my mommy has. My dad says it's the baby blues, and sometimes women go crazy after they have a baby."

I found the girl's explanation believable. Mrs. Clark was always talking about her new baby, and there was no doubt in my mind that she did seem crazy at times.

The other students were quick to forgive Mrs. Clark for her outbursts but were constantly on edge, knowing she could blow her stack at any time. I went along with the class and forgave her too, but deep down, I didn't trust her. She frightened me.

I hoped things would go better for me this year than they had gone last year in the second grade, but as I quickly discovered, third grade reading and writing was extremely difficult for me. I tried desperately to get a grasp on it and catch up to the rest of my classmates but to no avail. After about a month and a half of school I was scared and just barely treading water. It felt like I had concrete blocks attached to my legs. Not only was I fighting to keep my head above water, I was fighting to keep the other kids from noticing that I was about to drown.

As I sat in class each day, I felt more and more like an outsider. I wasn't able to keep up, and the boredom was maddening. At the same time, I was constantly anxious and on the edge of my seat, hoping that I wouldn't get called upon and be embarrassed in front of the class.

Being such a curious kid, I craved knowledge, and since I couldn't find it at school with all the "normal kids," I unwittingly created my own classroom outside of school with the unsuspecting characters of McAlisterville as my teachers.

On the days I walked home from school, I often stopped and looked through the big windows of Shirley's Restaurant to see if my pal, Walter, was sitting at the counter. And if he was, I went in for a lesson.

Old Walter Dunn could be found most afternoons drinking coffee at Shirley's. He was so lonely and bored that he hardly knew what to do with himself.

"I get up in the morning with nothing to do and go to bed half-finished," he often joked.

Walter was the oldest person in McAlisterville. He was so old he remembered holding my grandfather on his lap when my grandfather was just a baby — and my grandfather was old!

On Walter's ninetieth birthday, Shirley baked him a cake, and a newspaper man came out from Mifflintown to take his picture cutting the cake.

But what Walter wanted more than anything was just to tell stories. That's why he went to Shirley's Restaurant every day. He hoped to find someone who wanted to listen. Everyone liked Walter, but most folks just seemed too busy to sit and listen.

I, on the other hand, couldn't get enough of what old Walter Dunn had to say.

Walter's patchy white hair was never combed. He had quite a few fingers missing, and it took two trembling hands to hold his coffee cup. It wasn't uncommon to see old guys minus a few fingers from farming or timbering accidents.

He'd see me coming and smile that big smile that was minus a few teeth. I'd sit down beside him and say, "C'mon Walter, say it. I want to hear ya say it!"

"Nelson, I've said it for ya every day this week. Ya ought to know it now by heart."

"I do, Walter, but I like it best when I hear you say it."

His face lit up as he said, "OK, I guess I can say it again."

He'd take a big slug of coffee and a deep breath. "Neither snow nor rain nor heat nor gloom of night stays these couriers from the swift completion of their appointed rounds."

I loved when Walter rattled that off.

Walter Dunn, with an immense sense of duty and a wagon hooked behind a team of mules, began making his appointed rounds in the year 1905.

For forty-five years, in the worst blizzards, in the most torrential rains, on days when the sun could blister a man's skin, and often late into the night, the United States mail got through. Walter Dunn, United States mail carrier, at your service.

Old Walter told stories 'til we were both worn out, and he seldom told the same one twice.

As I stood up to go home, Walter often slipped me a dollar bill.

"Nelson, give this dollar to your daddy and tell him to buy me a bottle of port wine when he gets to Mifflintown," he'd say. "Have him hide it in the usual place in Jake Knouse's shed, and for heaven's sake, don't let my wife find out."

Dad always laughed as I handed him the dollar bill. The last time a bottle of port cost a dollar was probably back in the 1920s. But Dad didn't mind, he enjoyed keeping Walter in wine.

It was common knowledge among townspeople that Walter

sneaked into Jake Knouse's old board-and-batten shed about 1 p.m. every afternoon to enjoy his glass of port. One hundred or so years earlier, sometime after the Civil War, the shed was built to house horses and a carriage. Back alleys in small towns like McAlisterville were full of them. One by one, the sheds fell down, burned down, or were torn down. But this particular one, just like Walter, stood the test of time. Sure, it was rickety. It looked like a good windstorm could come along at any time and take it down. I suppose going in there, shutting the door, and enjoying a glass of port returned Walter to a place and time when the world made more sense to him.

Townspeople peeked through their curtains and snickered as the daily drama between Walter and his wife unfolded.

Mrs. Dunn, a five-foot-tall, hundred-pound ball of fire, could see Jake's shed from her back porch. Day after day, she'd watch and wait for Walter to slink into the shed and latch the door behind him. Day after day, hell-bent on giving Walter a piece of her mind, she'd scamper up the alley at full tilt.

She'd stand outside, beating her cane on the locked wooden shed door, hollering, "Walter Dunn, I know you're in there!"

She'd furiously admonish him on the evils of drink — and yet somehow he must have been able to turn it all off as he sat there enjoying his port. He often referred to their marriage as "seventy years of wedded bliss."

My insatiable curiosity about everyday people, like Walter, was fast becoming my education. It filled the void.

As fall turned to winter, third grade was becoming more difficult every day, and I was receiving failing marks across the board.

My classmates had mastered printing their names in the second grade, a task I was still struggling with. If someone asked me to spell my first name out loud, I could rattle off N-E-L-S-O-N. But getting that from my head and down onto paper was a struggle. And spelling or printing my middle and last name was extremely difficult. Every so often I got it right; most of the time I didn't. And even when it was correct, it was hard for me to tell the difference.

In third grade, we had moved on to cursive, which to me looked mostly like scribble.

Mrs. Clark handed out worksheets every morning with the usual directive, "Write your name in cursive on the top of your paper."

It wasn't enough just to write our first and last names on the paper. She insisted we write our middle names, too. I concentrated and really tried, but every day my name came out as a jumble of illegible chicken scratch.

Mrs. Clark came up with a plan that I guess she felt would encourage me to try harder.

I clearly remember the first morning she implemented her plan. We all arrived for school and were busy hanging up our hats, gloves, and coats as prescribed while Mrs. Clark was busy writing something very big the whole way across the blackboard.

We took our seats and looked at the curious etchings on the chalkboard. Mrs. Clark tapped her pointer on her desk several times to get everyone's attention.

"Class, class," she said. "Does anyone know what I have written on the chalkboard?" Nobody seemed to know. "Well, let me inform you," she continued. "This is how Nelson Charles Lauver lazily scribbled his name on his paper yesterday."

Classmates were called upon, one at a time, to try to pronounce the illegible writing.

"Nezon Chass Liver," one girl thought out loud. The room erupted in laughter and chanted, "Nezon Chass Liver! Nezon Chass Liver! Nezon Chass Liver!"

Mrs. Clark instructed the class, "This is what you are to call Nelson for the rest of the day until tomorrow when I'm sure his name will be something different."

I laughed along on the outside so as to seem unaffected, but on the inside, I was thinking, *I hate you, I hate you for this. Why are you doing this to me?*

It was a pivotal moment in my life. *Lazy?* I wasn't lazy. I had been trying so hard to understand. I wanted to learn!

I realized I needed to do something. I said to myself, *Nelson, you have a choice. You can either look like the dumb kid who everyone makes fun of, or you can be the bad kid.* At that moment, I chose to be the "bad kid." The thought of being the "dumb kid" — and how other kids teased and taunted them — made it feel like the only choice.

I didn't want to be the "bad kid." I wanted to be the good kid and get good grades! Throughout school, so far, I admit I had been a bit of a button-pusher at times, but I was never disrespectful to my teachers. Now I knew I had to pour it on.

I knew there would be ramifications. I was aware this new persona would invite unpleasant punishments like paddling, slaps, and ruler cracks from angry teachers. Life was so much better in the first grade, and I wished Mrs. Parsons were still my teacher. I saw her in the hall every day but couldn't bring myself to look at her. I wondered what she must think of me now. It was a very small school. Surely, she and Mrs. Clark would have talked. And surely, Mrs. Parsons must have felt she had wasted her time on me. The thought of letting Mrs. Parsons down saddened me.

In keeping with my new "bad kid" persona, I capitalized on Mrs. Clark's crazy-button and pushed it at opportune moments. Things like making a face at her, making an inappropriate remark, acting indifferent, or just ignoring her helped in that she'd choose not to call on me for the sake of her own personal sanity. I became very successful at making Mrs. Clark dislike me. She often sent me to the hallway with my desk and chair so I would not disrupt the class. It was embarrassing because anyone who entered the school for any reason could see me sitting there alone. But, regardless of how embarrassing it was, it could never have compared with the embarrassment of being the dumb kid.

A remedial reading teacher came to the school several days a week to work one-on-one with kids who were having a hard time keeping up. As I was a student who was obviously not keeping up and had become a behavioral problem, Mrs. Clark arranged to have the remedial reading teacher see me for a session during late winter of my third-grade year. He knocked on the classroom door and called me out for our meeting. I knew that this teacher quietly helped kids get caught up. I was happy to get out of class and was secretly hopeful that this could be my opportunity to get help in making school work easier to understand.

The remedial reading teacher took me into a room, sat down next to me at a long library-style table, opened a book, put it in front of me, and asked me to read. As I tried, I stammered, stuttered, and struggled to pronounce the words. I had to keep going back to try again and again. It took what seemed forever, but I managed to hack through two sentences before he closed the book and pushed it away. He then pushed the table away and said, "Turn your chair and face me like a man," as he turned his chair toward mine. "This is the result of not paying attention in class," he sharply scolded. "You have no one but your lazy self to blame for your reading troubles." He spent the rest of the session berating me for being a "goof-off." I didn't say a word for fear it would only make him nastier.

I knew I wasn't lazy. I knew he was wrong, but he scared me. In my little boy mind, it became clear. I was on my own. There was nobody to help me. It solidified my resolve that the best option for getting through school was by being the "bad kid."

My number one goal as the "bad kid" in elementary school was to make sure no teacher wanted me back the next year because the most embarrassing of all things would be to flunk. If, on occasion, Mrs. Clark did call on me, I would disrupt the class. The easiest option was to throw something — a book, a pencil, a tablet. Throwing things was completely against the rules and got the most effect. I got in trouble often and was frequently sent to see the senior teacher and disciplinarian, Miss Marybeth.

All of the other kids addressed her as Miss Stoner, but seeing as she was my dad's first cousin, I was permitted to call her Miss Marybeth.

Miss Marybeth was in her fifties. She was a solid woman with a sturdy center of gravity, strapping arms and shoulders, a ruddy complexion, and not a touch of makeup. She had never been married or had a man in her life. Her thick, blonde hair was neatly wrapped up in a bun, atop of which sat her ever-present prayer covering. She was a pious woman, a member of Grandpa's flock, who could recite the Bible cover to cover. She strongly believed in every word, including "spare the rod and spoil the child."

Miss Marybeth's disciplinary "office" was a desk inside the janitorial storage room. Beside her desk was a chair where she counseled children right before the proverbial "rod" — or "big wooden paddle" in this case — was taken down from its hanging place. The construction of the paddle was well thought out and bore all the efficiency that could be crafted in a Pennsylvania Dutchman's woodworking shop. Miss Marybeth's paddle followed the age-old standard design. The handle accommodated a double-fisted swing. A dozen or so three-quarter-inch holes had been drilled through it to ensure it whistled through the air with maximum velocity. The whistling sound served another purpose, too — striking terror into the heart of the child who was about to be anointed with the sting of hellfire. Miss Marybeth's personal mission was to ensure no child would be spoiled under her watch.

I was sent to see Miss Marybeth for my first counseling session after I hurled a book at Mrs. Clark. Incidentally, that was the last time she wrote my name on the blackboard as a means of discouraging my "laziness."

I devised a plan as I sat in the chair of counsel, waiting for Miss Marybeth to arrive and warm my ass with religion. It was a brilliant plan, I might add, and one of which I'm still secretly proud. I decided to place the onus of my bad behavior on someone else. I would lay the blame squarely at the feet of another.

Finally, Miss Marybeth presented herself to deal with my book-hurling infraction. She took the paddle down from its hook on the wall and laid it on the desk as she prepared to counsel me. I handed her a note from Mrs. Clark. She examined it, refolded it, and laid it on top of the paddle.

"Nelson," she said with a thick Pennsylvania Dutch accent. "What do you have to say for yourself?"

I looked down at my shoes and quietly said, "I didn't do it."

"Speak up! What did you say?!"

"I said I didn't do it!"

"Oh, I see, Nelson, then perhaps you'd like to share with me who the actual culprit was who threw the textbook at Mrs. Clark? I suppose you are going to tell me it was Danny Aucker?"

"No, Ma'am, it wasn't Danny."

"I know it wasn't Danny. He's a good Christian boy! I think you threw the book, Nelson. Didn't you?"

"No, it wasn't me."

"Then do tell, Nelson. Who was it?"

I swallowed hard for effect and kept my eyes focused on my shoes. After a dramatic pause and one more coaxing from Miss Marybeth, I softly uttered, "It was Satan."

Miss Marybeth gasped and pushed back in her chair. She hurriedly recited a passage committed to memory for warding off the dark angel.

"Oh, dear heavens, Nelson!" She inquired, "Did you hear a voice in your head?"

"Uh ... uh ... yeah ... yes ...YES. I heard a voice, and it told me to throw the book at Mrs. Clark."

"Oh dear, oh dear, oh dear," she said as she instinctively adjusted her prayer covering. "Did the voice say anything else?"

"Yes!" I told her, now confident that she was buying what I was selling. "Yes, yes, Satan said he wants you to paddle my backside until it turns purple."

She sprang to her feet in defiance, uttering a passage that included something about "the protective blood of Jesus." She hung the paddle back on the wall and boldly proclaimed, "I will not!"

She was still wringing her hands as she sent me back to Mrs. Clark, who was clearly disappointed she did not hear the crack of a paddle on the delicate flesh of my tender bottom echoing through the halls of the elementary school.

I was soon making regular visits to Miss Marybeth for various infractions. All that was necessary for me to do to avoid a serious ass-fanning was the utterance of one word: Satan. Miss Marybeth would nod in agreement and send me back to class.

It was clear, based upon everything I knew about Hell, poor behavior was guaranteed admission. Minding your teachers and never back-talking your parents were prerequisites for having St. Peter show you favor and swing open the Pearly Gates of Heaven. But Miss Marybeth's big, wooden paddle was clearly in the here and now. I feared the near-term threat my actions bore far more than the eternal, unrelenting fires of Hell.

I tried really hard to keep Mom and Dad in the dark about my poor behavior at school, but being such a small town, word sometimes made it back home.

Mom was not pleased when she found out about my "shenanigans." She said, "I swear to God, you're going to Carson Long Military School if you don't straighten up!"

The sheer mention of "Carson Long" struck terror into my heart.

Carson Long Military Institute in the little town of New Bloomfield was about twenty-five miles or so south of McAlisterville.

When Mom was near her breaking point, she would repeat the name "Carson Long" over and over while nodding her head as if she had found a solution for out-of-control sons.

On occasion, she would throw the phone book open to the letter "C" and run her finger down the page while repeating, "Carson Long, Carson Long, Carson Long," as she searched.

If she really wanted to scare the living daylights out of my brother and me, she would pick up the phone and start dialing the number.

"NO MOM, NO MOM — DON'T CALL CARSON LONG. WE'LL BE GOOD, WE PROMISE!"

The thought of being "hauled away" to a military school was terrifying. My brother, Carl, didn't help matters much with his stories of new recruits being hazed by the formerly delinquent and incorrigible older boys, who were now being "whipped into shape" as Carson Long Cadets.

With a solemn face and a trembling voice, Carl said, "They get new kids there and do terrible things to them! Mostly, though, they stick all kinds of things up the new kid's ass! They stuck a stick of dynamite up one kid's ass, lit it, and blew him to kingdom come!"

Every time I brought my report card home covered with F's, my mom would look at it and just keep repeating "Carson Long, Carson Long," as she nodded her head. "Those kids don't even get to come home for Christmas," Carl told me.

According to my brother, we, like all other Carson Long Cadets, could be sent to fight in the Vietnam War. Carl said, "Most end up as prisoners of war, and their families never see them again."

Every time we went somewhere in the car, I couldn't help but wonder if maybe we were going to be dropped off at the gates of Carson Long.

Carl said doctors in white coats meet parents at the gates, jump in the car, and give the new recruit a shot that "knocks them cold," so they can be easily dragged into the compound.

I was sure I would eventually be "hauled away" to Carson Long. It seemed to me that it was only a matter of time.

I formulated a plan in my head for a Carson Long escape, just in case, and I was sure it would work.

I figured I'd have to wait a few years 'til I was old enough to get on the Carson Long football team — and hopefully, not be sent to fight in the war in the meantime. At an away game, I'd sneak off when nobody was watching. I'd quickly make my way to the mountains and hide out there living off the land for the rest of my life as an AWOL fugitive from justice.

My mother's threat of Carson Long, combined with the threat of "If you get in trouble at school, you're going to get it double when you get home," kept me tight-lipped about everything that happened in the classroom.

There was no longer any enjoyment to be found in school, and home was a frantic, disorganized bundle of chaos with two very tired parents. Mom was still working shift work, and Dad's oil business had continued to grow by leaps and bounds. He was now working six or seven days a week. He left the house early in the morning and didn't arrive home until late in the evening.

My favorite escape from the stresses of being the "bad kid" was riding with Dad on the oil truck after school. There was nothing better than hanging out with Dad. He was my hero.

One afternoon, I was sitting across the desk from my dad in his office waiting to go along with him on the oil truck. The buzzer on the front door announced a visitor. Dad and I could hear the familiar voice of the Coca-Cola deliveryman saying hello to the bookkeeper at the front counter. Dad went out to exchange pleasantries and a few laughs, and of course, I padded along. The gregarious Coca-Cola man wore spit-shined shoes, well-pressed blue pants, and a snappy red-and-white striped shirt.

Dick Roush also came out of his office, smoking his pipe. Dick had an office in the oil company building to meet with customers for his insurance business. Dick was a tall, well-dressed man who drove a Lincoln Town Car and had all the airs of success. I had always admired him. He lived down the street from us with his lovely wife.

Dad and the Coke man were laughing and joking when my dad uttered his signature line, "If you have a minute, I've got a great story." The Coke man replied, "Sure, I always have time for a great story." Dick Roush, standing off to the side, caught the Coke man's eye and gave him a wink. It was one of those belittling winks, and it spoke volumes. In his wink to the Coke man, Dick was saying, *"This Clair Lauver sure is a pain in the ass with all his GREAT stories."*

Dad told the story masterfully, and the Coke man burst out in side-splitting laughter.

Dick went back into his office without saying a word. I thought Dick was our friend, and I was puzzled by his attempt to belittle Dad. It hurt my feelings and made me angry.

I changed my mind about riding on the truck with Dad that day.

Instead, I got on my bike and rode downtown to Shirley's Restaurant. I sat at the counter and drowned my upset in an ice-cold Coke with two squirts of Cherry Smash.

Soon, the bell on the restaurant door jingled, and in walked the funniest man in town, Dad's pal Peanut. Peanut sat down at the counter next to me and knew something was eating at me.

"Who rained on your parade?" he asked. I explained the whole Dick Roush winking thing.

"Oh, old Winky Dick got to you, did he? Don't pay no nevermind to him. He's just jealous that your dad's a great storyteller."

The bell on the door jingled again, and in walked Doc and George the Banker. Peanut explained to them that I was having a bad day and why. "Yup," George said. "Winky Dick can't tell a good story to save his life."

Doc took a big gulp of coffee and nodded in agreement. George lit up one of his nickel cigars and, shaking the flame from the match, said, "Nelson, your dad's the best storyteller around, and anyone who says different is wrong, including Winky Dick." Doc took another gulp of coffee and again nodded in agreement as he swallowed.

The friendship between Dad, Doc, Peanut, and George was based on storytelling and making each other laugh. Their get-togethers were mostly impromptu. If not at Shirley's Restaurant, they often took place at my dad's oil company office.

After hours, at Dad's office, they gathered mismatched chairs from the secretary's desk, the bookkeeper's desk, and wherever else they could find them — and arranged them in a circle. They set out a few bottles, mixers, ice, and stir sticks. Dad kept glasses in his office, and in no time, they had their makeshift bar fully stocked and operational.

Peanut preferred his whiskey straight up and said, "Mixing whisky with soda is as senseless as putting milk in beer."

If I happened to be with Dad at his office when one of these impromptu events occurred, I considered myself very lucky. I didn't want to sit in the circle, nor would I have been allowed to. I sat back out of the way where I was soon the forgotten observer. Sometimes, I'd even hide under Dad's desk. The more they drank, the more outrageous the stories became. I sat quietly and listened, the proverbial fly on the wall.

They all told stories. Funny stories, traveling stories, hometown stories, and even gossip.

"Did you hear about Guy Schmidt?"

"No, what about Guy Schmidt?"

"Well, Guy Schmidt's wife was getting all dressed up every night — putting on makeup, jewelry, perfume … the works — just to go to the grocery store. Or so she said. So what do you think Guy Schmidt does after a couple weeks of this? He gets into the trunk of the car so he can figure out, once and for all, what the hell his wife is up to. So, sure enough, he's in the trunk for about half an hour and starts to hear voices! The next thing you know the car is rocking and shaking — Guy Schmidt pops out of the trunk to find Butch Ward on top of his wife in the backseat!"

"No!"

"Yup!"

"Guy Schmidt says to Butch Ward, 'Do you want to marry her?' Butch says 'Hell no, I don't want to marry her!' And Guy tells him, 'Well, then get the hell off of her, she's *my* wife!' Guy Schmidt gets behind the wheel with his wife still naked in the back seat and drives off, leaving Butch Ward five miles from home with no clothes!"

"No!"

"Yup!"

Peanut howled, and Doc laughed. George slapped his knee, and my dad shook his head. Their favorite saying after each story was, "Somebody should write a book about this town!" And they laughed some more. ❧

Chapter 6

The Bad and The Good

THIRD GRADE BEGAN TO TAKE ITS TOLL on me socially. I became guarded and distrustful. I disconnected from the other kids in class. Sure, I was friendly and turned my "bad kid" antics off with them, but I didn't want to get too close. They often talked about school subjects, and I was afraid I'd say or do something that would prompt someone to say "you're dumb."

I stopped participating in class altogether. As I put in my time, there were painful, daily reminders that something was wrong with me. Surely there were other kids who were struggling, but I couldn't imagine their struggles were as serious as mine. All I could see were the successful, perfect students like the Kaufman triplets. They were bouncy, happy, enthusiastic girls — always dressed alike — and always with the right answer to every question. They seemed to do everything perfectly, and I was just the opposite. I couldn't do anything right, except, as I was finding out, be the "bad kid." Throughout third grade, I continued to perfect my craft.

Back in second grade, I'd begun wearing glasses to correct my distance vision and allow me to see the board better. By the third grade, those glasses became my ace in the hole. The convenience of breaking or losing my glasses became a solid excuse for my lack of participation.

"I just can't see anything," I'd tell Mrs. Clark.

Of course replacing my glasses became a new frustration for Mom. She'd proclaim after every new pair, "If you don't stop losing glasses, I'm going to wire those goddamned things to your head!" I always apologized, "Sorry Mom." I felt bad, mostly because I knew I would have to come up with another excuse for losing my glasses.

I guess Mrs. Clark and Miss Marybeth eventually theorized that maybe I was using my habitually lost glasses as an excuse for not participating in class. So, they sent me to the school nurse for an eye test. I failed it — purposely. Whatever letter Nurse Rhodes asked me to read on the chart, I'd just call out a different letter. If it was an "A," I said "C." It seemed like a good plan. Regardless, I was permanently moved to the front row right in front of the blackboard.

On days I was wearing my glasses in class, I had to get creative and pull something from my "bad boy" bag of tricks. I hated doing this. It was generally unpleasant, but the thought of the humiliation I would face otherwise made it a necessity. One day when handing out worksheets, Mrs. Clark handed me mine and, with a harsh whisper, said, "You will do this worksheet, or you will face the consequences."

She went back to her desk and sat with her head down, correcting papers or doing some other teacherly task. I had a sick feeling in the pit of my stomach. I knew I wasn't going to try to fill out any part of the worksheet for fear she would hold my paper up in front of the class and embarrass me. I also knew that, by doing nothing, I could provoke a standoff with her. It wasn't so bad when she called me up to her desk and quietly berated me. But if she were to berate me in front of the class for doing nothing, it would be embarrassing, and I would have to come up with something argumentative and disrespectful. I'd try to turn it around with something like, "I didn't want to take your stupid test," hopefully getting the class to laugh and Mrs. Clark to back off quickly.

On this particular day, I folded my worksheet into a paper airplane and gave it flight, landing it squarely on Mrs. Clark's desk, right under her nose. She looked directly at me, gritted her teeth, shook her head, and promptly sent me off to see Miss Marybeth, where I explained that the paper airplane was the work of Satan. The ever-pious Miss Marybeth was still buying it.

My decision to "quit school"— show up, put in the time, but not participate — was like being struck out at home plate. Strike one came with the laughter and humiliation of trying to read out loud in class for Mrs. Williams in the second grade. Strike two came when Mrs. Clark wrote my chicken scratch name on the blackboard morning after morning. Strike three came when the remedial reading teacher refused to work with me any further because of my "laziness."

There was some good news, though. My bad-kid plan was working. I had finally managed, using my newly developed poor behavior skills, to persuade Mrs. Clark to simply ignore me in class since the consequences of calling on me or asking me to participate were simply too disruptive to the rest of the class. I had a feeling that Mrs. Clark wouldn't want me around for a second year and would promote me to the next grade to be someone else's problem. I was right. I passed third grade.

School had started out being so much fun, and Mrs. Parsons had made me feel like a great success. After such an early positive experience, I would have never dreamed in a million years that I'd end up in this situation.

No one was happier to see the end of the school year and the beginning of summer break than I was. But just as summer was getting under way, an early season hurricane was forming in the Gulf of Mexico.

The Great Flood of 1972 remains the worst natural disaster ever to hit my home state of Pennsylvania.

Hurricane Agnes started her long journey some 2,000 miles away, near the Yucatán Peninsula of Mexico. When she hit the mainland way down south in Florida, she was only a category one hurricane, not much to worry about. That was our first mistake. As she moved up the East Coast, she was downgraded to a tropical depression — even less to worry about. That was our second mistake.

The big trouble came when Agnes stalled in the atmosphere over the Middle Atlantic states. Not expecting Agnes, the "perfect storm," to stall above us was our third, and deadly, mistake.

The skies opened up, and in a period of twenty-four hours, the rains of Agnes created a magnitude five-hundred-year flood. In other words — based upon scientific projections and weather history — a flood as intense as Agnes comes along only twice in a millennium.

Approximately 220,000 Pennsylvanians lost their homes. By some estimates, as many as five hundred people lost their lives, but an accurate death count still remains unknown.

Babbling brooks turned into killer rapids. Dry valleys became raging rivers. Homes, farms, and businesses were swept away in the blink of an eye. Luckily, our home was spared.

Dad managed to get me and Carl to Mifflintown, nine miles away on Route 35, so we could see for ourselves the Juniata River out of its banks at levels never before recorded. We stood safely up the hill from the river on Bridge Street along with hundreds of other people and watched in awe as billions of gallons of water, that looked more like chocolate milk, flowed over the platform of the river bridge. The big steel canopy of the bridge stuck up out the water and acted as a catch-all for debris floating south.

I watched a house trailer floating, almost as if in slow motion, toward the bridge. Onlookers huddled into a circle, held hands, and prayed no one was inside. With the power of the current behind it, it smashed into the bridge canopy with explosive force. Twisted metal, broken glass, and anyone inside quickly disappeared into the raging chocolate milk. Never before or since have I personally witnessed anything equal to the power that Mother Nature unleashed in the rains of Agnes.

The National Guard was deployed, and helicopters brought supplies. The waters receded, and the good people of Pennsylvania put on hip boots and waded into the muck and debris to salvage what they could.

We put lives back together where almost all was lost. We hung on together. We stood up beside each other. We dug graves and buried our dead.

Although our home and family were safe, the plant where my mother worked was destroyed. All employees lost their jobs.

I was only nine years old but knew someone had to get in touch with President Nixon and tell him about the flood in Pennsylvania. I just assumed he didn't know because he was surely very busy being the president and all — not to mention he was fighting with some guy named McGovern who was trying to wrestle his job away from him. I figured it was up to me to take action and let the president know how bad things were in the aftermath of the flood.

A nice girl from down the street acted as a secretary, and I dictated a letter to President Nixon. I started the letter Dear P.N. — P.N. for

President Nixon. I told him that we had experienced a terrible flood, many people died, and that my mother and her co-workers lost their jobs. I told him he had to come to see for himself, because words could not describe how bad the situation was. "There's a large farm field behind my house where you can land your helicopter. Pick me up, and I'll show you around."

The letter wasn't just an invitation to the president; it was a declaration that we needed him, and we needed him now. I took the letter to the McAlisterville Post Office with a stamp and an envelope. Dean, the always-friendly postmaster, addressed it for me and sent it off to the White House.

I began to watch the skies from the back porch of our house. I was sure P.N. would be landing soon. A week went past with no sign of the president's helicopter. And then one late summer afternoon, I was playing football in our backyard with the neighborhood kids. The wooden screen door on the back porch of our house screeched open and slammed against the banister with a ferocious slap.

Out popped my mother, screaming with utter shock and disbelief in her voice. "NELSON CHARLES LAUVER, GET IN HERE, AND GET IN HERE NOW! THE *WHITE HOUSE* IS ON THE PHONE!"

I ran up the back steps and into the kitchen. I was sweaty, grass-stained, and out of breath as I picked up the phone. I stuttered, "Hel… he…hello?"

A man with a distinctive and authoritative voice identified himself as "Brigadier General George A. Lincoln, calling from the Oval Office of the President. "I'm in charge of emergency preparedness, and President Nixon wanted me to call and review with you what we are doing to help the fine people of Pennsylvania."

As he spoke, I continued to stutter and agree with everything he said … yeah … uh-huh …. yup, yup, okay, yup, yup okay, okay. My heart raced with the notion of speaking to a man who said he was standing in the White House! I shook from head to toe and needed two hands to hold the receiver that I felt could slip from my sweaty palms at any moment.

General Lincoln wanted to know, "Nelson, did you see the news footage last week on television of the president touring flood-damaged Scranton?"

Even though I hadn't seen it, I replied, "yeah, ahaa, yes, yup …."

"Nelson, President Nixon wants you to have my direct phone number here in Washington in case you have any more concerns. Do you have a pen and paper?"

"Yeah, ahaa, yes, yup …."

I tried to scribble down the number as he rattled it off and got only part of it.

Then, we said our goodbyes. After hanging up, I was satisfied that I had done a fine job in delegating this assignment to P.N. and the General. Thanks to me, I thought, they were on top of the problem.

Mom hardly knew what to say. She dialed the phone for the oil company and handed me the receiver. "You'd better tell your father what just happened!"

I told Dad that Dean the postmaster helped me send a letter to Washington about the flood, and that I got a call back from the White House. Dad let out a big, proud laugh and said, "George Lincoln! Holy cow, I've seen him on the Today program!"

George the Banker, Peanut, and Doc agreed the next morning at breakfast that I was the most important person they knew. After all, I had a "phone number for Washington and the ear of the president of the United States."

The summer of 1972 wound down, and right after Labor Day, I started the fourth grade. For the first time, I had a different teacher for each subject.

I was very careful to avoid any situation that required my participation in class. I now solidly had the reputation of the "bad kid." If a teacher called on me I'd simply make an inappropriate remark toward her or some other kid in the class — whatever I could think of, I blurted out. Sometimes, if I couldn't think of anything, or just to mix things up a bit, I'd throw a book across the room.

I tried diligently to break the rules and get in trouble during recess, too. Punishment for playground infractions meant I would be forced to move my desk out into the hall during the next class. Being the "bad kid" was all I had.

I continued distancing myself from the other kids and became more of a loner. I just didn't think I had a lot in common with them and didn't have much to say. And since I was trying to keep a secret from everyone, it was just easier to stay on the periphery, observing.

Although I wasn't getting much out of school, outside of school, whether I knew it or not, I had set out on a course of self-education. I guess you could say I created my own alternative school.

My continued fascination and curiosity with the lives of villagers, neighbors, and customers on Dad's routes was becoming an all-consuming distraction. I followed the lives of locals and studied their histories like some people follow sports teams, players, and the trivia that surrounds it all.

I was fascinated by people and what prompted them to say and do the things they did. I wanted to understand their motivations. I gathered copious mental notes and tucked them away in my brain. Often, I lay awake at night connecting the dots in my head. Who was related to whom? Where did they come from? What made them decide to do the work they did? What tragedies had they survived? My list of questions and the need for answers went on and on. It wasn't hard to find the information I craved — it was a small town. All I had to do was observe and listen.

As I watched and studied the lives of hundreds of locals, I realized there was one man, Harold Kipp, who unwittingly acted as a central link to all of them. He was like the hub that secured the spokes of a wheel.

Kippy, as everyone called him, was the proprietor of Kipp's Market in McAlisterville.

Kippy's grocery store would seem old-fashioned by today's standards, but this small, two-aisle store was well organized and brimming with all the essentials for a busy, well-stocked, small-town kitchen.

Kipp's Market was a skinny building on the square beside Shirley's Restaurant. It was about twenty-five feet wide by one-hundred-feet long and didn't have automatic in and out doors. It had one door, and it was automatic only in the sense that the person going in held the door for the person coming out. In the front window was a spectacular green-and-red neon sign advertising "Aunt Nellie's Fine Foods Sold Here."

Kippy was a friendly, conservatively dressed man who took the grocery business seriously. Others had tried their hands in the grocery business in McAlisterville but soon floundered and fell by the wayside. Kippy's little grocery store hummed along with such efficiency that he could offer high-quality groceries at extremely fair prices. No one could compete with him.

Kippy was disciplined. He had a good head for numbers and managed his time well. He was up bright and early every morning and often worked late into the night. He developed a precise business model that worked for him and his customers.

Part of Kippy's model was his ingenious delivery system. Mothers sent their kids to Kipp's Market for "this or that." Kippy allowed the kid to "pick out a free candy bar or pack of gum as a reward for helping your mom." In doing so, Kippy ensured no kid would ever say "no" when asked to "go to the store for a gallon of milk, a loaf of bread, and get some eggs — don't drop 'em — and while you're at it, you might as well bring home a frozen pizza." Kippy had at least a hundred "delivery boys and girls" living in McAlisterville.

For as well disciplined and ingenious as Kippy was in the art of running a grocery store, he had one habit that defied all business logic. The empathetic Harold Kipp was very generous in extending credit to locals who had fallen on desperate times.

Families in our tiny village each seemed to take their turn at going through hard times. Fire, loss, tragedy, and disease were every bit as common in McAlisterville as in other small towns across America.

Almost every family in the area had a story about hard times that included the sentence, "If it wouldn't have been for Kippy, we would have starved."

Our family also had a personal story about hard times and the kindness of Harold Kipp.

Things didn't go quite as planned when Dad left his job as a railroader to go full time in the oil business. Cash flow became a problem, and things were so bad at one point that Dad went without income for nine months.

Even when it looked as if Dad wasn't going to make it in business, and his dreams were about to collapse, Kippy allowed my parents to continue buying groceries on credit. He told Mom and Dad that he had no doubt that he'd get paid when things turned around for our family. Mom, like countless other McAlisterville moms, still tells the story of how "we would have starved if not for Kippy."

I don't think Kippy ever realized how important he was to the citizens of McAlisterville, and if he did, he would never have admitted it. In many ways, Kippy was the glue that held our town together. More importantly, he was often the glue that held families together in hard times.

People such as Kippy — all the people about town for that matter — fascinated me, but nothing fascinated me more than my own family.

When I think back on my childhood, the central characters in our house were Mom, Dad, Carl, our dog Brindle, and me. My sister, Susan, being about a dozen years older than I, wasn't a big part of my young life. She married and moved out right after she graduated high school in 1969, so I have few memories of her at home.

Our house was chaotic, disorganized, and had no schedule or structure whatsoever. Dad worked long hours and Mom worked odd hours. Carl and I fought endlessly. Mom and Dad bickered constantly. Mom frantically hollered at Carl and me, "Settle down or I'll peel your little asses like a peach!" The telephone rang off the hook. People who wanted to place an order for oil or gas after business hours or on weekends knocked at the front door, making the dog bark incessantly. And the volume of the TV roared to compete with it all. The best way to describe our house is to say it was four walls and a roof, filled with madness.

The stress of our household was hard on everyone, but I think it affected Dad the most. Sometimes when he couldn't take it anymore, he said, "Come on. We're all going for a ride in the car!"

Often it was just around bedtime. Carl and I, wearing our pajamas, would crawl into the backseat with our pillows and a blanket.

I loved feeling the air blowing in from Dad's driver's-side window at night. Carl and I giggled as if we were getting away with something, riding in the car instead of going to bed.

"Roll up your window, Clair!" my mother barked. "That night air will catch the boys their death of the croup!"

A nighttime ride like this meant one of two things: We were either going to listen to the bullfrogs sing at the Cocalamus Dam or we were going across the Westfall Hill to Thompsontown to park along the railroad tracks and watch the big trains clickity-clack on past. Given the choice, I would have never been able to make up my mind between the two.

Going to the Cocalamus Dam took us past East Juniata High School. "That's where the big kids go to school! We'll go there some-day," Carl said with great excitement.

Dad pulled in near the dam, and we listened to the big bullfrogs sing. There were hundreds of them, all taking their turn. Dad named them each time they croaked.

"There goes my favorite, Satchmo Armstrong. I think that one is

Frank Sinatra…. Oh, Dean … Dean … where are you, Mr. Martin?" Mr. Martin answered, giving us all a big laugh.

On the driving nights that we didn't go to listen to the bullfrogs, we went to the tracks to watch the trains. Dad loved trains and knew their schedules like the back of his hand from the years he had worked on the Pennsylvania Railroad after he came home from the war.

From our house, it was seven miles or so over to the tracks in Thompsontown. We sat quietly in the car with the windows down and the motor off, waiting to see who could be the first to hear the big loco-motives chugging west on the main line of the Pennsylvania Railroad.

Carl and I jumped up and down in the backseat with anticipa-tion as soon as we heard the engineer throttling the mighty engine and blowing his whistle from about ten miles out. Soon enough, his light pierced the darkness. He was coming around the bend. Before long, he was blowing his whistle at us as he passed. We plugged our ears with our fingers and giggled with unbridled delight. Our joy was indescrib-able as the thundering vibrated our Ford.

We counted the cars — usually about one hundred. The caboose brought up the tail end. Dad flashed his headlights, and the man in the caboose flashed his lights back.

"Wow, Dad! Is the man in the caboose your friend?"

"Yup. He'll be all the way to Chicago by morning."

Carl and I always fell asleep on the way home, and Mom and Dad carried us up and tucked us into bed.

I loved those special moments — naming the bullfrogs and blinking the lights at the man in the caboose. But my favorite family time was when the electric power got knocked out. In the summertime, it was usually lightning from a big thunderstorm hitting a transformer. In the winter, it was most always an ice storm that brought the lines down.

Life came to a grinding halt when the electricity went off. We had candles on hand for just such an "emergency."

In the wintertime, we built a roaring fire in the fireplace to keep us warm. I asked Mom and Dad if this is what it was like in the olden days when they were kids.

"Yes," they replied, and the storytelling of how they grew up filled my mind with images of what life must have been like during the Great Depression.

Without the distraction of electricity and all the modern conveniences it powered, our house took on the qualities of a home. The usual bickering and arguing were replaced by kinder, hushed tones. The timbre of every voice became truer to the personality that directed it. In the candlelight and glow of the fire we had everything, in that we had nothing but each other. 🌿

Chapter 7

Grandpa

A S WINTER 1972 ARRIVED, the typical small-town excitement of the holiday season was in full swing, and things were starting to resemble normal again after the great flood.

I was well into the fourth grade, and things were going better, at least in the sense that I didn't have as much stress about school anymore. I had settled into a routine and accepted the fact that I wasn't like the other kids. The initial shock of being different had passed. I wasn't sure what made me different, I just knew I was — and there didn't seem to be anything I, or anyone else, could do about it. What I cared about most was making sure nobody, my parents included, thought of me as the "dumb kid."

Kippy had a model for running his grocery store. Dad had a model for running his business. It seemed like everyone had a plan. I had a plan too. My business model was simply the "bad kid" model, and I could switch it on and off at will.

Teachers seldom called on me anymore because they knew I would disrupt the class, leading me to feel like I had the school thing figured out. They hadn't flunked me yet, and I was pretty sure they would keep passing me from grade to grade.

Teachers often warned their classes, asking, "What will become of you if you don't study, do your homework, and get good grades? If you don't do well in school, don't expect to do well when you grow up and go out into the world."

It was a hard pill to swallow, but I had come to realize I'd never be a lawyer or a broadcaster. *How would I be able to make sense of legal mumbo-jumbo or anything in the complicated world of broadcasting if I can't even make sense of simple third and fourth grade stuff?*

I thought about quitting school for good but had done some asking around and learned I couldn't drop out until I was at least sixteen years old.

I was preoccupied with the thought: *What will become of me? I suppose I'll be in the oil business like Dad when I grow up. He doesn't have a high school diploma. Or maybe I'll be a farmer like Grandpa. He only went as far as the sixth grade.* Those realizations weren't particularly comforting; they were more like a consolation prize.

I started watching closely as Dad shifted gears in the big truck. I thought, *I'll be able to reach the pedals and drive the truck when my legs get longer. If I decide to become a farmer like Grandpa, I guess I'll have to learn to drive the tractor, but that surely wouldn't be any harder than driving the oil truck.*

I hadn't seen much of Grandpa lately. He never picked me up after school anymore. After having thirteen kids of his own and tons of grandchildren, he and Grandma must have been sick of kids. I was sure Miss Marybeth, being his niece, had told him I was possessed by the devil. Or maybe she had kept that nugget to herself, because Grandpa hadn't said anything to me. You would think, being a preacher and all, he would have tried to get the devil out of me — or at the very least, would have said something about it to my parents. I suppose Grandpa had his own problems to worry about. According to Dad, Grandpa was going to die soon.

Some time back, I had answered the phone at our house. It was Grandpa, and he wanted to talk to Dad. He asked Dad to come over to his house the next evening. He had something very important to talk to him about. Dad agreed to meet Grandpa at seven.

I was lying awake in bed that night when Dad came home from Grandpa's. He sat down with Mom in the kitchen and told her about the conversation they'd had. I could always hear whatever they talked about in the kitchen very clearly from my bedroom.

"Pop's ready to lay down and die," Dad told Mom. According to Dad, Grandpa started the conversation off with, "The time has come, I'm being called home to Heaven."

Dad said he argued with him and told him, "But Pop, you seem good to me!" To which he replied, "That's irrelevant. I'm ready, and I must go. I'm being called home, and there is nothing more to discuss regarding that fact."

Dad asked him, "Did you want me to come over here to tell me you're dying, Pop?"

"No," he said. "I called because I have a favor to ask of you."

Dad said, "Sure, Pop. Whatever you need."

Dad said Grandpa leaned into the conversation and quietly asked so that Grandma, who was working in the kitchen, wouldn't hear, "Clair, will you look after your mother when I'm gone?"

Dad told him, "Well, of course I will, Pop. That goes without saying."

"Good, good. That was my big worry. I'll put it out of my mind and think of it no more," he told Dad.

Over the next few weeks, Grandpa tied up loose ends. He wrote his own will in long hand on a simple piece of paper. He took it to Attorney John Welsh in Mifflintown with intentions of having it typed up and properly worded in legalese. Attorney Welsh read over it, handed it back across the desk, and told Grandpa that his will was so eloquently written that it would be a pity to have any lawyer hack at it. He suggested that Grandpa take it directly to the courthouse and record it as is, in his own handwriting, which he did.

Several weeks later, shortly after the holidays, Grandpa had a heart attack and died. He was seventy-six years old.

I got the word at school through Miss Marybeth, who informed me, "Nelson, your Grandpa has gone home to Heaven." I wasn't surprised after what I'd overheard from Mom and Dad's conversation in the kitchen.

As I walked home from school that afternoon, the world felt different, emptier than before.

I'll never forget this day, I promised myself. I felt that the best way to honor Grandpa was to never forget the time, day, and date that I had learned of his death: 10:35 a.m., Tuesday, January 16, 1973.

Mr. Stuck, the funeral director, did a nice job laying Grandpa out in his casket. The funeral home was just a few doors down from our stone house. It was customary to have loved ones in the ground three days after their death, but in Grandpa's case, a decision was made to wait four days instead. Three of Dad's sisters lived in the Midwest, two in Kansas, and one in Oklahoma. Waiting the extra day to bury Grandpa gave the families driving east more time to get to McAlisterville.

In the meantime, Dad went over to the funeral home several times a day and sat with Grandpa for fifteen minutes or so. He was having a hard time coming to terms with the fact his father was gone. He asked me to come along on one of his visits. It was the first time I'd seen Grandpa since he died.

"He looks good. Doesn't he, Nelson?"

"Yeah, he looks pretty good considering he's dead and everything."

Dad leaned down and gave Grandpa a little peck on the forehead. "Nelson, do you want to give Grandpa a goodbye kiss?"

"I didn't kiss him when he was alive, why would I kiss him now that he's dead?"

Dad chuckled. "I'm sure Grandpa, before he left us, would have just appreciated the thought that you would want to give him a goodbye kiss before they close the lid on him. After all, it's a Pennsylvania Dutch custom."

"Yeah, I know that's what everybody does, but I'm still not kissing a dead person."

Dad chuckled again and I smiled. It was sort of a funny moment, albeit a bit morbid.

The night before the funeral, at the family visitation, people stood in line to walk past the casket and pay their final respects.

I swear Grandpa's forehead was like the Blarney Stone. Everybody had to kiss it. Well, maybe not everybody, but a few dozen people anyhow.

It wasn't the first time I had seen people kiss dead loved ones, but it still didn't make sense to me. *Kissing the dead is creepy!* I thought.

And if the kissing wasn't bad enough, people brought their cameras, for God's sake!

There were plenty of photos to go around of Grandpa when he was alive. Why did people feel the need to take pictures of him laid out in his casket? It just seemed so weird! The thought of people having a picture of my dead Grandpa on Kodak Living-Color Film seemed very ironic.

The next morning at the funeral, Grandpa's church was filled to capacity with mourners. We were packed into the pews like sardines. I sat tight up against Dad and could feel his sides shake as he cried. I had never seen him cry before. I felt sympathy for Dad and my aunts and uncles, too, but most of the sympathy in my heart went out for my grandmother.

I didn't feel as if I was taking Grandpa's death as hard as everyone else. I clearly understood what death meant. I realized I would never see him again and, of course, I would miss him. But he had been very adamant that he had lived as long as he had wished to and was ready to go. I took him at his word that this was what he wanted. I understood why Dad cried. It was memories of his father — memories that turned bittersweet the moment Grandpa died — that made Dad break down.

I understood Grandpa had been a man on a mission. For years and years, he looked forward to the day he would reap the reward he believed was promised to him at death. I watched as he fervently preached, reassuring what he believed, to countless mourners, that the "Great Reward" was now a promise fulfilled to their dearly departed.

After a lifetime of preparation, Grandpa finally reached his goal — eternal salvation.

Several mourners gave testimony at the funeral to the humble greatness of the Rev. Harvey S. Lauver. One man said, "Harvey Lauver was as close to being the perfect man as there ever was." I leaned forward and looked hard to my left, past Dad, to see Mom's reaction to that statement. She sat in the pew stone-faced, but I knew what she was thinking. I was sure she was thinking back to the time Grandpa chided her for praising FDR for his greatness. If I knew my mother, she was thinking, *If FDR wasn't worthy of such praise, well then neither is anyone else, and that includes the Rev. Harvey S. Lauver.*

The funeral concluded at the graveside, and that was the last we saw of Grandpa.

It was hard to imagine Grandma without Grandpa. They were a team, joined at the hip, two peas in a pod. Grandpa drove the car. Grandma never had a driver's license. Grandpa paid the bills, wrote the checks, did the banking and grocery shopping.

After Grandpa died, my grandmother, with the exception of learning to drive, mastered all the things that had traditionally been Grandpa's duties. She was proud of herself. I was proud of her, too.

Grandma and Grandpa had met in the early part of the twentieth century. The Lauver farm was famous for the Christian Love Feast.

The faithful came from far and wide for the annual celebration. To refer to the gathering as a "feast" was an understatement. Plates were heaped high with ham, beef, and chicken. There was ample corn, tomatoes, greens, mashed potatoes, and beans. Pickled eggs with red beets and cabbage slaw were favorite sides. And, to top it all off, there was PIE! Pie of every kind was baked in a large, outdoor, wood-fired brick oven. The oven was so large it could accommodate ninety pies at a time!

A week ahead of the baking, a fire was built in the hearth of the oven. Wood was added constantly to fuel the fire and heat the bricks to the desired temperature. The red coals were then scooped out of the hearth, and the bricks held the heat for days.

Finally, on "baking day," the pies were slid into the baking chambers on long wooden paddles. The breeze through the valley carried the wonderful aroma of pie. Perhaps the Lauvers' magnificent outdoor, wood-fired, brick pie oven, reserved strictly for the Love Feast, was the only one of its kind and size anywhere in the world.

My grandmother, as a teenager along with her parents and siblings, boarded a train some hundred miles west in Altoona and made the annual pilgrimage to Juniata County for the Love Feast.

Grandpa was smitten with Grandma, and a long-distance court-ship via love letters and postcards ensued. But there was a problem. Grandpa's father didn't want Grandpa to marry Grandma. She had a harelip. It had been surgically corrected, stitched together, and was hardly noticeable, but Grandpa's father was concerned it was a genetic problem that would be passed down to offspring.

Grandpa was a young man in love, but at the same time he wanted to be obedient to his father, the Rev. Solomon "Hellfire and Brimstone" Lauver. Grandpa decided to pray on the matter. After careful consult with God, Grandpa announced to his family that he felt confident in asking for the hand of the girl he loved. He explained to his parents and others, "God has assured me, no children born of our marriage will suffer a harelip."

Harvey and Ruth Lauver were married in 1919. None of their thirteen children had a harelip. ❧

Chapter 8

Big Fish, Deep Water

OUR NEXT-DOOR NEIGHBOR, MR. YEISLEY, returned home every day from his job as a federal meat inspector and immediately found comfort in a stiff drink. When Dad returned home, sometimes late in the evening, he joined him for a belt of booze.

I don't know why for sure, perhaps it was Mr. Yeisley's commanding presence, but Dad was adamant that Carl and I refer to the Yeisleys as "Mr. and Mrs." We knew Doc as "Doc," Peanut as "Peanut," and George as "George," but Frank and Nancy were "Mr. and Mrs. Yeisley."

I also spent a lot of time hanging out with Mr. Yeisley. He was ten years older than my dad. His sons were grown and off living their lives. One was a very successful businessman down South, and the other had a classified job with the federal government. Mr. Yeisley treasured being a father more than anything else in the world, and with the absence of his own sons, I became somewhat of a surrogate son to him. He took an interest in me and went out of his way to make time for me.

Mr. Yeisley was a tall, strapping man. He was handsome and could have easily been mistaken for a captain of industry. He was well-groomed and carried himself with an air of sophistication. People who didn't know him well might have thought of him as aloof. Mr. Yeisley was anything but aloof. He was a private man who valued family and loyal friends above all else.

Mrs. Yeisley, on the other hand, was happy-go-lucky. Her appearance was typical of a Methodist lady in the 1970s. She was a tall woman of average build and spent one day per week in the beauty shop having her salt-and-pepper hair "set" in the style of the day. She wore golfing attire in the summer and bundled up like an Eskimo in the winter. Mrs. Yeisley sported the most up-to-date eyewear and enjoyed showing off her latest jewelry and makeup purchases from the local Avon lady.

The Yeisleys moved into the house next door a few years after we'd moved into the stone house. Mrs. Yeisley's first official act as a neighbor was asking to borrow my mother's Sears & Roebuck catalog, as she couldn't find hers anywhere among her boxed-up belongings. She didn't ask *if* Mom had a Sears & Roebuck catalog, she simply inquired if she could *borrow* her Sears & Roebuck catalog, assured that Mom had one. She was correct in her assumption. Mom did have one. Every household in America had a Sears & Roebuck catalog.

The Yeisleys were in their late forties when they moved to McAlisterville. They had come from a similar-sized town in the northern part of the state, where they had operated a small grocery store. In a mid-life re-evaluation, Mr. Yeisley saw the handwriting on the wall. Large supermarkets were springing up everywhere. He knew the day of the Mom-and-Pop corner grocery would soon fade into history. In his words, "I got out while the getting was good."

Mr. Yeisley accepted a job with the USDA as a meat inspector. It was that job that brought the Yeisleys to McAlisterville. Mrs. Yeisley, now a housewife, quickly ingratiated herself into the community. She played cards with the ladies of town, became an avid golfer, and attended church regularly. Mr. Yeisley threw himself into his work.

Mom and Mrs. Yeisley — Nancy — became fast friends. Mom tried to get eight hours of sleep after her shift. Regardless of when she finally got up and around, she placed her stainless-steel percolator in the kitchen window, directly across from Nancy's kitchen window. It was a signal for Nancy to come on over for a cup of coffee and to catch up on the latest gossip. Day after day, they spent hours together — coffee was the excuse, friendship was the reason.

The spring after Grandpa died, Mr. and Mrs. Yeisley invited us for a long weekend three-and-a-half hours upstate to their vacation cottage on Tingley Lake.

Mom, Dad, Carl, and I made the jaunt in Dad's latest car, a big, white Chrysler New Yorker. We arrived late in the afternoon on Friday. The weatherman was calling for sunshine and warm temps. I was traveling light. All I had was a fishing pole, a simple tackle box, and a brown paper sack with a change of clothes.

The Yeisleys had a fabulous supper waiting for us when we got there, and we spent the evening talking. There were no phones ringing, televisions blaring, radios crackling, or people knocking at the door. There was just talk and laughter in a cozy little white cottage on a lake.

I was up bright and early the next morning. I scrambled through the woods, thirty yards or so, down to the dock where Mr. Yeisley had promised I would catch fish.

I stood on the small, red plywood dock with my fishing line simply dropped in along the side. The water right off the dock was teeming with little fish.

Mr. Yeisley seemed to be the only one who cared that I was down at the water by myself.

At nine years old, I was an excellent swimmer. Unless some big Loch Ness-type monster were to come boiling up out of the water to eat me alive, I was relatively safe as far as my parents were concerned.

Mr. Yeisley brought me a sandwich and a drink at lunchtime so I could keep fishing. He had a box of Tiparillo cigars, skinny cigars with a plastic holder on the end.

"Now, look, I'll give you three of these cigars, but they're just to keep the bugs away. You can bite down on the plastic holder and let the cigar burn. If you draw the smoke in, you're going to get sick and that will be the end of the fishing."

Mr. Yeisley was always right about everything, and besides, fishing was a lot more fun than throwing up.

"Okay, I won't smoke them," I said.

Every hour or so, he hollered from the porch of the cottage, "What's the count, Nelson?" I'd holler back with the official tally. I'm sure Mr. Yeisley's hourly inquiry was really just a way of checking to see if I was okay.

I fished all day Saturday until dark, ate supper, and crawled in the bottom of the bunk beds that were reserved for my brother and me.

Sunday morning I was up before anyone else with no care at all about breakfast. I grabbed my fishing pole and sprinted for the dock. Mr. Yeisley was soon out of bed and kept a distant watchful eye on me. I had no idea what the rest of my family was doing with their time at Tingley Lake, nor did I care. I was a million miles away from school, and all I cared about was the thrill of catching fish. Just like the day before,

Mr. Yeisley brought me a sandwich for lunch and continued to give me a holler every hour or so as I hollered back with the official count.

Finally, as the sun was starting to sink below the tree line, Mr. Yeisley came down to the dock and stood for a minute or so, watching me fish. I could tell by the way he was standing there, with his hands in his pockets, whistling a tune, that I was about to be taught one of Mr. Yeisley's famous life lessons, or metaphors, as he liked to call them. I figured I should listen because these nuggets of wisdom were probably why his sons grew up to be so successful. Mom always said that Mr. Yeisley's one son had "a whole shit-pot full of money."

"Nelson, you've just been dropping your line over the edge of the dock and catching little fish," Mr. Yeisley said.

"I'm afraid if I cast too far, Mr. Yeisley, that some big fish out there in the deep water will break my line and get my hook and sinker."

"Well, Nelson, you have more hooks and sinkers, don't you?"

"I have at least ten of each," I replied.

"May I borrow your fishing pole?" he asked. The tall, powerful Mr. Yeisley cast my line halfway out across the lake, and just as I figured, the philosophy lesson began.

"Nelson, if you want to catch big fish, you have to cast your line into the deep water. Or, you can just fish off the side of the dock if you're satisfied with catching little fish for the rest of your life."

Mr. Yeisley's metaphor wasn't lost on me. I got exactly what he was saying.

Soon, my bobber disappeared below the water and the drag mechanism on my fishing reel spun with a big zin-n-n-n-ng sound.

Mr. Yeisley yelled for everyone at the cottage, "Come on down here to the dock! Nelson has hooked into a monster of a fish!" It took a good twenty minutes to reel it in, and everyone cheered my skills as a fisherman.

Mr. Yeisley gently removed the hook from the fish's mouth and put it back in the water. It quickly swam away.

It was getting dark and was time to go back up to the cottage. We were leaving in the morning after breakfast. School started again on Tuesday.

Why can't I stay at Tingley Lake for the rest of my life? I thought.

With the long weekend over, I was back at school. I continued to show up because I had no other choice, and as usual, I followed my model of the non-participating "bad kid."

The last month or so of fourth grade was rather uneventful and terribly boring. I fidgeted around in my seat and watched the clock, waiting for recess, lunch, and the end of the day.

Miss Marybeth informed me on the last day of fourth grade that I had passed and was headed to fifth grade in the fall.

I had six-and-a-half years to go until I could quit school. I could hardly wait.

Right after Labor Day that summer, I started the fifth grade. Miss Marybeth had just retired from teaching, and the new disciplinarian at the school was Mr. Jones — the only male teacher in the school.

"Jonesy," as we called him, was one of my teachers. He was a husky sports fanatic with wire-rimmed glasses and a moderate case of adult acne. He was a loner who lived down Route 35 with his parents, drove an old pickup truck, and seemed to have trouble finding a girlfriend. He was a somewhat friendly fellow who possessed all the attributes of your run-of-the-mill serial killer.

One day, Jonesy called me to the front of the class along with several other students. He instructed each of us, "Pick up a piece of chalk and write…." That was the last thing I heard him say. I could see his mouth moving with further instructions, but I had entered a state of terror and panic and couldn't hear his voice for my own that was screaming inside of me. *Oh Christ, I'm not going to write anything on the chalk board! It'll look like chicken-scratch, and all the kids will laugh at me!* I didn't pick up the chalk as instructed. Instead I just stood there at the board, said nothing, and started to sweat.

Upon realizing my blatant insubordination, Jonesy turned red with anger and came at me with outstretched arms and hands. He grabbed me by the neck and started to choke and shake me. He grabbed and shook kids all the time but never to this degree. I knew by the look on his face that he had lost it. I couldn't breathe; I was starting to see spots from lack of oxygen and knew I would soon pass out. I thought, *JESUS CHRIST HE'S GOING TO KILL ME!* Just as I felt the tension in my body release and my muscles go limp, he dropped me on the floor.

I gasped for breath and worked to orient myself while my heart furiously pumped blood to my brain and adrenalin to my muscles.

I gathered myself up off the floor and stumbled in the general direction of my seat. I found my desk and tried to calm down and get my mind around what had just occurred.

Mr. Jones continued with the lesson as if nothing had happened. I have no memory as to the reactions of the other students. I was too preoccupied with the trauma of the event to gauge their response.

As my faculties returned, my fear turned to anger. I sat in my chair thinking about getting even with Jonesy. *You no good bastard … I'll get you, I'll get you if it's the last thing I do on this earth.*

I lay in bed that night thinking about how close I'd come to dying in Jonesy's death grip. My anger turned back to fear.

Up until this point, being the "bad kid" had been unpleasant. It meant lying, pushing buttons, getting yelled at, and feeling like a jerk sometimes. It's one thing to get paddled, scolded, or have your desk put out in the hall. It's another to be violently choked to the verge of unconsciousness. The stakes had just gotten much higher. Being the "bad kid" had now become much more complicated and worrisome.

How can I protect myself against Jonesy? I thought about it all night. *What if he goes off on me again, doesn't let go, and I die?*

My dad didn't own any handguns. He had lots of rifles and shotguns, but they were too big to hide in a jacket or down my pants. I had a pocketknife, but it would take too long to get it out of my pocket and open it to defend myself.

Borrowing an idea from Mom's playbook, I settled on the idea of a long hat pin. I fastened it under my shirt on a seam where no one could see it. I made up my mind that if Jonesy ever came at me again to put a death grip on me, I'd pull out the hat pin, stick him with it wherever I could and then run like hell and hide inside the Presbyterian Church across the playground.

The next day at school, Mr. Jones was as nice as could be, but I wasn't about to let my guard down. I took the concealed hat pin with me to school every day for the rest of the year.

Recently, when I spoke to my mother about the incident with Jonesy, she told me that she and Dad knew he had choked me. She remembered seeing hand marks on my neck.

I don't recall telling my parents, as the last thing I wanted to do was let them know about any trouble I got into at school. For as much as I was frightened of Jonesy, it paled in comparison to the terror I felt with the threat of being sent to Carson Long as a result of my poor behavior at school.

I wonder if Dad might have found out through the grapevine why I had a bruised neck. Perhaps another student told their dad and that dad told my dad.

For the rest of the year, Mr. Jones didn't call on me again. And his nice-as-pie demeanor toward me made me suspicious that Dad went to see him for a man-to-man.

By today's standards, if a teacher choked a child, the police would be at the school in no time to place him in handcuffs. An incredulous Nancy Grace would be sticking an accusatory microphone in his face and asking, "Why'd you do it?" It would be a big deal. The local DA would bring charges, and the media would follow the trial. In the end, the teacher would make a deal and get some time in jail and lose his teaching credentials.

In 1960s and 1970s McAlisterville, probably like many other rural parts of the country, physical assaults by angry male teachers surely happened far more frequently than they do today. It was accepted by many in the community as a way of keeping order in the schoolhouse.

McAlisterville Elementary was nothing like East Juniata Junior/Senior High School when it came to severe punishments. Every kid who had an older brother or sister attending East Juniata had heard the stories of male teachers and administrators slamming kids against the wall, getting in their faces, and working them over. Occasionally, parents went to the school in protest but seldom had the wherewithal or resources to do anything about it. And forget about calling the state police in those days. Because Juniata County was so rural, it was one of the counties, if not the only county, in the state without a state police barracks. In order to get the state police involved in anything, you had the call one of the neighboring counties — and the desk officer would often tell you they didn't have jurisdiction in our county. Juniata County, as far as law enforcement was concerned, was a no-man's-land where people were left to settle their differences among themselves. 🌿

Chapter 9

A Time to Try Again

LATE SUMMER 1974: Having made it through the fifth grade without any more major trouble with Jonesy, I was now less than five years away from being able to drop out of school. I considered that I was just past the halfway point: six years of school behind me, five more to go. That thought gave me some comfort. The idea of finally being able to drop out at age sixteen felt liberating. At the same time, there was the nagging concern about what my future would hold. I kept telling myself, *Everything will be okay. I'll be able to make a go of it in Dad's oil business or as a farmer.* I just needed to do the rest of my "time" first.

The last few weeks of summer before the start of sixth grade would have been a glorious time if not for an indiscretion that got me grounded for two weeks.

It all started when eighty-four-year-old Mrs. Heintzelman stopped at Dad's oil company to buy five quarts of motor oil. Every 3,000 miles or ninety days, whichever came first, she changed her own oil. She said she wasn't about to pay anyone a "plug nickel" for anything she could do herself.

"Hello, Mrs. Heintzelman. You're looking lovely as always!" Dad said.

Mrs. Heintzelman batted her eyelashes and replied, "Oh, Clair Lauver, you devil! I know you say that to all the girls!"

Her face was wrinkled and weathered from years of working beside her late husband, Roscoe, on the farm. Her hair was wispy grey, and she wore a tattered flannel shirt with the sleeves rolled up past her elbows. She wasn't a bit bashful about smiling and displaying the only tooth she had left in her head.

"Now, let's see, Mrs. Heintzelman. You have a birthday coming up, and I believe you're turning thirty-seven this year, right?"

"Oh, Clair Lauver, you're nothing but a goddamn liar. You know full well I'm in my eighties!"

"You can't be in your eighties!"

"You're just buttering me up thinking you can hornswoggle me into paying full price for this motor oil!"

"Oh, absolutely not, Mrs. Heintzelman. You get the pretty girl discount of twenty percent."

"Twenty percent, my ass! That's still highway robbery! I want a thirty percent discount!"

Funny thing is that Dad would have given her the motor oil at any price, for free even, if she would have asked for it. Dad loved making an old lady's day and went out of his way to make Mrs. Heintzelman feel special. He got a kick out of it; it made him feel good. Besides, any eighty-four-year-old woman who changed her own motor oil should be celebrated as far as Clair Lauver was concerned.

"Okay then, a thirty percent discount it is. Now, Mrs. Heintzelman, don't you need an oil filter, too?"

"Well, hell yes, I need an oil filter! How much are you gonna rock me for that?"

"Filters are free today, Mrs. Heintzelman, with the purchase of five quarts of oil."

Mrs. Heintzelman smiled and paid her bill. "Hell's bells, Clair Lauver, you're a bigger goddamn bullshitter than my husband was."

Dad thanked her for the compliment and counted back her change.

I was on my way out the front door at the same time as Mrs. Heintzelman. Being a kid and not thinking, I darted out the door in front of her and carelessly allowed it to spring closed in her face.

Dad yelled for me to come back in and hold the door for Mrs. Heintzelman. Then he took me into his office, closed the door, and informed me I was grounded for two weeks. Dad was terribly disappointed in me.

"We're Lauver men, and we always hold the door for a lady, *especially* an old lady," he admonished me.

I knew he was right to ground me — I had it coming. *But, oh God, why does it have to be at the end of summer break? I want to go to the carnival!* It was a painful lesson, and one I never forgot.

I was paroled just in time for the start of the sixth grade.

Even though the sixth grade was still considered elementary school, my class was bused to East Juniata Junior/Senior High because McAlisterville Elementary was bursting at the seams and out of space for the sixth-graders.

A regular-sized classroom at the high school was originally designed to accommodate about thirty students. However, our sixth-grade class comprised fifty-five. To create two manageable groups of about twenty-some students, our single, cramped classroom was divided in half, right down the center, with a thick wooden accordion door.

On each side of the big wooden curtain was a teacher. The teachers divided up the subjects to be taught, and the sixth-graders rotated for lessons between the two.

On one side of the divider was the desk and classroom of the young, vivacious Mrs. Eyler. I knew from the very first second I met her that she was special. She had a genuine smile and bubbled with enthusiasm. Mrs. Eyler was a breath of fresh air. We had chemistry; she had chemistry with the whole class.

It wasn't enough to instruct her students; she wanted to know the details of our lives, in and out of school. She wanted to know what made us tick so she could better reach us.

Every morning when I walked into her class she made it a point to say hello to me. I liked that. I replied, "Good morning, Mrs. Eyler," and smiled as I took my seat.

I made up my mind that I was going to give up my "bad kid" persona and try with everything I had to please Mrs. Eyler.

On the other side of the divider was Miss Hood, who was starkly different from Mrs. Eyler in her attitude and teaching style. I guess the best way to describe her is to say that she was not Mrs. Eyler. Miss Hood was sour and always seemed to be in a bad mood. I couldn't figure out why she put in all those years at college only to take a job she seemingly hated. She was in a bad mood before she ever got to school in the morning — and it only got worse as the day went on.

Miss Hood and I did not share any chemistry. She took a disliking to me from the start, and the feelings were mutual.

Even though I'd decided to give it my all in Mrs. Eyler's class, I still got failing grades. Mrs. Eyler was a very verbal teacher, so I was able to retain information from classroom discussions. I participated and even raised my hand to answer questions, but when it came time to take a test or a quiz, I did poorly. And I never did homework, because I couldn't read and write well enough to understand the assignments.

One day, Mrs. Eyler pulled me aside and asked quietly, so the other students wouldn't hear, "Nelson, will you stay in from recess so we can talk?" She had just given a quiz that morning, and the paper I handed in, as usual, was filled with illegible chicken scratch.

"Of course I'll stay in if you need me to," I said.

Mrs. Eyler could have asked me to jump off a bridge and I would have said, "Sure, of course. I'd be glad to."

I sat in a chair beside her desk, and she gave me the same quiz again, this time orally. I got every answer correct.

She looked at me and said, "Nelson you're very, very smart. Why is it so hard to take tests and quizzes and do homework?"

"It's easy to talk and listen, but it's hard to read and write." I told her.

She sat at her desk looking puzzled. "You can go outside and play with the others now if you want."

It felt so good to hear Mrs. Eyler tell me that she thought I was smart. I was happy that at least one person thought so, but I tempered her comments about being smart with the fact that I only got the answers on the quiz correct by listening and talking. It seemed like the easy way out. And people always talked about the easy way out being a bad thing. To be able to read a book was hard work and struggle.

Try hard, work hard, study hard. Hard, hard, hard. Everything about school was supposed to be hard, or it wasn't real learning. Listening, remembering, and talking came easily for me, so that must be wrong, it all must be cheating, I thought.

But it was obvious that Mrs. Eyler could see my struggle and was trying to figure it out. No other teacher had ever given me an oral test.

Simply by giving me my quiz orally, Mrs. Eyler was a teacher years ahead of her time, working in a school district that was years behind the times and allocated little, if any, resources to help kids like me. She must have been as frustrated as I was. I don't think she had anyone to turn to for aid in helping me.

No matter how hard I tried, I wasn't making progress.

I rode the bus home after school every day and went straight to my room and locked the door. I dove onto my bed and took deep breaths in an attempt to calm down. I had always refused to let anyone see me cry, but in the privacy of my room the tears came easily. I just wanted to be like everyone else. Why did school have to be so hard? I continued to agonize over my future. I buried my face in my pillow to muffle the sounds of my sobbing.

While Mrs. Eyler and I had a good relationship in spite of my learning problems, Miss Hood from the other side of the wooden curtain had no time for my "laziness." She and I were going nowhere fast. I didn't like her, and she didn't like me.

By this time, I knew how the system worked. I was going to the seventh grade next year no matter how poor my marks were. The only reason I tried so hard in Mrs. Eyler's class was because I knew she cared about me. I cared about her too and didn't want her to think she was wasting her time on me.

I think Miss Hood must have been talking with Mrs. Eyler and learned of my success in taking an oral quiz.

Miss Hood announced one morning in front of the whole class, "Nelson Lauver, you will be staying in at recess to take an oral quiz." At least Mrs. Eyler had been discreet and kind enough to ask me quietly instead of embarrassing me in front of the class.

Miss Hood had been giving the class a talk on the native tribes of Mexico. Now she was keeping me in from recess to give me an oral quiz to see how much I was paying attention. I was doing well until she asked the question: "What did these native people use for building materials?" I wasn't sure. Miss Hood had gone on and on in her classroom discussion about how much gold one of these ancient tribes had. From her talk it seemed as if they had an endless supply of gold.

"I'm not sure, Miss Hood."

"Well, we talked about it in class and you were there, Nelson!"

"I just don't remember."

She threw the history textbook open. "Read this paragraph!"

I picked up the book and pretended I was reading. After about thirty seconds she loudly demanded, "What's the answer, Nelson?"

I hesitated. I knew in my gut that I was in a no-win situation.

She ripped the book from my hands and slammed it, spine down and open, on the desk. She pointed to a word.

"RIGHT THERE IT IS! SAY IT, NELSON!"

Looking back today, I assume the word was "adobe." But with my limited literacy skills, I had no idea what the word was.

I had to say something, so I said, "Gold?"

"I'VE HAD IT WITH YOU, NELSON LAUVER! YOU STAY HERE. I'LL BE RIGHT BACK!"

I sat there waiting. I was pretty sure she was making arrangements to either paddle me or have me paddled. When you're eleven years old waiting to be paddled feels like waiting on death row for the high executioner to come and lead you away to an unpleasant end.

She returned about five minutes later with a high school teacher. I wasn't in a position to argue with him. I was scared. He was large and looked as if he could break me in two. I was hoping Miss Hood would be swinging the paddle and not him. East Juniata High was a big school compared to McAlisterville Elementary, and I didn't know this man. I didn't know most of the teachers, especially since my class was cloistered in a single room.

The male teacher, as it turned out, was there as a witness — a policy sometimes adhered to when paddling students. "BEND OVER AND GRAB YOUR ANKLES!" Miss Hood said, with a tone that clearly reeked with satisfaction. She swung the paddle like she was a batter at home plate.

WHAM … WHAM … WHAM … WHAM … WHAM ….

She was winding up for wham number six when the witnessing teacher said, "That's enough!"

It's a good thing he was there, or I think Miss Hood would have swung all day.

I righted myself. My backside was on fire and my legs were rubbery, but I wasn't about to give her any satisfaction that pounding my ass with a piece of lumber had any effect on me. But it did have an effect on me. My dislike for her turned to pure hate. I hated her with everything I had.

Several weeks after the overzealous punishment, the worst possible thing that could happen did happen: Parent Teacher Night.

Mom, Dad, and I first arrived in Miss Hood's classroom, where she started off by lambasting me in front of my parents. She said the same thing that many other teachers had been saying for years now: "Nelson, you're lazy and refuse to apply yourself!"

I despised teachers who said that. It was as if they were saying I was a loser, and I knew I wasn't a loser. It made me angry, and I kept pushing that anger down deep where it added to the toxic stew boiling inside me.

Later, we met with Mrs. Eyler on the other side of the room. She tried to be positive and put the best spin that she could on my failing marks. I understood that she was trying to be kind. She told my parents that she believed I was very smart, but schoolwork did not come easily for me. I didn't expect her to lie, and I appreciated when she said she enjoyed having me as a student.

"Well, we've got to get to the bottom of this, once and for all," my father said at the end of the meeting, having concluded that I should undergo a complete physical and mental evaluation at the renowned Geisinger Medical Center in Danville, Pennsylvania.

I didn't want to go, but I had no choice. I was sure they were going to delve into my problems and officially conclude what everyone else professed to know. I was sure they would say that I was a dumb, lazy kid.

Doc Yoder set it all up, and when the day finally came, I was poked, prodded, stuck, gagged, pinched, palpated, peered into, peered at, peered on, and peered up. They took blood, and I had to pee in a cup. Electrodes were pasted to my head and chest to see if I had a brain and a heart. No orifice of my body was safe from the inquiring minds and digits of the experts at Geisinger.

After the physical evaluation, I sat down for an hour with a psychiatrist who asked many questions, took copious notes, and replied "Hmmm" and "I see" to all my responses.

By the end of that day, I had been exposed to the curiosity of the best minds the prestigious Geisinger Medical Center had to offer. The conclusion was that I was a healthy eleven-year-old boy who, based on school report cards, was well below average in intelligence and seriously lacking motivation.

Today, as I look back, I shake my head when I think that not once did any of the esteemed medical experts ask me to read or write anything. Not once did any of those towering intellectuals even consider exploring the possibility that I might have dyslexia.

I am sure my parents never gave serious thought to whether I could read or write. They weren't book readers; books just didn't play a big role in our home. My parents read the newspaper every day and leafed through magazines from time to time. I, myself, glanced through the paper looking at the pictures and trying to discern what I could out of the captions. I guess my family just assumed I was reading.

The Geisinger findings affirmed the horribly misguided assumption that schools of the time were made up of three student subsets: smart kids, average kids, and kids like me. This assumption was simply accepted as fact by many parents, teachers, and schools all over the country. Unfortunately, as good and decent as my parents were, they too could be included among the millions of parents who bought into the flawed thinking of the time — if for no other reason than just not knowing any better.

When Mom and Dad met to review my results with the psychiatrist at Geisinger, he explained to them that I needed "structure, discipline, and responsibility." He told them in the brief meeting that, if they failed to get a handle on my "laziness," I would surely grow up to be a "great disappointment" to them. He informed them that there wasn't much they could do about my "low intelligence." According to him, I was born with that problem.

"But as far as the laziness his teachers report, you are the only people with the power to change that," he informed them.

In the summer between sixth and seventh grade, Dad decided it was time to follow the doctor's prescription and put me to work.

Dad had recently purchased a gas station about thirty miles from home, in the village of Port Treverton. Port Mobil Gas & Repair sat smack dab, front-and-center on a major highway, U.S. 15. The gas station was always busy.

There were three gas pumps out front: regular, premium, and unleaded. The building had two bays for repairs and oil changes. The back room was where everything from fan belts to motor oil was stored. The most important room of all, the front office, was home to the cash register.

The cash register sat behind the candy counter and was the central nervous system of the gas station. An ice cream cooler was filled with Popsicles and half-gallon cartons of Hershey's ice cream. An upright cooler with a glass door was well-stocked with cold soda.

It wasn't like the gas station/convenience stores of today — it was far more basic. But it was a full-fledged gas station at a time in history when it was still free to put air in your tires.

The front office had floor-to-ceiling windows so the attendant could see the pumps.

When a car pulled up for gas, it ran over a black air hose that sent a blast of air to a bell that dinged, informing the attendant a patron was at the pumps.

Most gas tank fills were under the car's back license plate in those days. The license plate bracket had a hinge on it that swung down to reveal the gas cap.

I met people from all over the world at Port Mobil Gas & Repair, and I met the locals too. There was the two-dollar guy who always got two dollars when he pulled up to the pumps, and the five-dollar guy also. Most people either got ten dollars worth of gas or a fill-up. Old-timers didn't order by dollar amounts; they ordered by gallons.

Dad taught me how to use the cash register, state-of-the-art for its time but highly antiquated by today's standards. In spite of the fact that I was a terribly poor student, I was able to master the cash register in a matter of minutes.

A patron would pull up to the pumps, get a fill-up, a quart of oil, a 3 Musketeers candy bar, and a can of Coke. Then, click, click, click, click, click, DING! I could add it all up on the cash register like nobody's business. And unlike the cash registers of today, which tell you how much change to give back to the customer, with ours you had to do the math yourself. But that was okay, I could count back change like a seasoned bank teller. I was a money whiz!

Within two weeks of starting my new job, I could be left alone to run the gas station all by myself for a full shift. There could be as many as a dozen customers at a time, and I had no trouble handling them all.

My success at the gas station proved two things that I knew deep down in my heart. I wasn't dumb, and I wasn't lazy.

If Dad asked me once, he asked me a thousand times: "Nelson, why is this so easy and school so hard?"

"Because Dad," I answered. "It's different here. It's real, not make-believe like school. There's nobody accusing me of laziness. Learning has a taste, a feel, a smell. And besides, this is money numbers. We don't talk about money at school."

I guess my answer didn't make sense to him because he never stopped asking. Dad, of all people, should have understood the mystery of my success at the gas station because, although he didn't know it at the time, just like me, he was dyslexic too. 🌿

Chapter 10

A Brand New World

THE FIRST DAY OF SEVENTH GRADE was a brand new world for me. I was no longer an elementary student. I was now a member of the student body at East Juniata Junior/Senior High School, a.k.a. E.J. Even though I had been bused to the high school building for sixth grade, we'd spent that year confined to our room and we were never allowed to mix with the older high school kids.

As the buses pulled into E.J. on the first day of school, hundreds of country kids got off and filed into the auditorium. Some were wearing brand-new clothes purchased for them at Dank's Department Store for the new school year or from the shopping mall an hour away in Selinsgrove. Others obviously had on hand-me-downs that were ill-fitting and tattered. Some of the kids were still in their barn clothes — bib overalls and boots that they wore to milk the cows before coming to school.

After the seven-hundred-seat venue was filled to capacity, Principal Morgan took the stage. He was a big, tall man who was bald on top with a fringe of dark hair on the sides. His clothes fit him poorly, and he constantly fumbled with the waistband of his pants in an attempt to keep his wrinkled oxford shirt tucked in.

His voice was deep, booming, and voluminous. As he stood at the podium, he proudly pushed the gooseneck microphone out of his way, as if to say, *A man with my oratory skills needs no microphone.* He was correct. His authoritative voice thundered throughout the auditorium.

He was there to "start the school year off right" by laying down the law and placing the fear of God into us. It was a sobering talk about rules and consequences.

It was obvious that Principal Morgan was a devotee of Jerry Falwell. I couldn't help but notice that he emulated the televangelist. His gestures and facial expressions were almost like a *Saturday Night Live* parody of the TV preacher. The disingenuous smile that occasionally turned up Principal Morgan's lips when he spoke of unpleasant topics was the same smile made famous by the Rev. Falwell. Principal Morgan had Falwell down to a T. A dramatic cymbal crash punctuating each of Principal Morgan's edicts would have fit in well with the talk.

"If you are sent to my office by a teacher for discipline, you are GUILTY until proven innocent!"

"If you are sent to my office by a staff member for discipline, you are GUILTY until proven innocent!"

"If you are sent to my office by a bus driver for discipline, you are GUILTY until proven innocent!"

"East Juniata High School is not a democracy. It's a dictatorship!"

"If your parents don't want you to be physically disciplined, they will need to come to the school and sign a form to that effect."

"Once you graduate from this school, do not use me as a reference on a job application. My mother always told me that if you don't have anything good to say about someone, don't say anything at all. Chances are I may not have anything to say about you!"

The rules went on for an hour. But the one that got everybody's attention was the one Principal Morgan spent the most time talking about. Principal Morgan had a great disdain for hats. He was absolutely adamant that hats must be taken off before entering the building in the morning and put on only after exiting the building in the afternoon. I could clearly understand that it would be inappropriate to wear a hat during the school day or to a class. But jeez, what was the harm in wearing your hat, gloves, and coat to your hall locker in the morning and then taking them off where you could properly hang them up? Or getting yourself bundled up at your locker at the end of the day so as to be well-braced against the harsh Pennsylvania winter when you stepped outside?

Principal Morgan went on to inform us, "The only individuals permitted to wear a hat in this school building are police officers or members of the military who are carrying a firearm." He reasoned that police and military personnel were exempt from his hat rule, because having a hat in their hand could interfere with their ability to reach for their gun. *Why would soldiers or police officers need to come to our school with guns?*

Truth be told, I was scared of Principal Morgan even before I got to school that first morning for his speech. Susan, my sister, often told the story of a frightening episode that she witnessed when she was a student at E.J. One day Susan was walking from one class to another in a crowded hall. A boy she knew well and was good friends with came up beside her and put his arm around her shoulder. Principal Morgan saw this from some yards away and came running. He grabbed the young man and slammed him against the wall with such force that he knocked him unconscious. Susan said that when the boy hit the wall his eyes rolled back in his head, and he slowly slid down the wall. My sister said she was terrified and kept walking.

In a rural area like Juniata County, many would have felt that Principal Morgan's actions were appropriate. After all, the boy had broken the rules. It struck terror into my heart every time I heard my sister tell that story, because I knew that someday I would have to deal with Principal Morgan.

My brother, who was two grades ahead of me, also told stories about Principal Morgan's legendary temper. He said he once saw him grab a boy by his long hair and shake his head frantically before throwing him to the hallway floor. I heard stories from other kids also, not just about Principal Morgan, but about certain male teachers beating up kids.

I heard stories of bloody noses, fat lips, and corporal punishment that crossed the line. One angry male teacher was purported to have hit a boy countless times with a metal-edged yard stick, leaving numerous deep lacerations in his skin.

But perhaps the punishment that frightened me most of all was "the vault."

I had first-hand testimony regarding the vault from a "prisoner" who had been inside. When I was a sixth-grader being bused to E.J., Mrs. Eyler arranged for me to be given the responsibility of raising the American flag in the morning and lowering it at the end of the school day for an entire week. After taking the flag down, I folded it and returned it to the school office. One afternoon while returning the flag, I saw an older boy sitting in a chair by the secretary's desk. The school secretary had stepped out for a moment, and he was in the office by himself. He didn't look well and his eyes were swollen, as if he were sick or had been sleeping.

I asked, "Are you all right? Do you need a drink of water or something?"

"No, thank you," he said.

"Are you feeling okay?" I asked.

"Yeah, I'm okay. I just got out of the vault a few minutes ago, and I'm trying to adjust my eyes to the light," he said pointing over to a big black metal door with a silver combination dial on it.

"Oh my God, you were in there?"

"Yeah, it's *in-school suspension*," he replied.

"How long were you in there?"

"Today was my second day. I have to go back in tomorrow morning — tomorrow's my last day."

"Oh my God. What did you do?"

"Principal Morgan caught me smoking in the restroom."

The vault was a real fireproof/burglarproof vault similar to a bank vault but not as sophisticated. It was basically a small seven-by-ten-foot masonry room with a heavy-duty steel door and an impressive combination locking mechanism.

The vault's original purpose was to store cafeteria money, locker keys, and anything else that was worthy of such security. But now, in the hands of Principal Morgan, it was the perfect jail cell to incarcerate incorrigible youth. Now that I was a seventh-grader, I felt terrified of what could happen to me at East Juniata.

After Principal Morgan's talk on that first day of school, we seventh-graders were called out, assembled in a group, and taken to our homerooms. The homeroom teacher called the roll, and when students raised their hands he gave them each a sheet of paper with their class schedule on it.

"Nelson Lauver?"

I raised my hand. He walked over and handed me my schedule.

"Are you Clair Lauver's boy?"

"Yes, Sir."

"Your father is a fine gentleman — I trust you will be a fine gentleman here at E.J."

"Yes, Sir."

I looked at the strange schedule. I knew I was supposed to use this piece of paper to navigate the halls and figure out where my classes were, but I couldn't make sense of it. It was a small sheet of paper with tiny blue mimeographed type and some sort of chart filled with an overwhelming amount of information. I'm sure it made perfect sense to everyone else, but to me it was an intimidating jumble of letters and numbers. Just looking at it gave me a feeling of dread because I knew that if I had to use this thing to figure out where I was supposed to be, I was in trouble from the get-go.

The bell rang for first period, and I found myself in a sea of students who were hurriedly trying to get to their classes in the allotted three minutes. Soon the hallways emptied again, and there I was, alone, without direction. I stared at my schedule as if looking at it long enough would somehow help me to make sense of it. I walked up one hall as if by magic I would be lured into the proper room. When I wasn't, I walked down another hall, and then another, and another.

After twenty minutes or so, a voice thundered from a corridor away, "Young man! What are you doing in the hallway?"

It was Principal Morgan! I froze and said nothing. As he walked toward me, I started to tremble. *Oh my God, he's going to put me in the vault,* I thought.

As he got closer, he said, "Where are you supposed to be?" I didn't say a word and handed him the paper.

"Lauver, Nelson," he read aloud. "Are you Clair Lauver's boy?"

"Yes, Sir."

He smiled. "You are supposed to be in Room 107. Follow me."

I couldn't believe it. Principal Morgan was friendly! *He seems like a nice enough man. I think he likes me — he even smiled at me.* I took an empty seat in Room 107, and twenty minutes later the bell rang for second period. Again, I found myself in the hustle and bustle of the halls. It seemed everyone else knew where they were going, but I didn't have a clue. I was afraid to ask for assistance and felt completely helpless. Soon enough, I was alone again. The only noise in the halls was the echoing of my heels as I walked aimlessly, searching to stay out of trouble.

Principal Morgan came to my rescue for a second time.

"Mr. Lauver, are you lost again?"

I nodded my head yes, and he led me to the proper room. After finding me wandering the halls for the third time that day, Principal Morgan took me to the office and sat me in a chair. His demeanor had turned from friendly to frustrated.

He left me alone for a time, and I worried. *He's looking for a paddle to hit me a good one. Either that, or he's going to stick me in the vault for wandering the halls when I should have been in class.*

Principal Morgan returned fifteen minutes later with a sheet of paper. "Do you know Curtis Seiber from McAlisterville?" he asked.

In a small, frightened voice I said, "Yes, I know him."

"Good, he has the exact same schedule you do. Follow him everywhere he goes."

Principal Morgan took me to where I belonged, and for the next two weeks, until I got my schedule committed to memory, I never let Curtis Seiber out of my sight.

A month or so of seventh grade had now passed by, and with the exception of wandering lost in the halls the first day of school, I had been flying under Principal Morgan's radar.

I have less than four years to go until I turn sixteen and can drop out. How am I going to avoid Principal Morgan for four years? He was a nice enough guy when he helped me on the first day of school, but I for sure don't want to get on his bad side after all the stories I've heard about his temper.

Then it happened. I knew in my heart of hearts it was just a matter of time. My English teacher, Mrs. Rogers, was having students read aloud in class one afternoon. My heart raced with anxious anticipation that she might call on me to read. My mouth was dry, my face felt hot, and I could feel myself trembling.

"Nelson, would you like to read the next two paragraphs for the class?" she asked pleasantly.

I took a deep breath and said, "No, Ma'am."

"What?"

"No, Ma'am, I wouldn't like to read the next two paragraphs."

"Why not?"

"Because I don't want to."

"You will read the next two paragraphs, or you will go to Principal Morgan's office."

I said nothing and looked down at my desk as a feeling of dread overtook me. Mrs. Rogers hurriedly scribbled a note and ripped it from a pad of paper.

"Have it your way, Mr. Lauver," she said as she handed me the note to give to Principal Morgan.

It was the last period of the day. Instead of going to Principal Morgan's office, I hid in a stall in the boy's restroom. When the bell rang, I went to my locker and hurried out of the school to my waiting bus.

I tossed and turned all night in bed, wondering if I could really get away with it. *Wouldn't Mrs. Rogers have talked to Principal Morgan after school to find out what my punishment was for not participating in class? But, then again, it's a big school. People are busy, maybe it never came up.*

The next morning during homeroom, an announcement came over the loudspeaker: "Nelson Lauver, please report to the principal's office. Nelson Lauver, please report to the principal's office."

Principal Morgan paddled me for not coming to the office as instructed by Mrs. Rogers. He didn't lose his temper like everyone said he would. He wasn't an out-of-control maniac who wanted to throw me against the wall and knock me unconscious. He just gave me one very light swat with a paddle. It was really no big deal, and the swat didn't even hurt. But I think it made everyone involved feel better, especially me, because the worrying about what might happen was over.

Two weeks later, when Mrs. Rogers asked me to read aloud in class again, I wasn't frightened at all to tell her "no." After all, I'd much rather get a light swat from Principal Morgan than be embarrassed in front of my classmates for my inability to read. Mrs. Rogers again sent me to see Principal Morgan with a note, and this time I went without hesitation.

I presented myself in the school's office along with my reason for being there. Principal Morgan's secretary led me back to his private office where he gestured for me to have a seat across the desk from him. He matter-of-factly examined the note from the teacher and inquired, "Why did you tell Mrs. Rogers 'no' when she asked you to read aloud?"

"Because, Sir, I didn't want to participate."

I was hoping he would just give me my swat, and we could get this over with. My answer agitated him, and he said, "Well, Mr. Lauver, there are many things in this life we don't want to do. For instance, I don't want to pay income tax, but every year I pay more and more. What should I do about that? Tell President Ford that I don't want to participate?"

This was something with which I actually thought I could help. Taxes were a constant topic of conversation between Dad and his friends, and since starting my job at the gas station I had become fascinated with everything having to do with business, money, and finance.

I was completely sincere as I said, "Maybe you should try using the same tax guy my dad uses from Harrisburg. Dad says his guy is tops."

Of course, it soon became obvious that Principal Morgan's question was more rhetorical in nature, and he had no interest in soliciting the advice of a twelve-year-old kid who had recently discovered a love for commerce and capitalism while learning to make change at his family's gas station. I don't think he saw my answer as the least bit helpful.

I finally got to see Principal Morgan's temper, and it was everything it had been billed as.

His face turned red, the veins on his bald head popped out, and he became enraged. Everything on his desk rattled as he slammed his fist down. He rose up out of his chair and bent forward, leaning across his desk on the palms of his hands. I could smell his hot, stale coffee breath, and saliva flew from his mouth as he screamed in my face.

I had never seen anyone that angry in my whole life! His eyes looked as if they were going to pop from his head. His voice went from a deep authoritative tone to the hoarse oxygen-starved rant of a madman. It was plain to see that he had no control over what was happening to him. The strain on his body, mostly his face and head, was obviously painful, but he was unable to turn it off.

I was scared out of my wits and couldn't move. I sat there, just gripping the arms of the chair. I was so frightened I couldn't process his words, and I don't think it mattered because I don't think he knew what he was saying anyway.

The rant lasted about a minute, which is a long time to have someone screaming in your face. Afterward, Principal Morgan lowered himself to his chair. We both sat there dumbfounded for a moment. He calmed his breathing and finally said, "You're a punk. Go back to class!"

I moved quickly for the door, turned the handle, and got out of there. The secretary in the outer office sat at her desk busily working as if nothing had happened.

On my brisk walk up the hall I thought, *I don't think Principal Morgan swore at me.* I tried to remember what he said. Nothing stood out except the thought that he hadn't sworn at me. I was amazed that anyone could be that angry and not use any swear words. *He did call me a punk ... that's a bad sign.*

My hopes of flying under Principal Morgan's radar had been dashed.

Two weeks later, a kid threw a chalkboard eraser at me in morning homeroom. The teacher walked in the door just as I was throwing it back. I was sent to the principal's office with a note. This time, there wasn't any talk or screaming or swats with the paddle. Principal Morgan didn't even examine the note. He simply used the collar of my shirt to direct me toward the vault. He pulled the vault door open and pushed me in as he grunted, "Three days in-school suspension, punk."

He didn't shut the vault door the whole way closed. There was a crack letting light in. I was instinctively drawn to sit at a small chair and desk that was obviously placed there for prisoners. I could see the silhouette of a small safe and a filing cabinet. On the ceiling of the vault there appeared to be a light. I stood up and started running my hands over the concrete walls looking for a switch. Twenty minutes of searching yielded no results. I concluded the light must be controlled from outside the vault.

Soon I heard a grumbling Principal Morgan coming again. As he walked past the vault on his way to somewhere else, he pushed the door shut and I heard the mechanism latch. I was entombed.

Trapped in the dark, alone with my thoughts, I couldn't distinguish between five minutes or two hours — time ceased to exist inside the walls of the vault.

Why did I throw that eraser back at that stupid kid?

I wonder if there is enough air in here to keep me from suffocating.

What if they forget about me in here and go home at the end of the day? I'll die for sure.

What if I have to go to the bathroom?

Who the hell ever heard of a twelve-year-old giving tax advice to the principal of his school?

If they bring me lunch, they have to open the door, and that will mean more air.

I wonder who knows I'm in here.

My first-grade teacher, Mrs. Parsons, is married to the guidance counselor. He will surely go home and tell her I'm in the vault, and she will know she wasted her time on me.

I am not going to cry.

I am NOT going to cry.

I wonder if my parents really love me, or if they see me as more trouble than I'm worth.

What a stupid idea thinking I could someday become a lawyer or a broadcaster.

What if I get tired from lack of oxygen, fall asleep, and die?

I wonder if this is what it's like to be buried underground when you're dead.

I've heard of people being buried alive; this must be what it feels like.

I can't hear anything through the vault door. I think they went home.

What if I pound on the door and Principal Morgan hears me and knocks me unconscious?

What if I die in here and Principal Morgan has to dispose of my body, and my family never sees me again?

I wonder if there are roaches in here.

I wonder if there are rats or mice in here.

I wonder if this room has ever been cleaned. It smells like someone threw up in here.

I'm getting sleepy. I wonder if that means I'm going to die.

What if I die here, and I wake up in Hell? Surely, I will go to Hell if I die. There's no way I could get into Heaven with as much trouble as I've been in.

I fell into a deep sleep and had no idea if it was minutes or hours. I woke up in a panic in the pitch black, not knowing where I was. I started crying as I desperately crawled on my knees fumbling around feeling for something familiar. Finally, I felt the desk and remembered where I was. I told myself, *Stop crying, Nelson, stop crying. You'll use up more oxygen if you cry.* I found the chair and sat down, calmed myself, and then measured my breathing, taking only half-breaths to preserve the oxygen. Sometime later, I heard the mechanism move and the door slowly opened.

It was Alice, the study hall monitor. "Go get your lunch, Nelson, bring it back and eat it in the vice principal's office. When you're finished, take your tray and plates back to the cafeteria, use the restroom, and then back in you go."

As I was coming back for the second half of the day in the vault, I confirmed that the light switch was on the outside and that I had no control over it. If only I could have turned the light on, the vault wouldn't feel like being in a grave.

After lunch, the door stayed open a crack the rest of the day.

I could hear the bell ring, denoting the end and the beginning of another class period. I could hear the secretary answer the phone and see visitors to the office through the crack of the vault door. I spent the next two school days in the vault with the door open a crack. Thank God for that crack of light.

After serving my three days, I returned to classes. My stint in the vault gave me a lot of time to think, and I came to a rather solemn conclusion. If I had to choose between the vault or being laughed at by my classmates for not being able to read, as horrible as it was, I would take the vault any day.

As seventh grade continued, there were more confrontations and more days in the vault. I refused to participate, and teachers didn't like my attitude.

I tried my best to dodge confrontations, but if a teacher got angry with me, I became defiant and often belligerent if I had to. I locked eyes with the teacher and refused to back down. *I can't back down, I can't give in, I can't do what they ask of me, or they will figure out that I can barely read and write and think I'm dumb. What are they going to do to me? I've been in the vault, and I've been swatted with the paddle. What's the worst thing that can happen beyond that?*

The problem was that this belligerent kid wasn't at all who I wanted to be — it was who I felt I had to be to get to the end of the day.

I spent my nights tossing and turning in bed, frustrated and angry about my situation. *I'm stuck with no way out for now. What will happen tomorrow? Who will confront me for not participating in class, and what will I have to say or do? I hate being considered a joke and worthless by the teachers.*

I took it one day at a time by doing whatever it took to get through the day... to get through the year ... dreaming of the moment I'd be old enough to drop out.

History had taught me that the school district would continue to promote me to the next grade, despite my failing marks. I fought my way through the seventh grade and in the fall of 1976, I started the eighth grade.

Just three years left to go until I can drop out. 🖎

Chapter 11

Click, Click, Buzz

IT WAS DURING THE LAST TEN MINUTES of Mrs. Collins' eighth-grade English class. It started as usual with a click-click, followed by a slight buzzing noise. It was the telltale sign that the intercom system had just been turned on. The intercom could be set up to broadcast to the entire school or simply to communicate with one classroom. Every kid in the class got a look of impending doom on their face each time they heard click, click, buzz. Often click, click, buzz was followed by a request from Principal Morgan's secretary to have so-and-so report to the office. You prayed to God when you heard click, click, buzz that you wouldn't be the next student summoned to witness the veins popping out of Principal Morgan's angry bald head.

"Mrs. Collins," the secretary said.

"Yes, Wilma?"

"Mrs. Collins, is Nelson Lauver in your class?"

"Yes, he is, Wilma."

"Good, will you please have him come to the office?"

The class sighed a collective sigh of relief that it was me and not any of them being called to the office. I often sighed in relief when it wasn't me, so I could hardly blame them for being honest and showing their relief.

My heart pounded and my mind raced as I walked down the hall toward what I was sure would be an unpleasant punishment. I thought to myself, *I'm not sure what I did this time, but God, I hope I don't get the vault again.* So far, since starting junior high, I had been placed in the vault approximately a dozen days. Before my junior high career ended, I would find myself a prisoner of the vault many more times.

But, on this occasion, I didn't even have to see Principal Morgan. I just had a message delivered to me by the secretary. She informed me that I would be participating in a remedial math class three days a week — Monday, Wednesday, and Friday — right after lunch. "The class will be held in the vocational agriculture building," she told me.

The Vo-Ag building was an odd place for a math class, I thought. The building had a classroom as well as a shop filled with industrial tools. It was detached from the rest of the school because of the noise made by the saws, drills, and lathes.

There were six or seven students who showed up for the first day of remedial math. The Vo-Ag students went to the second lunch period, and their classroom became ours for the better part of an hour. I was embarrassed to be there because it meant someone had figured out that I was a "dumb kid."

The teacher, Mr. Brookfield, a special education teacher, towered above our class of eighth-graders. He had thick dark hair and stood over six feet tall with a muscular, athletic build. He seemed like a giant.

"Welcome to Remedial Math," he said with a smile, while holding a pointer in one hand and gently tapping it into the palm of his other hand.

"Let me tell you how this class works. I'm here to teach you your times tables. I'm going to stand up here and point my trusty pointer at one of you and call out a times table. It is your job to give me the correct answer."

Directing his gaze at my classmate Paul, Mr. Brookfield said, "For instance, if I point to you and ask, Paul, what is six times six? It would be of great benefit for you to know, without hesitation, that the answer is thirty-six. Do you know what will happen to you, Paul, if you don't know the answer?"

Paul shook his head and said, "No."

Mr. Brookfield used his pointer to point to "Mr. Helper."

"Mr. Helper" was a large wooden paddle perched atop the chalk tray. This wasn't just any paddle, this was a monster paddle made of walnut, with a double-fisted handle. It was approximately one inch thick and well over two feet long. Being constructed of walnut, it was extremely heavy and was much more like a flat club than a paddle. Whoever designed it — perhaps Mr. Brookfield himself — put a great deal of sinister thought into it.

Mr. Brookfield continued, "Paul, if you hesitate in answering or answer incorrectly, you will come to the front of the room and nicely ask Mr. Helper to wake up from his nap and help you remember that six times six is thirty-six."

I now realized why the Vo-Ag building had been chosen as the venue for this class. The crack of the paddle and the screams of students, just like the sound of industrial tools, were out of earshot of the rest of the school.

With the instructions clearly stated, the class started immediately, with me as the first contestant.

Mr. Brookfield stared down his pointer at me, and my skin instantly went clammy, my breathing stopped, and my stomach did a somersault.

"Nelson Lauver, what is seven times nine?"

"Fif... six...sixty, sixty-one...."

"Well, Nelson, I guess you will have the privilege of being the first student to wake up Mr. Helper."

I sat in my chair not knowing what to do.

"Come on, Nelson. Wake him up."

Mr. Brookfield grabbed me by my shirt with a sadistic smile on his face and hauled me out of my chair. He pushed me toward Mr. Helper.

"Ask him to wake up, Nelson!"

"Wake up, Mr. Helper," I said, in a low, frightened voice.

"I don't think he can hear you, Nelson. Say it louder!"

"WAKE UP, MR. HELPER!"

"That a boy. Tell Mr. Helper why you need him to wake up."

I didn't know what to say. I stood in front of Mr. Helper, trembling but determined not to cry in front of my classmates. "Nelson, ask Mr. Helper to wake up and help you remember that seven times nine is sixty-three."

"Mr. Helper, will you wake up and help me remember that seven times nine is sixty-three?"

"OH MY, LOOK AT THAT. MR. HELPER IS AWAKE!" Mr. Brookfield said.

I looked back at my fellow students sitting in the chairs with a look of panic in their eyes.

Mr. Brookfield was a Vietnam veteran and a self-ordained minister in his spare time. He grabbed the paddle with one hand and a piece of chalk with the other. He sat down on a chair and wet the chalk on the end of his tongue.

He then used the chalk to draw a smiley face on the paddle at just about the place he expected it to connect with my backside — all the while whistling, "*Jesus loves the little children of the world.*"

"Bend over and grab your ankles!" Mr. Brookfield instructed me. With my hands on my ankles there was nothing to brace against. "If you get knocked off your feet, you get double the swats."

I clenched my teeth, closed my eyes tight, took a deep breath, and swore to myself, *I will not cry.*

WHACK!

With each whack I exhaled and prepared for the next by again clenching my teeth, closing my eyes tight, and taking a deep breath.

WHACK!

WHACK!

WHACK!

WHACK!

"Stand up, and go back to your seat!"

I righted myself and tried to regain my composure. I couldn't have cried even if I wanted to. I was shaky and light-headed and thought I might pass out.

Paul Yeater was next to go through the ordeal of waking up Mr. Helper. Mr. Brookfield went through the same routine with the delighted sadistic smile, the chalk, and the whistling.

WHACK!

WHACK!

WHACK!

WHACK!

WHACK!

Paul didn't fall over, nor did he cry. It felt like a small victory.

"Nelson Lauver, seven times four?"

"Thirty twent seven eight…"

I woke up Mr. Helper again and got more smiley faces on my blue jeans.

WHACK!

WHACK!

WHACK!

WHACK!

WHACK!

It was frighteningly clear that Mr. Brookfield was enjoying himself.

Remedial math with Mr. Brookfield was different than any other class I'd ever been in. There was no arguing, there was no running away, there was no pleading your case, there was no defying him. He owned us. During our fifty-five-minute class, we were his prisoners.

On the days I had to attend remedial math, I woke up with a sick feeling in my stomach. In getting ready those mornings, I'd put on two pairs of pants, hoping it would give me some protection from Mr. Helper. But when I think about it, getting hit wasn't the worst part of remedial math. It was the anxious walk to the class that was the most nerve-wracking experience of all. The anticipation made me shake from head to toe.

There was never any teaching done in Mr. Brookfield's remedial math class, and there were no tools to help us learn our times tables. You simply had to try to remember a correct answer that may have been given by another student and try to fire it back quickly. My time learning to do math in my head at the gas station was of no help to me here. When Mr. Brookfield turned his pointer in my direction and fired off a question, I was so panic-stricken, even when I knew the correct answer, I couldn't get it to come out of my mouth. And there was certainly not enough time to try and calculate in my head.

As a young boy, I felt what was happening in this class was wrong and unjust. But in my head, I rationalized that he was an adult, and kids who didn't do what adults want them to do get smacked around — it was a fact of life for many in Juniata County.

Today as an adult, I look back and realize that Mr. Brookfield's class had nothing to do with teaching students — rather it was simply about satisfying a sadistic need.

One of my punishments from Principal Morgan for my continual non-participation in school was carrying all my textbooks all day long and then taking them home with me on the bus in the afternoon. The customary protocol for students at E.J. was to carry the necessary textbooks for the morning classes and to make a locker stop at lunchtime and exchange your books for the ones needed in the afternoon. Carrying all my books was a pain, but compared to the other possible punishments I could receive, it wasn't so bad.

I frequently had such an unmanageable armful of books that I ended up dropping them, especially when trying to put them down on a school desk or pick them up from a desk to go to my next class.

One day, upon entering remedial math class and trying to take my seat, I dropped my books along with an oak cutting board I had made for my mother in woodshop. The calamity startled Mr. Brookfield, who had been in deep concentration, working at his desk with his head down. He looked up and quickly discerned I was the one responsible for the ruckus.

A sick smile formed on his face, and his eyes lit up as if he had just won a prize. He stared at me for several seconds and then jumped from his seat as if he were on fire. I was trying to show I was making an effort to pick up my books. He grabbed me with one hand and the handle of my mom's new cutting board with the other. He shoved me, face first into the wall. Dazed, I slid down to the floor. He recollected me and threw me on top of a waist-high bookshelf, my head hitting the wall a second time. As my head connected with the wall, I heard a loud pop in my neck that made my ears ring. For a split second, I thought my neck was broken, but fortunately, it wasn't.

Using the cutting board I had made for Mom, he hit me over and over, relentlessly and with all his might. As quickly as the attack started, it was over, and I stumbled back to my seat for the beginning of class — during which, as usual, I found myself connecting with Mr. Helper at least a half dozen times. After class, I threw the cutting board in the trash in the boys' restroom. I couldn't give it to my mother after what had happened.

A few weeks later, at the end of another school day, I stopped off at the boys' restroom, removed my extra pair of "remedial math" pants, and placed them in my gym bag. I went to my locker and worked to organize myself to catch the bus back to McAlisterville. Besides all my books that I was required to carry home, I had my bag full of gym clothes, a towel, and my extra pair of pants. I was also trying to incorporate into the load a salad bowl for mom that I had just gotten an A+ on in woodshop. It was the only A+ I ever got in my whole life. It was the dead of January and I had a heavy coat, gloves, and a hat. I was well aware of Principal Morgan's no-hats-in-the-building rule, but I felt confident I could slip out of the building this one time to my waiting bus. With my hands and arms full, it would seem sensible to anyone that I would put my hat on in preparation for the frigid outdoors.

I should have known better.

I was still feeling shaky all over, and my legs were rubbery from a bunch of double-fisted whacks from Mr. Helper in remedial math class just two hours earlier. I was foolish for taking this chance now.

As luck would have it, I was confronted by two teachers, Mr. Fairfax and Mr. Clay.

Mr. Fairfax pulled my hat off, balled it up in his fist, and gave me a slug to the jaw. The two men pushed me into an empty classroom. I tried to fight back because I knew what was coming. There was no time to think or voice an opinion about what was happening. My primitive fight or flight mechanism had been triggered, and there was nowhere to run. My books went everywhere. The wooden salad bowl I made Mom lay broken on the floor.

Principal Morgan quickly appeared as if to confirm they had me and then disappeared from sight. A third teacher, Mr. Summers, stood outside the classroom door, acting as a lookout while the assault continued.

Mr. Fairfax took a large double-fisted paddle from his closet and handed it to Mr. Clay. It was every bit as menacing as the paddle in remedial math class. Mr. Fairfax stood off to the side of me clamping my hands with his to the chalk tray and using his knee in my groin to push my backside out for targeting while Mr. Clay swung the paddle.

At one point, I broke free and tried to turn and run. As I did, the edge of the paddle hit me below the elbow and an agonizing pain shot up my arm and traveled through my shoulders.

The abuse of this episode, combined with what I had received just hours earlier in the remedial math class, proved to be too much. I don't know if I blacked out or simply went into shock. At the very least, events became fuzzy, and I ended up alone in a heap on the classroom floor.

As I tried to get up and gather my thoughts, another man appeared. I immediately sensed that he wasn't there to harm me, but to help.

Mr. Leister was an elderly man who had retired from the school as a janitor. He had a gaunt, ashen face with silvery-grey hair and wore a flannel shirt and blue workpants. He was probably at the school to pick up his wife, who was the head cook in the cafeteria.

The halls had cleared and the buses had left. I was several miles from McAlisterville.

He knelt down beside me. "Don't try to get up," he said. He gently pushed on my rib cage. "Does that hurt?"

"No," I answered. "My arm. I think my arm is broken."

Mr. Leister helped me get my coat off.

"Those sons of bitches, they've been pulling shit like this for years," he said.

He looked at my arm. "I don't think it's broken, but it looks like you took a hell of a whack. Okay, I want you to try to stand up." I stood up and got light-headed and lowered myself back to the floor.

"My car is out here at the side of the building," Mr. Leister said. He picked me up, looked to see if the hallway was clear, then carried me down the hall and out the side door to his car, leaving my books and broken salad bowl strewn across the classroom floor. I wasn't a very big kid at thirteen, but where the old man got the strength to cradle me as he hurried for a side exit amazes me to this day. He put me in the backseat, got in the front, and we were off.

"You're Clair Lauver's boy, Nelson, aren't you?"

"Yes, Sir."

"We've got to go talk to your dad about this."

"No, Sir. Please, please, don't tell my dad. He'll be so disappointed that I'm getting in this much trouble at school. Please, Sir, please...."

"I've known your daddy since he got home from the war. He's one of the best men I've ever met. If I tell him what happened, he'll go to the school and eat every last one of those sons of bitches for breakfast, including Principal Morgan himself!"

"No, Sir, please, you've got to promise me. My mom and dad can't know about this. Please, Sir, I beg you. If they know how much trouble I'm getting into, they might send me away to military school. They've already talked about it. Please, Sir!"

He stopped in front of the stone house.

"Do you think you're okay to walk now?"

"Yes, Sir. You're not going to tell my dad and mom, are you, Sir?"

"No, I won't, but I think you should, Nelson."

That evening, sure that my arm was broken, I put a washcloth between my teeth to bite down on, in anticipation of the pain, and pushed my forearm with even pressure against a door jamb in my bedroom, hoping to set the bone if it was broken. I wrapped it with an Ace bandage and hid it under a long-sleeved shirt.

The next morning, my books were neatly stacked and waiting for me in my locked locker. There was no sign of the broken salad bowl. Weeks went by, and my sore arm was a constant reminder of what a mistake it was to put my hat on in the hall.

About a month after the incident, I saw Mr. Clay, the one who swung the paddle, walking into school wearing his hat. That's when I realized I was simply scheduled for a beating to keep me in line. I would have been beaten that afternoon regardless of whether I'd had a hat on my head.

The eighth grade continued to be filled with unpleasant punishments, and then one day there was a great victory.

Click, Click, buzz.

"Mr. Wright?"

"Yes, Wilma?"

"Is Nelson Lauver in your class?"

"Yes, he is, Wilma."

"Please send him to the office."

With a smile that said, *Ha, looks like you've got one coming*! Mr. Wright motioned for me to go. "Okay, Wilma. He's on his way."

"Thank you, Mr. Wright."

As I made the now-familiar walk to the office, I wondered, *What have I done this time? Some teacher probably reported me for not participating in class. Will I get the vault, or a beating, or am I going to have to smell Mr. Morgan's coffee breath as he screams in my face?* To my relief it was none of those things. When I entered the office, Wilma simply informed me of a change to my class schedule.

"You will no longer be going to remedial math Monday, Wednesday, and Friday. Instead, you are to report to study hall," she told me.

The remedial math class had been canceled, and it wasn't until many years later that I learned why. My classmate, Paul, had been taking a bath one night before bed. When his mother saw the bruises on him, she demanded to know what had happened, and Paul reluctantly explained to her how the remedial math class worked.

The very next morning, Paul's infuriated grandfather was in Principal Morgan's office expressing his outrage and demanding an end to the brutality.

Amazingly, of the half dozen or so kids who were subjected to Mr. Brookfield's sadism, not one of us, to my knowledge, willingly told our parents about it. What might be even more difficult to comprehend is the notion that, perhaps, some of the kids did tell their parents, and no one took action to stop it — except for Paul's grandfather.

For me, the choice had been easy. Either put up with people like Principal Morgan and bad guys like Brookfield, Summers, Clay, and Fairfax, or face the possibility of being sent to Carson Long Military Institute to be "whipped into shape" or, even worse, revealed as the "dumb kid."

Of course, not all teachers at East Juniata were abusive. It was just this small handful of bad guys. There were good teachers who had entered the field of education long ago and were every bit as passionate about shaping young lives now as they had been then.

Mike Wilson, the boys' gym coach, was one of those teachers. He was well-meaning when he invited me into his office for a good old-fashioned "talking to."

Mr. Wilson's office was dark and mysterious. Prior to this trip inside, I had only ever viewed it from the outside, looking in the windows of the small room from the cavernous banks of benches and lockers in the steamy, musty boys' locker room.

I had never seen Mr. Wilson come or go from his office. From outward appearances, it seemed more like a storage closet than anything else.

"Mr. Lauver, I'd like to see you in my office."

Oh shit, what did I do now? What could he possibly want out of me? I show up for gym class twice a week, put on my old smelly gym shorts and a T-shirt, run around outside chasing or kicking a ball in sub-freezing temperatures, come back in, take off my gym clothes, and enter the never-ending humiliation of the boys' gang shower, where everybody tries to sneak a peek at everybody else's ding-dong to see if they measure up or not. I dry off, get dressed, and go on my way, happy that ding-dong check is over, at least 'til Thursday, anyway. What more could he ask of me?

Mr. Wilson leaned back against the wall with the sole of his right shoe propped up on the wall behind him. I stood against the opposite wall, six feet away, thinking, *Wow, his office is smaller than the vault. No wonder he doesn't spend any time in here.* The dim light of the dank locker room barely peeked through the narrow blinds. I wasn't afraid. I didn't have to worry about Mike Wilson putting a beating on me or slapping me around. He didn't belong to that group of bad guys who, out of a need for control, sadistic pleasure, or an outlet for rage, regularly behaved in ways that would, by today's standards, get them arrested.

Mr. Wilson was even-tempered. He quickly pointed out that my performance in gym class wasn't a problem, but what was a problem was the overall negative reputation I had earned throughout the faculty.

I hardly knew what to tell him. It was obvious that this good, old-fashioned talking to had a fatherly quality to it. I rather appreciated that he took the time, but to confide in him in any way would have given up the secrets of my inner struggle and, ultimately, my fear of being thought of as the "dumb kid."

I suppose Mike Wilson was the appointed mouthpiece for a collective of reasonable and caring teachers who had seen, or had knowledge of, the heavy-handed punishments I had endured at the hands of lesser educators.

I stood quietly in his office, putting on an air of apathy to ensure that he realized what a "pain in the ass" I thought he and every other teacher at East Juniata was. I felt rather ashamed of myself for not showing my heart and thanking him for taking the time out to try to help me. But, at the same time, I was very pleased with his unwitting confirmation of my label as the "bad kid" and not the "dumb kid."

The eighth grade was coming to a close in another month or so. It had been the most unpleasant year of school yet, but at least remedial math was over and done with, and my arm was pretty much back to normal.

The one really bright spot of school, especially now that spring was in the air, was being able to put on a light jacket, go outside, talk to a few schoolmates, and enjoy the sunshine for twenty minutes or so after lunch.

Greg was a seventh-grader with a big, toothy grin. He'd just finished his lunch and was coming outside, delighted with the fact that he had some big news.

"Hey, Nelson. Did you hear the latest?"

"No, what's the latest, Greg?"

"Doc Yoder dropped over dead!"

I turned and walked away without saying anything, but in my head I was thinking, *It's not true, it can't be true. That stupid kid doesn't know what he's talking about. I just saw Doc yesterday at Shirley's Restaurant. He was trying to find homes for a bunch of kittens that had been born under his porch. How could he be dead?*

I walked down the hall toward the payphone in the lobby of the school. The bell rang, and I should have been going to my class, but I had to know if Doc was dead or alive.

I dropped a dime in the phone and started to roll the rotary dial, plugging my index finger into the holes and twisting the numbers for home.

My mom answered the phone. It wasn't a good sign that she sounded wide awake, considering she had worked eleven to seven the night before.

"Some stupid kid at school said Doc dropped over dead. Is that true?" I asked her.

"Yes, I'm afraid so, Nelson. The bookkeeper called me from the oil company and said your dad has himself locked in his office. She said he won't come out, and he won't talk to anyone."

"I'll try calling him," I told her. I knew Dad's office was his sanctuary.

I hung up the phone, dug through my pocket for another dime, then dialed J.V. Oil Company. The bookkeeper answered the phone.

"Hi, this is Nelson, may I talk to Dad?"

"Oh, Nelson, he's not in a good way. You heard about Doc, right?"

"Yes," I said.

"I'll go over and knock on his door and tell him you're on the phone, and we'll see if he picks up."

"Thanks."

Dad picked up and tried to say hello as if nothing were wrong.

"Hey, Dad, I heard about Doc."

"Yep, it's hard to imagine the world without old Doc," he said as if he weren't affected. I knew better. I could tell he was hurting. There was a long pause of about thirty seconds, and neither of us said anything. A teacher came along and gave me the evil eye for being on the phone. I covered the mouthpiece and quietly said "Family emergency." That seemed to settle the matter quickly. Kids weren't allowed to use the payphone unless it was an emergency.

Finally, Dad was the first one to talk again. Trying to add a little levity, he said, "There will never be another Doc, will there, Sir Nellie Boy?"

"No, Dad, there sure won't."

We both chuckled as we remembered the day I'd gotten even with Doc for calling me Sir Nellie Boy.

"I'll come down and sign you out of school for the rest of the day. I have a couple of barrels of motor oil to deliver to a sawmill over the mountain," he said. "I could use the help anyway."

Dad didn't say much as he drove across the mountain to the sawmill. The radio was off, and the only sound in the truck was Dad, tapping the band of his Masonic ring on the gear shift.

Tap, tap, tap … tap, tap, tap … tap, tap, tap….

I suppose the tapping of the ring was an unconscious thing as Dad reflected back all those years ago to when he first stuck out his big, callused hand and welcomed the young doctor to McAlisterville. They were not only great pals, they had become business partners. When Dad had the idea to start the oil company, Doc stepped right up and said, "I want to be an investor."

It had been a great investment for Doc, and the sale of his oil company stock would help to keep his family comfortable after his passing.

Dad and I arrived at the sawmill and got out of the truck. I knew the drill: put two old rimless tires on the ground, one on top of the other as a cushion, and roll each fifty-five-gallon barrel of oil off the back of the tailgate; let it bounce down onto the tires, then roll it on its side to wherever the saw-miller wanted it.

Dad took the bill into the office while I moved the oil barrels. He came back out, and we were off again.

Tap, tap, tap ... tap, tap, tap ... tap, tap, tap....

Dad told me the story of how some months earlier he'd ridden along with Doc to the Milton S. Hershey Medical Center. While Doc was inside the hospital, Dad said he'd waited in the car and pulled the brim of his Mobil Oil cap down low, reclining the passenger seat to take a nap. About an hour later, Doc returned to the car with a fistful of rolled-up papers. He was laughing as he opened his doctor bag and threw the papers inside.

"Well, I finally did it!" Doc told Dad.

"Finally did what?" my dad inquired as he straightened the brim of his hat and returned to consciousness.

"If and when I die, my body will be donated to medical science."

My dad sank back into his seat and pulled the brim of his hat down over his face again, as he chuckled, "I don't know what the hell anybody would want with that ugly damn body."

"You go to hell, oil man, you're just jealous!"

The two laughed, and up the road for home they went in Doc's big old doctor's car.

The morning Doc died, he had been riding an exercise bike in his basement while his wife was making breakfast. She called for him, but he didn't come. She ran down the steps and saw him lying on the floor. She called Dad at the oil company, and he rushed right up to Doc's place.

Dad said Doc must have known it was coming because he got off his bike, lay down on the floor, and crossed his hands on his chest. Dad said it was obvious that Doc wanted to be found in a dignified manner. Doc had been aware that he had an inoperable aneurysm and that it was only a matter of time.

The coroner came and officially pronounced Doc dead. Within a few hours after his death, a specialized refrigerated truck showed up to take his body away, and it was the last anyone in McAlisterville ever saw of Doc, one of the most wonderful characters that ever lived in our little town. There was a memorial service a few days later at the Presbyterian Church, but there was no body to view.

I had been to lots of funerals, but this was only my second memorial service. With the exception of bad car or farming accidents, every time somebody died there'd been a viewing the night before so that everyone could see the body for themselves. I guess that's what funerals are for, to give people the chance to see the person's body and help them accept the fact that the person is gone.

There must be something to it because, even to this day, I have a hard time accepting that Doc is gone. I think it's because I never got to say goodbye to him.

Medical science was finished with Doc's body about a year after they received it. What was left was cremated and sent back to McAlisterville. His ashes were buried in the Presbyterian Cemetery.

Doc was the first of the McAlisterville Rat Pack to go, and after that, each time Dad, Peanut, and George got together, it just wasn't quite the same.

"I can't believe the bastard ran out on us like that," Peanut once said. Dad and George laughed and agreed, "The old son of a bitch should have stuck around to fight with us some more." There was one less rat in the pack.

Even my mom, who called him "that goddamn pill pusher," shed a tear at his memorial service. Of course, she cared for him. Everybody liked Doc. 🌿

Chapter 12

A Fork in the Sidewalk

I STARTED THE NINTH GRADE in the fall of 1977. I was fourteen years old.

During the previous summer, I'd worked long hours at the gas station and started my first business too: *Nelson Lauver Scrap Metal*.

Using money I saved from working at the gas station, I bought dead car batteries from auto salvage yards, repair shops, gas stations, and farmers. I resold them for the scrap value of the lead inside the batteries. Business was good. I had found a lucrative outlet for my batteries that none of the other small scrap dealers in the area seemed to know about. The scrappers I competed with were only paying fifty cents per battery. Then they had to load them up into a big truck and haul them forty miles to a smelting plant. After all that work, the smelting plant only paid them about $1.25 per battery.

I worked directly with The Mobil Oil Company's TBA (tires, batteries, accessories) Division. They paid a premium, three dollars for scrap batteries, and even sent their own tractor-trailers to pick them up.

I bought junk batteries for a dollar and made a two-dollar profit on each one. When the word got around that Clair Lauver's boy was paying a dollar for batteries, people showed up from near and far with their pickup trucks filled with them.

I quickly ran into a cash-flow problem. The big Mobil truck came only every three months or so to pick up my batteries. In the meantime, I had to bankroll the cost of inventory. The need for working capital quickly ate up my savings. I needed more cash to run my operation. I asked Dad for some help.

"You're a businessman now, Nelson. Do what businessmen do when they need operating capital."

"What's that, Dad?"

"Put on a suit, shine your shoes, and go to the bank for a loan!"

Dad's pal George had retired from the bank. There was a new guy who I didn't know very well, but he must have liked the shine on my shoes because he gave me $2,500 on my word that I'd pay it back — that, plus my dad's co-signature. I tripled the money in three months and paid the banker back his share with interest.

One of my first business purchases was a calculator. I had learned, if not mastered, basic math at the gas station and could calculate dollars and cents in my head as well as most people. But on paper, the dyslexia made it very difficult. With my trusty calculator, there was no math problem I couldn't solve.

I became consumed with everything having to do with commerce. I had long conversations with Dad about how business works. I watched everything I could on TV that had anything to do with finance and the markets and asked questions of every local businessperson I could find. I used my profits from the scrap metal business to buy stock in Pennsylvania Power and Light, IBM, and General Motors. It was easy to make those purchases. I just walked into the bank and told the banker what stock and how many shares I wanted, and they took care of the paperwork. All I needed to do was sign my chicken-scratch signature.

Even though I was having wonderful success as a small business-man, I was still floundering in school.

Punishments for my lack of participation in class continued to be severe at times. There were more days in the vault and more assaults from the thug teachers. There were still frequent corporal punishments that sometimes crossed the line and became heavy-handed. All in all, for as ugly as it could be at times, it was still better to endure the punishments than be embarrassed by the fact that I could barely read and write.

Later that school year in the spring of 1978, as ninth grade was winding down, I was struck by the fact that there was a great change in the manner in which my teachers were dealing with me.

I haven't been paddled in at least a month. No teacher has grabbed me by my shirt and slammed me into a locker lately. I haven't been sent to the office to have Principal Morgan scream in my face or throw me in the vault. This is wonderful!

I welcomed whatever caused this truce, but it was obvious that the gang of thug teachers who had made my life hell were not happy with whatever brought this change about. Not one bit happy. I couldn't help but notice the nasty looks I was now getting from them as I passed in the hallway — but that's where it ended, just nasty looks. There were no threats or abuse.

As the school year drew to a close, it was becoming more and more evident that I was simply being ignored — and that was just fine by me. I reciprocated by being on my best behavior. I still didn't participate in class for fear of being embarrassed by my deficiencies, but I certainly appreciated the ceasefire and wasn't about to push any hot buttons.

The sands had shifted. A new day had dawned for me. Other kids were still getting smacked around and paddled. There had not been an overall change in discipline techniques at the school except where I was concerned. It was obvious that something had happened causing a change in the way I was being dealt with ... and I'm quite certain that "something" had to be a "someone." Sometimes, I like to imagine all the people who may have come to my rescue. I weigh the possibilities in my mind.

Maybe it was my dad. Maybe he found out what was happening at the school and took action to stop it.

Maybe Mr. Leister, the janitor who came to my rescue when I was beaten for the hat incident, finally talked to my dad about what happened. And maybe Dad went to the school and had a "Come to Jesus" with Principal Morgan. If he did, he would have kept it to himself so that I didn't think I had a license to misbehave. That's just how Dad was.

Maybe my dad had nothing to do with it at all. Maybe it was Mr. Leister himself, whose sense of justice compelled him to finally take a stand on my behalf.

Sometimes, I like to imagine it was our next-door neighbor, Mr. Yeisley, who might have heard through the grapevine what had been happening to me at E.J. Mr. Yeisley had been like a second father to me. He was the one who told me not to be afraid of going after the big fish in the deep water.

I can just imagine Mr. Yeisley pulling up in front of the school in his elegant Chrysler, walking inside, and diplomatically presenting himself and the reason for his visit. Mr. Yeisley's commanding presence itself would have been sufficient in getting his message across. There would have been no need for shouting or yelling. Mr. Yeisley would have simply made his declaration, and people would have adhered to it.

Some days, I enjoy wondering if it might have been my first-grade teacher, Mrs. Parsons, who remembered the kid who gave her the thumbs-up every day after school. Maybe she went to the high school madder than a hornet, vowing consequences if they failed to cease their criminal behavior.

As my mind considers all the far-out possibilities, I quickly dismiss my mom as my rescuer. If she had been the one to confront Principal Morgan, there would have been a crime scene with yellow police tape, forensic investigators collecting samples of evidence, and a chalk outline of Principal Morgan on his office floor.

Maybe it could have been my sixth-grade teacher, Mrs. Eyler, who told me I was "very smart." Maybe she stood up to the powers that be and said, "no more!"

What if Mr. Wilson, the boys' gym coach, or some other reasonable teacher in the school finally expressed their indignation when it came to my heavy-handed punishments? But what about the other kids who were still being manhandled?

It might be completely possible that the "someone" who came to my rescue was a person I didn't even know. Maybe it was the parent of another student or a community leader. Maybe it was a local plumber or carpenter who, in their younger life, lived my story. Maybe it was the school secretary who had finally seen enough.

I'll probably never know for sure who it was, but someone was responsible for sending the message: "enough is enough." The one thing I know for sure is that the "someone" found the guts to stand up and be my voice when I didn't have a voice of my own.

I've always been inspired by the thought of everyday ordinary people finding the courage to stand up and challenge injustice. I suppose I like imagining all these different people stepping up in my defense because

I like to believe that's how the world works. When someone needs help fighting injustice, others will rally to the cause. I still believe what I believed all those years ago when I ordered my Superman suit from Santa for Christmas in 1967 — Truth, Justice, and the American Way.

At the end of that school year, it came as no surprise to me that I would be a sophomore in the fall.

On the first day of tenth grade, after the usual tired assembly where Principal Morgan laid down the law — strongly admonishing students that "hats in the hallways will result in swift punishment" — I went to my homeroom and waited for the bell to signal the beginning of the end.

I gave a quiet sigh of relief as I thought, *This will be my last year. I'll be sixteen next June, and I'll finally be able to drop out.*

Dropping out of school wasn't my first choice, but it seemed like my only choice. Dropping out was plan B. Of course, plan A had been a career as a lawyer or broadcaster. Plan B included someday taking over the oil business. But first, I thought, I'll keep myself busy and plied with cash via my modest scrap metal business. Besides buying and selling batteries, I was now making money with scrap iron, copper, and aluminum too. It was a good little business, and part of my plan B was to expand it even more.

The bell rang, and I entered what I believed would be the home-stretch of my schooling.

The no-punishment policy remained in effect, but the tension was ever-present. Tenth grade was definitely easier than seventh, eighth, and ninth, but the possibility of trouble rearing its ugly head at any moment was constantly on my mind. I was now over six feet tall thanks to a summer growth spurt, and I couldn't help but think it worked to my advantage.

As the school year went on, I tried not to bother anybody. I showed up for class and put in my time. Teachers seldom called on me, and I didn't offer any participation. Principal Morgan and I seldom made eye contact, and when we did, I could see his disdain for me. He, along with his band of thug teachers in the school, had grown to dislike me very much, maybe even hate me.

Mr. Brookfield and the rest of the thug teachers had earned my disgust. It wasn't just what they had done to me; it's what they had done and were still doing to other kids too. Now that I was a few years older, I was starting to understand that what had happened to me in the remedial math class, the vault, and various other over-the-line punishments was wrong.

Granted, I was no angel, but the punishments didn't fit the crime. I was now beginning to become more aware and concerned about the abuse other kids were getting — other kids who had essentially taken my place. A small voice was growing inside of me, wanting to scream out for justice, but it didn't yet have the maturity to come to anybody's rescue. I was still struggling to get through my own day-to-day life.

In May, the high school yearbooks came out. My brother, Carl, was graduating, and his picture was in the full-color section reserved for seniors.

I'd always dreaded yearbook time. It was customary to pass yearbooks around to friends and classmates and ask them to write something in it. Each time someone would ask me, I'd die a little. I tried to be as brief as possible, sometimes only making the scribbly line I had practiced endlessly as my signature. You never knew when someone would say, "sign here." At least I could do that with some proficiency.

When just signing my name in a classmate's yearbook wasn't

enough, I concentrated with all I had, trying to use one-syllable words as much as possible, in a brief message of "Good luck."

One-syllable words were manageable, two-syllable words were very difficult, and three-syllable words were only achieved with great luck. I hated yearbook time because it was the one time I couldn't avoid having people see me using a pen. It was gut-wrenching to think of someone seeing my illegible chicken scratch — the type that could only be expected from a second-grader, or a doctor.

After all these years of school I could read and write just enough to embarrass myself, and I tried with great creativity to avoid it. I had come up with a convenient excuse at yearbook time — a "broken" index finger with a splint on it. It worked, and helped classmates understand why my writing appeared so poor.

On the last day of tenth grade, I boarded the bus for McAlisterville. Debbie was on the bus too. I still cared for her as much now as I had all those years ago in the first grade. We were friends and talked often, and I was sure she had forgotten that I once asked her to be my girlfriend via good old reliable Curtis Seiber.

As we casually talked on the ride home, I wished things could have been different. Debbie was kind and caring, and my heart secretly ached for her closeness. I rehearsed in my mind what I would say if I only had the courage to speak up about my feelings.

Debbie, I'm in love with you, and I always have been. Maybe I'm not the best student, and sure, I've had my share of troubles. But I promise you, God as my witness, no one has ever or will ever love you as much as I do.

Even if I could have found the courage to say that, I wouldn't have. She had big plans for the future, and I loved her enough not to mess with those plans. The last thing she needed was a guy who had no intention of returning to school in the fall.

The bus stopped in front of her house, and she smiled and said, "See ya around, Nelson." I smiled back and said, "So long, Debbie."

The next morning, I went to work expanding my scrap metal business. I wasn't yet old enough to drive, so I hired a local guy to drive me around to farms and sawmills throughout the countryside looking for junked equipment I could buy. Farmers and millers were hungry for money and deals came easily. I paid them in cash and made arrangements to come back with a crew of teenage boys eager to tear something apart and get paid for it. Soon the scrap would be loaded in pickup trucks and off to the smelter.

Everywhere I went, I heard, "You're Clair Lauver's boy, ain't ya?" Based on the good faith from knowing my dad, everyone seemed eager to shake hands and make a deal.

My sixteenth birthday was coming up at the end of June. In anticipation of getting a driver's license, I bought a 1976 Ford pickup for $2,600 with the money I made scrapping. It was a fine truck.

I quizzed everyone I knew who had recently gone for their driver's test as to the protocol for obtaining a driver's license. I was trying to figure out without actually asking if reading and writing was required for the test. Everyone I talked to said it was a piece of cake. Apparently, all that was required for a learner's permit was an eye test and answers to three or four verbal questions regarding the rules of the road before hopping in your car with a cop and driving around a test track without screwing up. Repeat the process in thirty days, and presto, you had a driver's license.

First, though, you had to obtain an official Pennsylvania Driving Manual and study the questions and answers in the back of the book.

There were dozens of questions, and the cops could pick out any three or four at random for the oral quiz.

I asked a girl I was dating if she would drill me on the questions and answers. I don't think she knew I couldn't read or write very well. If she did, she never let on. She gladly helped me by reading off the questions and telling me the answers. She continued drilling me until I had the answers memorized. Everyone was right; it was a piece of cake.

My new driver's license and pickup truck made my scrap business a lot easier. I no longer had to pay someone to drive me around to make deals. The summer was turning out to be quite profitable.

I hadn't stopped at the high school office yet to give the official word and sign the papers for dropping out. I figured I had all summer to do it, and I'd get around to it eventually.

I hated the idea of dropping out because it meant everyone who had ever said I was lazy and didn't apply myself would now have irrefutable evidence to back up their claim. Mom and Dad wanted each of their three kids to have diplomas, and I knew they were going to be heartsick when I dropped out. But from my perspective at age sixteen, two more years of sitting in school and not participating seemed like an eternity and a waste of time. I was ninety percent sure that if I stayed in school, Principal Morgan would eventually provide me with a diploma in order to get me out of his sight. After all, it was obvious they'd wanted to be rid of me since back when I was just a little guy, or else they wouldn't have pushed me through.

I kept telling myself I'd get around to stopping in at the high school office to sign the papers. My procrastination was only making the inevitable more difficult. I had waited so long that I couldn't wait anymore — the first day of school had arrived. I now had to face the music and sign on the dotted line.

I got in my truck and drove down Route 35 to the high school. I knew Principal Morgan would be busy in the auditorium that morning with his annual laying-down-the-law speech. Maybe it was cowardly, but I liked the idea that I could just give my notification to the secretary and wouldn't have to face Principal Morgan in the office.

I parked my truck in the student parking lot and walked up the sidewalk toward the school office. At the fork in the sidewalk, I stopped. Turning left would lead me to the administration office. Turning right would lead me to the auditorium and Principal Morgan. I stood there for a good ten minutes thinking about my mom and dad, how much I loved them, and how disappointed they would be in me for quitting school. Finally, I took a deep breath, turned right, and walked into the auditorium. After that, I went to homeroom and started my junior year at East Juniata High School.

Several days later, my class of just over one hundred gathered back in the auditorium for a meeting to pick class officers. Mr. Fry, the class advisor, asked for five nominations. The person with the most votes would be president, second most votes would be vice president, third most votes would be treasurer, fourth most votes, secretary, and fifth most votes, historian.

A number of names were shouted from the crowd and seconded. Among those names was one that clearly irked Mr. Fry. He hesitated as he wrote "Nelson Lauver" on the portable blackboard.

When the votes were tallied, I was voted in as treasurer of the Junior Class. The scowl on Mr. Fry's face indicated he was infuriated with the results. He immediately declared a re-vote. He didn't say why, but it was clear to me that he just couldn't accept me being a class officer. We recast our votes, and this time I was elected vice president. A very exasperated Mr. Fry dismissed the class without any further conversation.

I wondered what my class saw in me. Why did they nominate me in the first place and then make me vice president? Was it just to get a reaction out of Mr. Fry? I wasn't sure, but I was glad to be vice president instead of treasurer. Dealing with a checkbook and writing checks would have been an embarrassing task.

Later that day, I passed Mr. Fry in the hall and gave him a smile. He twisted up his face as he looked at me and mouthed the words, "Go to hell."

Outside of school, I was busy working at the gas station and running my scrap business. Many of McAlisterville's old-timers, like Walter Dunn, whom I had so admired as a small boy, were long gone. Most of the World War I soldiers had passed away, too. And the fellows who had entertained me endlessly with their stories from the horse and wagon days were almost all dead.

The eleventh grade was as boring as the tenth in that I participated as little as possible in the classroom.

Most of the teachers were decent, good-hearted people who, just like me, didn't want any trouble, especially with Principal Morgan. I put in my time at school and tried not to bother anyone. I could, however, feel the testosterone-laced tension between me and the thug teachers.

Even though I was still seething with anger over the punishments that had been visited upon me in seventh, eighth, and ninth grade, I optimistically hoped those days were behind me and that the thug teachers would keep their nasty feelings for me to themselves. It was still hard to reconcile the bad memories though. I secretly wished one of them would pick on the wrong kid and that that kid would teach them a lesson — or perhaps the father of that kid would come to the school and bring a bit of justice with him. I knew it wasn't right to think that way, but I couldn't help it. I wished for an incident that would make them think twice before doling out inappropriate and sometimes vicious punishments.

When I started to feel the tension thickening, I removed myself from the situation by skipping school for a day or two in hopes that the bad feelings would simmer down. Nobody ever asked for a written excuse. I think any day I wasn't in school was a good day for everybody.

Many mornings, instead of going to school, I would drive up into the Shade Mountain and disappear from sight back on a deserted logging road. I kept a pillow and blanket behind the seat in my pickup and often pulled them out for a nap, curling up on the bench seat of the truck. I usually woke up a half hour or so before noon and drove to one of the towns or villages on the other side of the mountain. I searched out mom-and-pop restaurants and cafes where no one knew my name or asked, "You're Clair Lauver's boy, ain't ya?"

Exploring far-flung, sleepy little towns that reminded me of McAlisterville kept my mind occupied. Most days while drifting from one hamlet to another in search of satisfaction for my growling stomach and endless curiosity, I felt a million miles removed from the trouble that boiled beneath the surface of East Juniata High School.

As the sun traveled west in the afternoon I headed back home. People were busy with their lives and nobody asked about my day.

I skipped approximately fifty days my junior year at East Juniata. Toward the end of the school year, something amazingly blatant happened.

It reinforced my hope that, if I were to simply hang in there, I would end up receiving a diploma to rid me from the system.

When the 1980 yearbook came out, I noticed that my longtime classmate, Delbert, had no photograph in the section reserved for our junior class. I was puzzled. I knew Delbert hadn't dropped out of school. I thought perhaps it was an accidental omission. The mystery would soon be solved. As I perused the color pictures in the section reserved for seniors, I found a photograph of Delbert sporting a jacket and tie. Not only had Delbert been pushed through the system for years (just like me and others), he was blatantly being advanced a full year to get rid of him! Delbert didn't seem to mind that he was getting his diploma a year early, and I understood why. I was even a bit jealous.

I had met Delbert on the first day of kindergarten back in 1968. We were the same age and went through elementary school together. When we got to East Juniata, Delbert joined his older brothers in the special education classroom — or, as the "normal students" shamefully referred to it, "The Sped Warehouse" — "sped" was a derogatory abbreviation for special education students.

The warehouse was where all special education students, grades seven through twelve, were "stored" 'til the powers-that-be could get them out of the system.

Some of the conditions that could land a student there included, as in Delbert's case, a family history of special education students. Delbert's father and older brothers had also been warehoused. An obvious mental, social, or emotional impairment could or could not, again depending on who your family was, land you directly in the warehouse room. Even one's lack of hygiene could be a direct ticket.

I considered myself fortunate that I somehow avoided spending my days in the abusive environment of the warehouse.

These students faced "paddle day" once a week, usually on a Friday. On that day they lined up, bent over, and were paddled for whatever infractions they may or may not have committed that week. The intensity of the paddling depended upon the memory of the teacher, who tried to keep track of who had misbehaved or performed poorly on a test that week. The power of the swinging paddle was ratcheted up or down accordingly.

The stories of survivors from the warehouse room at East Juniata are heartbreaking. 🌿

Chapter 13

A Small Voice Begins to Grow

I WAS NOW SEVENTEEN YEARS OLD and in the twelfth grade.
I continued trying my best to maintain a low profile. It may have
been wishful thinking, but it seemed to me that Principal Morgan and
I had an unspoken agreement to get me out of the system, and I didn't
want to do anything to rock the boat.

Even though I tried to drop my "bad kid" persona, it still followed
me throughout the halls of East Juniata. I was branded as a troublemaker. But now I had created a new shield to hide behind, and that
was simply indifference — indifference to everything regarding school.
I wanted every teacher to think that they were a pain in my ass, and
that I didn't have time for them. I know I came across as an arrogant
punk, but I just wanted to do the small amount of time I had left and
get out with a diploma.

Most teachers went along with the deal and made little effort to
encourage my participation in class. For those who did try, I simply
ignored them, hoping they would leave me alone, and for the most
part, they did.

For all those years as the "bad kid," I had anger boiling just under
the surface. I was angry at everyone — my teachers, the school, the
unfairness of life in general — but now as I reflected on my botched

education, my anger came to roost within me. I had matured to the point where I knew I had to accept my share of culpability; after all, I was the one who created the identity.

As a young boy struggling in school, I believed I had only two choices: to be the "bad kid" or the "dumb kid." But there was a third choice, the best choice; I had never been mature enough to consider it, until now. The third choice was to simply be Clair Lauver's kid.

Now as a high school senior reflecting on my decisions, it was clear that the best thing I could have ever done was to confide in my dad. "Look, Dad, this has nothing to do with me being lazy, or not applying myself, or being stupid, or anything else. There is something wrong inside my brain, but I don't understand how to fix it, and it scares me." If I would have gone to Dad and had the courage to really lay it on the line, he would have listened to me and moved heaven and earth to find a solution. Unfortunately third-graders don't necessarily think that way, nor do fifth, sixth, or even junior high kids. They're afraid of things like military schools. They take statements literally, like, "if you get in trouble at school, you'll get it double at home." I should have told my dad about the vault and Mr. Brookfield's remedial math class. Old Mr. Leister was right when he said, "We've got to talk to your dad about this." But logic seldom has anything to do with what goes on inside the mind of a frightened kid.

If I could have confided in my dad as a third-grader it would have been a game changer, or even as a sixth- or seventh-grader — but now it was too late. As a senior in high school, I believed my chance for an education was over. Now I had to suck it up and go out into the world and be a man.

In twelfth grade, just like in eleventh, I skipped school to avoid trouble. Although as hard as I tried, I continued to see trouble unfold all around me.

The annual three-day Senior Class trip to Washington, D.C. was scheduled for mid-November. It was paid for with the proceeds of a yearly magazine sales drive held by the school.

Dad had taken me with him on a number of Mobil Oil business trips to Upstate New York, Philadelphia, and Baltimore, but this was the first time I'd be visiting D.C. Ronald Reagan had just defeated Jimmy Carter in a landslide victory, and pictures of Washington had been on the evening news for months. I was looking forward to seeing the city for myself.

I was pleasantly surprised that Principal Morgan didn't exclude me from the trip. However, he did ensure that a particularly close eye was kept on me. I was the only student with an assigned seat on the bus at all times — right next to the chaperones, three male teachers.

Mr. Pierce, a business teacher at E.J. for years, sat in the seat next to me. He was considerably older than most of the teachers. All I knew about this tall, well-groomed man was that he was popular inside as well as outside of school and spent a lot of time on the golf course.

I never had him in class, and he only knew me by reputation, I'm sure. As we pulled out for Washington on the first morning, I could sense his distrust and dislike for me.

As our bus headed south, it was Mr. Pierce who struck up a conversation.

"You're Clair Lauver's son, aren't you?" he asked.

From there, the conversation flowed and quickly gravitated toward politics, stocks, finance, and business. As we talked, it was clear that his preconceived notion of me was changing. I saw a look of surprise, almost delight, on his face as he realized that I wasn't the kid he thought I was. I was a young man capable of intelligent, polite conversation.

We toured the Washington Monument, the Lincoln Memorial, the National Cathedral, the Tomb of the Unknown Soldier, Capitol Hill, and the White House. We even made a side trip to Mount Vernon. Visiting George Washington's home was the most positive experience of my school career. I loved history, and it came alive as I was able to imagine George Washington in his home, back in the day.

Just like at school, I was somewhat of a loner in Washington. I talked and laughed with the other kids, and they talked and laughed with me. Though, for the most part, I kept to myself. I enjoyed the trip and was sad to see it end.

After returning from Washington, I was stunned by what I learned the first morning in homeroom. Danielle, a long-time classmate, read a letter to me that had been placed in her locker by Mr. Fairfax, a forty-something English teacher.

The letter was romantic and suggestive in nature.

"I missed you while you were in Washington," he wrote her. She told me the letter was nothing new and that she had received a number of similar letters from him, all placed in her locker.

"You're not going to have anything to do with him, are you?" I asked.

"Of course not. He's a disgusting creep," she said as she rolled her eyes.

I never liked Mr. Fairfax. He had been one of the teachers who participated in beating me in the eighth grade for the hat incident.

I disliked him even more now that I knew he was a predator preying on one of my classmates. Mr. Fairfax had been teaching at the school since the '60s, and I wondered how many other girls he had stalked over the years. I knew from first-hand experience that he had a violent streak. I also knew that if he was brazen enough to plant love letters in a female student's locker, he was dangerous.

My immediate thought was, *I have to stop him,* but I knew the last thing I needed was to stir the pot this close to graduation. I came up with a plan. I would wait until the day after I graduate, if I graduated, to blow the whistle. I would contact the state police to tell them what I knew. They would haul Mr. Fairfax away to prison, I told myself.

Waiting was a mistake. I should have called the police right away. If I had, I might have been able to save an eleventh-grade girl named Gail. Gail Thomas was very quiet and timid. She was sweet in a shy way and never got in trouble. I liked her. We seldom spoke but I thought of her as a nice person. I saw her almost every day at the same time and place, passing in the hall. She would smile at me and then quickly avert her eyes back to the floor.

In a school as small as East Juniata, everyone knew everyone, and if a student was missing, even for a few days, it was noticeable. I noticed Gail's absence. It was obvious she was either very ill or had quit school. *But if she had quit school … why? Why would a girl as pretty and studious as Gail drop out?*

Soon, the halls were buzzing with the details. The news was horrifying and sent chills down my spine. In his pursuit of young girls, Mr. Fairfax had latched onto Gail. And that shy girl, who seldom spoke to anyone outside her small circle of friends, took the bait and a relationship started.

When the school administration found out about the relationship, instead of calling the police and having Mr. Fairfax arrested, the onus was placed on Gail. In a misguided attempt to put the best possible light on a bad situation, Gail was forced to quit school and marry Mr. Fairfax. Somehow, in a place like Juniata County, all seemed to be made right with a vow of marriage.

I knew little about Gail's home life other than the fact that she came from a poor family. I assumed her parents saw marrying a college-educated teacher, who was old enough to be her father, as a step up in the world for their child.

The thought of Mr. Fairfax climbing on top of Gail and getting all sweaty sickened me. She was just an eleventh-grade girl, and he was a creepy old pedophile.

The same day I learned of Gail dropping out, I passed Mr. Fairfax in the hall. He was standing outside his door, monitoring students coming and going between classes. He had a happy smile on his face as the teenagers filed into his classroom for the next lesson. I thought to myself as I tried not to look at him, *You are one sick son-of-a-bitch. Why aren't you in jail? Who is allowing you to remain a teacher?*

I was seething with anger but in my heart of hearts knew I had a measure of responsibility too, and perhaps that's what I was most angry about.

Why didn't I approach someone in a position of authority and share what I knew about Fairfax and his love letters to Danielle? When Danielle read Fairfax's letter to me in homeroom, why didn't I take the letter, march straight into Principal Morgan's office, slam my fist on his desk, and demand justice? Why didn't I? At that very moment I'd had the opportunity to stand up and become the voice of someone who didn't have a voice of her own. Why didn't I step up?

I'm nothing but a coward, I told myself. *I want a diploma so badly that I'm afraid to cause waves. I could have prevented a young girl from not only being raped by a pedophile but having her entire future stolen by a school system that is so screwed up, it became the pimp that turns out a child for the sexual gratification of a sick, twisted pervert.*

I skipped out of school early that day. I drove to McAlisterville and went into the bank where I exchanged a ten-dollar bill for two rolls of dimes. My plan was to call the state police barracks in the next county over and tell the commander what had happened to Gail Thomas. I figured if I called anonymously from the payphone in front of the hardware store, no one would be able to trace the call back to me.

I dialed 0. "This is the operator. How can I help you?"

"I'd like to place a long distance call to the Pennsylvania State Police."

"Is there an emergency?"

"No, Ma'am."

"Please deposit sixty-five cents for your first minute."

"This could take a while. How about if I drop a few dollars worth of dimes in the phone, and then you place the call? I want to be sure I don't get cut off. This call isn't an emergency, but it is important."

"I'll hold while you deposit the money," she said.

As I dropped my dimes in the top of the phone, I had time to think about doing the right thing. I realized the diploma I so desperately wanted wasn't worth making a coward out of myself any longer. I decided this would not be an anonymous call after all.

A deep voice answered the phone. "Pennsylvania State Police, Trooper Hamilton speaking."

"My name is Nelson Lauver. I'm calling from McAlisterville, and I'd like to speak to the commander."

"Lauver? From McAlisterville? You Clair Lauver's boy?"

"Yes, Sir. May I speak to the commander, please?"

"I'll put you through."

The commander answered the phone.

"Yes, Sir, I'd like to report a case of statutory rape in Juniata County of an eleventh-grade female student by a male high school teacher."

"Is that so?"

"Yes, Sir, that's so."

"Well, if I tried to arrest every man who is having sexual relations with an underage girl in Juniata County, I'd be busier than a one-legged man at an ass-kicking contest."

"Look, Commander, I hear what you're saying, but this is an eleventh-grade girl. A good, decent girl who was preyed upon. She's now dropped out of school and is living in the teacher's house. Any way you look at it, she's a prisoner."

"Maybe she likes that kind of thing, ya know. Maybe she has a thing for older men."

"Do you have children of your own, Commander?"

"Yes, I do."

"Well, Commander, how would you feel...."

"LEAVE MY KIDS OUT OF THIS!"

"I guess what you're saying, Sir, is it would be different if it were one of your kids?"

"Look ... Lauver is it?" the commander asked.

"Yes, Sir, Nelson Lauver from McAlisterville."

The commander continued, "If it was one of my kids, the pervert would never make it to the courthouse."

"Well then, Commander, why don't you step up and do the right thing and arrest this guy?"

"How old are you, Lauver?"

"I'm seventeen, Sir."

"Clair Lauver's boy from McAlisterville, huh?"

"Yes, Sir."

"Well, Lauver, give me the details. I'm not making you any promises as to what will happen, but I'll look into it."

I felt confident the State Police would investigate, but in my gut I knew they probably wouldn't do anything to help Gail. I also knew there was a good chance I had just sealed my fate regarding a high school diploma. I figured now, considering my phone call to the State Police, there was almost no chance of graduating.

At school, I went about business as usual. I kept my ear to the ground, waiting to hear any news on the arrest of Mr. Fairfax.

I wondered how Gail was doing. *Was she happy? Did she feel like she'd made a mistake and had no way out? Was she enjoying her days at home, alone in Mr. Fairfax's house? Did he have her locked in a room or chained to a heat pipe in the basement? Was he kind to her, or had his violent streak already come out? Did she get to see her parents and family? Was she allowed to have friends?*

I discreetly asked around and talked to some of the girls I thought she was friends with, but no one had heard from her. Several weeks went by and still no word on Gail.

At the end of school one day, as I was getting my jacket and hat out of my locker, Mr. Summers approached me and asked if he could have a word with me in his classroom. His tone was friendly and assuring, but I didn't trust him. He was one of Mr. Fairfax's closest friends and was the teacher who acted as the lookout when I was beaten for the hat incident.

I wondered why he wanted to talk to me but felt sure it had something to do with my phone call to the state police.

I was nervous but curious. I wondered, *Does he want to be a decent guy and reassure me that Gail is doing fine? Or, does he want to deliver a message from Fairfax, who I'm sure is fuming about my report to the police? Maybe he wants to try to scare me into minding my own business.*

As we walked to his classroom, I assessed Mr. Summers' short, flabby, out-of-shape physique. I was considerably taller than he was, and at my size, I didn't feel he posed a physical threat to me by himself. But what if some of the other thug teachers were waiting for me in his room?

I considered turning around and walking away before we got to his classroom. But I held out hope that maybe I could learn something from him about Gail Thomas and how she was doing.

"Nice weather we've been having, Nelson."

"Yes, it has been nice," I said as we walked toward his room.

"What would you like to talk about, Mr. Summers?"

"Let's wait 'til we get to my room."

We reached his classroom, and I said, "Please, after you." I stood at the door and looked in with great trepidation. I cautiously walked into his room and realized we were indeed alone. *Maybe he just wants to talk,* I thought. It was a short-lived and naïve thought.

Mr. Summers quickly seized on the letting down of my guard. He grabbed me by the back of the hair and pushed my face into the blackboard as he growled, "You're a troublemaker, Lauver." I immediately knew he was referring to my phone call to the police.

Mr. Summers grabbing me was a mistake. He overestimated his physical abilities and underestimated mine. For the first time, I retaliated.

I turned on him and plowed my right fist straight into his pudgy nose. It was a direct and solid connection. Blood splattered everywhere: on my face, hands, arms, and clothing. Summers' face and shirt were covered, and the blood kept gushing as he stumbled backward and fell on the floor between a row of school desks.

I panicked and bolted out of the room. There was a nearby exit, the same side exit Mr. Leister had carried me through just a few years earlier. I jumped in my truck parked in the student parking lot and drove away. I was consumed with fear. I raced down Route 35 heading for home.

I talked to myself as I drove. *Okay, he lured me under false pretenses to an empty classroom to start a fight, and I had a right to defend myself! But, who is ever going to believe my side of the story? It's going to look as if I went to his classroom after school and attacked him. And even if anyone does believe my version, I don't have a scratch on me and Summers has buckets of blood gushing out of his nose. I clearly went too far. When he pushed my face into the blackboard, instead of turning on him and punching him, I should have just turned around, pushed him out of the way, and walked out of the room. It's just a matter of time until the police come and haul me off in handcuffs for assaulting a teacher.*

I got home and parked in the driveway. I had the house to myself.

Mom and Dad were away for the week at the annual Mobil Oil convention, and Carl now lived across town with his new wife. I went inside the house and locked all the doors, took off my clothes, and threw them into the washing machine. I jumped into the shower to wash the blood off. I got dressed and waited for the police to come.

For years, I had felt that physically fighting back and winning would be a jubilant victory. When I couldn't fight back against Mr. Brookfield in the remedial math class, or Misters Fairfax, Clay, and Summers for the hat beating, or Principal Morgan when he forced me into the vault, or against the countless other times over-the-line punishments were visited upon me, I felt small and helpless. I always thought it would feel great to fight back and win. I was wrong because now I knew, as I sat alone in my family's home waiting to be arrested, that I had never felt as small and vulnerable as I did right now. To my great surprise and relief, the police never came.

I spent the next three days at home lying low and hoping for the best.

When I returned to school, there was a substitute teacher in Mr. Summers' classroom. The word was that Summers was out with a bad case of the stomach flu. Obviously, Mr. Summers thought better of reporting the incident to the police or school officials.

I wasn't called to the office on the matter, and if any of the other teachers knew anything about it, they weren't letting on. No one said a word. I walked the halls of E.J. as if nothing had happened. Everything seemed fine, except for the fact that there was still no word about Gail Thomas' well-being. Yet Mr. Fairfax was still at school every day teaching children proper English while he had a child at home who was learning nothing except how to be the victim of a pedophile.

Mr. Summers returned to school after his bout with the "stomach flu." He approached me again one afternoon at my locker and this time said, "I'm sorry, Nelson." And he kept on walking.

I can only speculate as to why he apologized. *Did he want the situation behind him as badly as I did? Were the other thug teachers angry with him for stirring up an already bad situation even more? Was he just as afraid of being arrested as I was?* Mr. Summers was the only one who knew the answer, and I certainly wasn't about to ask him.

I had hoped that this would be the last of my troubles and that I could coast clear to the end of the school year. However that hope was a little overly-optimistic on my part.

I was spending half my school days in a technical home building trade class taught by Mr. Fry. It was considered to be a good idea — by everyone except Mr. Fry and me — to keep me occupied for the better part of the school day. Mr. Fry didn't like my dad, and because of that, he didn't like me very much either. He lived across the street from our home. Mom had caught Mr. Fry's teenage son burglarizing our family home a few years earlier. Dad never pressed charges but in his polite, diplomatic way laid down the law to Mr. Fry and his son. Years later, on my first day in his class, Mr. Fry brought up the incident and said to me, "Your dad thinks he's the King of Siam and had no right talking down to me the way he did." Dad considered the incident over and done with, but Mr. Fry was still stewing over it.

One day in class, while building a bench, I retrieved a pipe clamp from the shelf and noticed that it was bent and inoperable. I took it over to Mr. Fry to show him the damage.

"Sir, the crank on this clamp is bent."

"HOW DID YOU BEND IT?"

"I didn't bend it, Mr. Fry. It was already bent when I took it down off the shelf."

Mr. Fry highly valued the tools in his shop. Students who damaged tools were held financially responsible.

"DON'T LIE TO ME, AND DON'T YOU TALK BACK TO ME, LAUVER!"

"Mr. Fry, I didn't bend the clamp. I'm just trying to point out that the clamp is damaged and can't be used for my project."

"I'LL HAVE NONE OF YOUR MOUTH!" Mr. Fry said as he rushed toward a large plywood box containing scrap lumber. He pulled out a discarded piece of two-by-four that was about three-and-a-half-feet long and raised it above his shoulder as if to swing it at me.

Mr. Fry had been a heavy smoker for the past twenty-five or thirty years. He hardly had the breath to pick up a two-by-four, let alone swing it with any amount of force.

I grabbed his wrist with one hand and took the two-by-four away from him with the other. He cowered as if I were going to bludgeon him with the piece of lumber. I told him, "Mr. Fry, my days of being the hitter or the hittee are over," as I put the two-by-four back into the scrap box. I think Mr. Fry would rather have had me club him to death than face the humiliation of having his weapon forcibly taken from him in front his students. I left the shop immediately. Mr. Fry's face had the look of a child who had just been scolded.

I knew I had to get out of Mr. Fry's class permanently. He would have spent the rest of the year trying to resurrect his masculinity at my expense. I went to the school office to see Principal Morgan.

"What's your problem, Mr. Lauver?" the principal asked.

"I need to have my schedule changed so I don't have to go back to Mr. Fry's class."

"Why is that, Mr. Lauver?"

"I took a two-by-four from him. He was going to hit me with it."

Morgan pushed back in his chair and chuckled. The chuckle spoke volumes; it said to me that Principal Morgan viewed a teacher's intent to strike a student with a two-by-four as humorous. I was already angry over how and why Gail Thomas had disappeared from the halls of East Juniata. And I was now old enough to understand that the brutality that often took place inside the walls of the high school was clearly wrong. I was no longer a frightened seventh-grader lost between classes. I was on the verge of my eighteenth birthday, the same age my father was when he went off to defend America.

Principal Morgan's chuckle flipped a switch that emboldened my sense of justice. At least for the moment, I had an impassioned voice. It was a voice free of fear and empowered with the steadfast conviction that I was on the side of right. I recognized the voice that had welled up inside of me. It belonged to the four-year-old kid in the Superman suit, the confident first-grader who belted out a song at the front of the classroom, the third-grader who threw a book at his teacher and said, "Don't you ever write my name on the blackboard again." It was the voice of the nine-year-old kid who felt compelled to invite President Nixon to land his helicopter in the field behind the house. It was the voice of the teenager who dropped the dimes in the phone and told the State Police trooper, "My name is Nelson Lauver from McAlisterville."

The voice came and went in my life, but at that very moment, it was definitely there, it was definitely on, and it was stronger than ever before.

I didn't care if Principal Morgan turned red and screamed at the top of his lungs. At six-foot-two, I could no longer be thrown in the vault or intimidated with violence. The only control Morgan had over me now was the diploma I had hoped for, but I had already resigned myself to the real possibility that I might not graduate. In my impassioned state, the right words came easily.

"Do you think that's funny, Mr. Morgan?"

"Well ya have to admit, old Fry picking up a two-by-four...."

"Do you think it is funny that a man who holds himself out as a professional educator picks up a slab of lumber with the intent of harming a student?"

"Now just you listen here a minute, Mr. Lauver!"

"Do you think it's funny, Mr. Morgan, when a kid gets beaten to a pulp because he broke one of your rules?"

"Don't you dare raise your..."

"Do you get a hoot on Fridays when the special education students are lined up for paddle day?

Do you think it is funny, Mr. Morgan, when you isolate a child in the vault?

Is it funny when a naïve eleventh-grade girl quits school and marries her pedophile English teacher?

Do those things give you a chuckle, too, Mr. Morgan? Do they?"

"I will not have you question my authority...."

"We've reached this point because of YOU, Mr. Morgan. YOU are the one who set the precedent that it's okay to slam a kid into the wall, or crack him across the face with your hand, or paddle him because he doesn't know the answer to a question. YOU, Mr. Morgan, the guy in charge, the leader. We got here because of YOU! Teachers who may have otherwise been great teachers ruined their careers by following your lead and example."

Morgan's face took on that smile that he only smiled when he was uncomfortable — his Jerry Falwell smile. "You know what I think your problem is, Mr. Lauver?"

"I believe your troubled life all stems from the fact that you have not accepted Jesus Christ as your personal Lord and Savior."

"If I were to agree with your assumption, Mr. Morgan, and I were to make this bond, would that absolve me of my sins?"

Morgan leaned forward in his chair, resting his forearms on his desk as he beamed with hopeful enthusiasm. God would surely bless him if he could somehow save and deliver a "troubled student" to the pews of the First Baptist Church, of which he was a deacon and lay minister.

"Yes, yes indeed, Nelson, it would. The blood of Jesus Christ would wash your sins away."

"Wow, Mr. Morgan, just think of all the rotten, nasty stuff I could do to people and still get a good night's sleep, free of worry that I'd have to answer for it."

"Oh, no, no, no, no, no, that's not how it works, Mr. Lauver. You must be Christ-like in your daily walk."

"Really, Mr. Morgan? I've always wondered how you justify it all. I'll stop in the office here tomorrow morning, and perhaps your secretary can let me know what my new schedule will be."

I left Principal Morgan's office and went to the lobby. I stood quietly looking out the front windows of the school. I reflected on the voice that had welled up inside of me. Expressing my voice was intoxicating. I realized now that this was the voice Mrs. Parsons heard all those years ago in first grade when she said, "Nelson, use your voice in the courtroom as a lawyer or across the airwaves as a broadcaster."

I could feel the sense of voice inside my chest. The voice had grown over the years but was not yet mature enough to be dependable. It had visited today in Principal Morgan's office, but I wondered, *Will it be here the next time I need it?*

The next morning, the secretary told me about my new schedule that removed me from Mr. Fry's technical home building class and placed me in study hall and of all things, speech class.

The time passed quickly, and my classmates and I were now in the home stretch to graduation. I had heard nothing about whether I would be participating in the graduation ceremony.

I opted not to order graduation announcements for fear that, in the end, Principal Morgan might call my bluff and invite me back for another year of school. I felt that would have been the ultimate irony, considering all the years I had been pushed along through the system. When the printer's representative visited the school displaying all the options and pricing for graduation announcements, I paid no attention. I was consumed with the thought of how embarrassing it would be if I sent graduation invitations to neighbors, friends, and family, and they all showed up only to realize I wasn't there. What would be even more embarrassing would be to receive all the customary gifts only to have to return them because I wasn't graduating.

My brother Carl had graduated two years earlier, in 1979. I paid him a visit and quizzed him on the details of graduation and what to expect. He wasn't much help.

"Just do everything they tell you to do. Beyond that, I can't help you much, little brother."

Carl's own graduation must have seemed, to him, a million years in the past. He was married to his high school sweetheart, and their post-high school life was now anything but sweet. Unlike me, Carl had become a fair student in later years and had earned the right to graduate. However, since leaving high school, his life had spiraled into low-wage work, drug abuse, and living in a dilapidated two-bedroom house-trailer. Carl was highly gifted in all things mechanical and automotive, but drug use was overshadowing his abilities. He dreamed of being successful and possessing material status. He told me, "Selling cocaine will get me there."

"Carl, that's crazy talk! The only thing selling cocaine will get you is a stint in the state penitentiary at Rockview."

He said, "Nope, little brother. I have a fool-proof plan."

"Okay, let's hear your fool-proof plan," I said, dripping with cynicism.

"First of all, I'm going to borrow some money from you, and don't tell me you don't have it because Dad brags about your scrap metal business all the time."

I wasn't about to loan him a nickel but allowed him to go on with his big talk. He showed me a pool cue. It was unusual and doubled as an ornate walking cane. I suppose he bought it for twenty dollars or so at the McAlisterville Carnival. It had a large ball-like brass grip on the top. Unscrewing that brass grip revealed a hollow center that stored a second piece. When the two pieces were screwed together, it became a pool cue.

Along with his mint 1969 Camaro, the mysterious pool cue was one of his prized possessions. Carl had little interest in the game of pool. He purchased the walking cane/pool cue with ulterior motives.

"I'm planning to make a little trip south of the border into Mexico," he continued. "I'll use the hollowed-out walking stick to smuggle cocaine back into the States."

Carl felt he could retail the coke in small packets to all his friends at a nice profit.

"ARE YOU NUTS? Have you seen the movie *Midnight Express?*" I asked him.

Maybe it was the drugs talking, or maybe it was the just the sheer confidence that comes with ignorance, but Carl told me he was sure he could get away with it.

"Carl, they have drug-sniffing dogs at the border. I've seen them on TV!"

But Carl was convinced that all he'd have to do is fill the hollow cane with coke, screw the grip on tight with pipe cement, and then give the entire outside several coats of clear polyurethane lacquer to seal it and make it airtight. "Surely," he said, "no dog will be able to smell through all of that."

"The first problem with your plan, Carl, is that I'm not loaning you any amount of money."

Carl drew back deep on a generic cigarette, "Well, little brother, I guess you're not the clever businessman Dad says you are, or you'd be smart enough to know I could double or triple your money in a week. Don't worry, Nelson, if you don't want in on the deal I'll find an investor who knows a good thing when he sees it."

"Good for you, Carl," I told him. "While you're at it, get your investor to pony up some extra cash for a case of Preparation H. You'll need it after you become someone's girlfriend in a Mexican prison."

I looked at Carl and his life and couldn't help but have concerns about my own future. I asked myself, *How far can I possibly go in this world considering my lack of literacy skills?*

The scrap metal business was doing well, but the secret had gotten out. Every teenager with a pickup truck was now driving around making deals with farmers and saw-millers on discarded farm and timbering implements. There was only so much scrap to be had in the ridges and valleys of Juniata County, and it was quickly running out. To make my future even more uncertain, Dad had just been made an offer by a much larger oil company across the mountain. The big oil company wanted to increase its market share in Juniata County, and the best way to do that was to make Clair Lauver an offer he couldn't refuse.

Several months before I was set to graduate, Dad accepted the offer and sold the oil company that he had built from the ground up.

With graduation approaching, there was a constant nagging voice in my head asking, *What will become of me?* 🌿

Chapter 14

Graduation?

THE CLICK ... CLICK ... BUZZ was switched on and directed to the three twelfth-grade homerooms.

"Attention seniors, this is Principal Morgan. After morning announcements, I would like you all to meet me in the auditorium to discuss the events surrounding graduation."

As we left our last official homeroom that June morning, on our way to Principal Morgan's graduation review, I walked down the hall with my classmate Kyle.

"Did you hear Rob, James, and Nick aren't graduating?" he asked.

"No, I didn't hear that," I said.

"They were called to the office first thing this morning and were told that they didn't have the grades. I'm afraid I'm next," Kyle said.

I didn't say anything. I was paralyzed with fear and couldn't utter a word. My heart pounded and I thought, *If these guys aren't graduating, there's no way that I'm going to be allowed to graduate. I'm failing everything!* I was frantically trying to figure out what might be in store for me. *When is Principal Morgan going to give me the news? Why hasn't he already done it?* I felt ill as a horrible scenario hit me like a ton of bricks. *He's surely angry with me for the blowout we had in his office. He's going to announce that I'm not graduating in front of the entire class and humiliate me. Why did I have to argue with Principal Morgan? Why didn't I keep my mouth shut? I should have just dropped out the first day of eleventh grade and saved myself all this time and avoided this embarrassment.*

I followed the herd into the auditorium and purposely sat in the back row of seats, just in case Principal Morgan chose to single me out in front of everyone to tell me I wouldn't be graduating. To embarrass me like that would be the ultimate revenge. At least I would be able to slip out the back door of the auditorium without anyone seeing the humiliation on my face.

One hundred or so of us were spread out across the seven-hundred-seat auditorium. Mr. Morgan stood on stage.

"Mr. Lauver," he called out with a motioning gesture, "Move down front here. Everyone, let's get into a tight-knit group so I don't have to strain my voice."

I moved closer, but I didn't trust him. If Principal Morgan ever wanted to embarrass me, now would be a good time. My heart thumped in my chest, and I had a lump in my throat. My face felt hot, and I knew it was red. I could feel myself trembling. When Morgan called my name, just before he asked me to move closer, I felt like my worst-case scenario was coming true.

Once the students in the periphery had shifted closer to the front, Principal Morgan started to speak. "Okay, graduates. Let me have your attention. First off, let me congratulate you on your achievement. As Mrs. Feathers passes out your tassels, I want to give you a brief rundown of how graduation night is going to play out."

It seemed straightforward enough. We were to bring our tassels on graduation evening and pick up our caps and gowns, which would be waiting on our homeroom desks. Next, wearing our caps and gowns with our tassels to the right, we were to make our way to the back hall of the auditorium and arrange ourselves, in alphabetical order by last name. Then, following the cue of our homeroom teachers, who were now graduation advisors, we'd walk onstage as a class and take our seats on the risers.

Principal Morgan continued his instruction. After the Rev. Givens from Niemond's Independent Church gave the commencement address, each student would be called to receive their diploma in alphabetical order from a representative of the board of education. Then, we were to circle back behind the risers and retake our seats on the stage. Finally, after everyone had received their diplomas, there would be the traditional cheering and throwing of the caps. After that, we were to be dismissed from the stage to form a reception line in the back of the auditorium to greet our invited guests.

Lastly, Principal Morgan delivered a stern admonishment to return our caps and gowns *neatly folded* back to our homeroom desks.

"After that, you will be free to go," Principal Morgan told the group.

He was pleased and smiled as the students giggled about the "free to go" statement.

Principal Morgan quieted the auditorium again.

"Ladies and gentlemen, ladies and gentlemen! If I can have your attention for just another moment, there is one more thing I would like to share with you."

The class quieted down and focused on Principal Morgan. I held my breath and thought, *Here it comes, he's going to announce I won't be graduating.*

"I just wanted to take a moment and share with you how important my personal relationship with Jesus Christ is," Principal Morgan said. "I'd like to give you each a book that I purchased with my own money. It's a gift from me to you. My hope, in giving you this book, is that you will read it, and in turn, make room in your hearts, as I have in mine, for the unconditional love that our Lord and Savior, Jesus Christ, teaches us to have for one another."

I exhaled. Of course he wanted to get in one last sales pitch. His constant reminders over the years about being "Christ-like in your daily walk" seemed so out of balance with the man who announced every year on the first day of school that graduating students should not use him as a reference because he would probably have nothing good to say about them.

His talk about Christian love was in stark contrast to the rage and injustice he had visited on so many students. Morgan, of all people, "spreading the word" just made no sense to me. In my mind, Principal Morgan was the epitome of hypocrisy.

With that we were dismissed for the day and didn't need to return until graduation evening.

I drove away from school thinking about the three guys who weren't going to graduate and wondered why I wasn't being held back, too. I couldn't help but think I wasn't out of the woods yet. *I won't believe I'm a graduate until I have a diploma in my hands. Maybe I'm just being set up for a cruel joke.*

The days leading up to graduation were filled with anxious anticipation. I had difficulty eating and sleeping. I tried to prepare myself for the worst. All kinds of thoughts went through my mind, including that I'd be walking across the stage in front of my family only to be told there had been a mix-up with my grading, and there was no diploma for me.

The evening of graduation finally came, and I did everything just as Principal Morgan had instructed. I retrieved my cap and gown from my homeroom desk and stood in line waiting to go on stage.

We took our seats and were applauded by the crowd. A few announcements were made and the commencement speaker, the Rev. Givens, was introduced. He was a friendly looking man and opened with the line, "Twenty years from now, none of you will remember a word I say here tonight." He went on to talk about his commencement speakers from high school, college, and seminary — and the fact that he couldn't remember one word any of them had said.

After he finished, the vice president of the Board of Education was invited to the stage. Graduates were called, one by one, and formed a well-spaced line. There was the walk, the handshake, the presentation of the diploma, and the tassel turn.

Then the announcer called the name "NELSON CHARLES LAUVER." With butterflies in my stomach, I stood up and joined the line, still unsure if I would really get a diploma. When it was my turn, the vice president of the board, who was a local farmer, reached out his big callused hand to shake mine and whispered, "You're Clair Lauver's boy, ain't ya?"

I smiled and nodded as he handed me a diploma, and I turned my tassel.

I walked behind the riser, but instead of retaking my seat, I slipped out behind the heavy black curtain on the stage. I hastily opened the leather-like booklet containing the document and examined it. It appeared official enough, and I was pretty sure it was the real thing.

I felt that as long as I was still inside the school my diploma could be taken from me. I had images in my mind of Principal Morgan grabbing it and tearing it to shreds in front of my face. I had to get out and get off school grounds as quickly as possible. Only then would I feel it was truly mine.

Gripping my diploma tightly in my hand, I sneaked out the back door of the stage and ran as fast as I could for homeroom. I tripped on my gown and went ass over tin cups but regathered myself and continued to run. I wrangled out of my gown, quickly folded it, and laid it on my desk. In my haste, I left behind what was almost as important to me as the diploma itself. I forgot to take the tassel off my cap.

With my heart pounding a mile a minute, I sprinted down the empty halls toward the front doors and straight to my truck in the parking lot. I got in, locked the doors put the key in the ignition and took a deep breath. I reflected for a moment and thought, *Thank God it's over*.

What I didn't consider at the time was how happy I should have been that they called us in alphabetical order to receive our diplomas. If they hadn't, everyone in the auditorium, including Mom and Dad, would have known that, out of 104 graduates, I was graduate 104.

I drove down the road, less than two miles, to an empty church parking lot. I pulled around to the back of the church, where no one could see me, and wept uncontrollably.

"I never have to step foot in a school again. Never," I told myself.

Eventually, as the tears quelled, relief, happiness, and an odd feeling of pride began to overtake me. I had escaped. I felt liberated. Even though I failed miserably in getting an education, I put in the time. My mom dreamed of her children receiving a high school diploma, and I didn't let her down — I considered that a victory.

I was street smart for my age, yet at the same time so naïve. I thought, *School's over. I'll never have to deal with difficult people again. I'm finally free, and no one will ever be able to control my life. Unless, of course, there's another Vietnam and I'm drafted.*

I drove home, changed my clothes, and apologized to Mom and Dad for missing them in the receiving line. They were still elated from the graduation ceremony and didn't seem to mind.

There was a big beer party later that night at a cabin in the woods to celebrate E.J.'s class of 1981. Someone's dad showed up and took everyone's car keys. We all acted annoyed about the whole thing, but the truth of the matter was that we really appreciated him showing up to keep us all safe.

I asked my classmate Kyle at the party if anyone had heard anything about Gail. He said, "No, not that I know of, and I don't think anybody will."

"What do you mean?" I asked

"Think about it, Nelson. Do you think he's going to let her go anytime soon?"

"No, you're probably right, Kyle."

I tried to put the thought of Gail out of my mind. After all, it was time to celebrate. I was finally free. But now with the celebration, and all the talk from my fellow graduates about college and opportunities and plans for the future, one thing was becoming clearer. I was facing some serious problems. I had to go out into the world and make my way as a functionally illiterate adult and wondered now, more than ever, *What will become of me?*

But that worry can wait — at least until tomorrow, I told myself.

I slipped away from the conversation at the beer keg and went to the porch of the cabin to collect my thoughts and courage. I had one more thing to do before I started my new life as a high school graduate.

Thank God for the confidence beer affords one in difficult moments. I thought about what I was going to say — and this time I walked right up to her and said it. It wasn't what I wanted to say but rather what I needed to say.

I wanted to pour my heart out to her and tell how much I cared for her, but it wasn't appropriate. She was going to school to become a flight attendant. It was her dream, and I wasn't about to mess with her dream or try to hold her back.

I walked up to her and said, "I want to wish you good luck and the best for your future."

She wrapped her arms around me and gave me a hug and said, "Thank you and good luck with your future too. I'm really going to miss you, Nelson Lauver."

I said, "I'm going to miss you too, Debbie."

It was the last time I ever saw her.

Chapter 15

Last Man Standing

I T WAS AUGUST AS I SAT WITH DAD in his brand-new, luxurious Oldsmobile. From the plush, gray velour seats and air-conditioned comfort, we watched as heavy earth-moving equipment prepared a site for a building pad and parking lot. Dad had just purchased the ten-acre parcel of ground nine miles from McAlisterville at the junction of Route 35 and US 322. A 15,000-square-foot metal building was on order, and the timeline called for opening the new business in just a few months.

My sister, Susan, and her husband, Barry, now married for almost a dozen years, were involved in the development of the new venture. In fact, they were the ones who brought the idea to Dad. In the late '70s and early '80s, roller-skating was all the rage, and Susan and Barry had become die-hard skating enthusiasts. With packed roller-skating rinks popping up all over the country, they convinced Dad that Juniata County was ripe for a flashy new skating rink.

So, shortly after Dad sold his oil business, he began building *Roller Junction*. It would be a family business with Barry and Susan at the helm calling the shots.

I appreciated the fact that the skating rink would provide me with a job and health insurance, albeit a minimum-wage job as a disc jockey and janitor, but I had concerns. My fascination with finance and the inner workings of business, sparked by my summers at Dad's gas station and my little scrap metal business, had continued to grow. I spent countless hours with my calculator, figuring out the numbers behind what made a business a success or failure. In the case of the skating rink, the numbers didn't look good.

Sitting alone with Dad in the car, watching the heavy equipment muscle through the once-green alfalfa field, felt like the opportune time to finally share the thoughts I had been keeping to myself.

"Are you sure about this, Dad?"

"What are you talking about? Sure about what?"

"Building a skating rink," I said.

"Well, Nelson, I'm committed now."

"No, you're not, Dad. You have thirty thousand in the land and another ten thousand in excavation. You can still get out of this with your shirt on. You can sell the ground for what you have in it and chalk this up to a bad idea. You're fifty-five years old and have enough cash from the sale of the oil company so that you and Mom will never need to worry about money. You can travel and enjoy life like you've always wanted to."

"What the hell are you talking about, Nelson? This skating rink is going to make a bundle of money!"

"I don't think it will, Dad — the numbers are no good. There aren't enough people in the area to support a skating rink of this size."

"What the hell do you mean? Skating rink owners all over the country are making money hand over fist!"

I went on to explain to Dad, pulling my calculator out of my shirt pocket to support my argument, that all of Juniata County only had a population of 20,000 people. The next town west, Lewistown, in a neighboring county only thirteen miles away already had an established skating rink. A small skating rink in Juniata County built for $175,000 or $200,000 would probably be mildly profitable. But the grand plans for this skating rink, based on the advice of Barry, could easily exceed, by 1981 numbers, half a million dollars.

"Dad, it will be overbuilt for the market by more than fifty percent."

The oil company had been sold on a structured payout and Dad was receiving a monthly check — so, of course, the skating rink would need a mortgage. The local bank would only go ten years on the mortgage and the interest rate in the early 1980s was almost twenty percent. The monthly bank payment on the skating rink would be almost $6,000.

And, although Juniata County had 20,000 people, it was ninety miles long. So, in actuality, only about half of the county could be considered the skating rink's market area. And because of factors like age, not all of the 10,000 people living in that market area could be turned into a regular skater. At best, twenty percent of the population, or about 2,000 people, could be considered ideal skaters.

Of course, the mortgage payment wouldn't be the only expense. There was payroll as well as advertising, insurance, supplies, maintenance, and utilities. All in all, expenses could easily average $25,000 per month. In order to make a worthwhile profit, every possible person who fit the ideal skater profile would have to be turned into a skating fanatic and patronize the skating rink at least once a week for eternity. Satisfying $300,000 a year in expenses and expecting a profit of $50,000 to $100,000 on top of that was a great deal to hope for from a market of only 2,000 potential roller skaters. To compound the problem, we were in a recession. The average hourly wage in Juniata

County was among the lowest in the state, and unemployment was among the highest. Even if people did want to patronize the business, many of them wouldn't have the money to do so.

Dad said, "I can't turn back now!"

"Sure you can, and if you're a smart businessman, you will. Besides, Dad, none of us knows anything about the skating business. Barry is a power company lineman, and you spent your life in the oil business. Heck, I don't even know how to roller-skate!"

I had another concern, too, but I kept it to myself. My sister's husband, Barry, was a hothead. When he was in a good mood he was a pleasure to be around, but his mood was volatile and he had an explosive temper.

Dad, on the other hand, valued Barry's opinion and said he was "a sharp guy." Barry had always talked about his dreams of being a businessman, and Dad was confident that Barry had "the right stuff."

"I don't want to hear any more of this negative talk, Nelson. I have committed to this and I'm going to see it through. I expect your support!"

What more could I say? I had voiced my opinion, but it was Dad's money, not mine, and at least I would have a job at the skating rink for however long it lasted.

The truth of the matter was that, although Dad was a fabulous salesman, he was not a great businessman. He had very little interest in details like feasibility or the numbers that tell the story of where a business is at the moment — or where it's headed in the future. Being a great salesman certainly worked to Dad's advantage with his oil business, but it was his trusted bookkeeper, Loretta, who kept the business end of things on track.

Loretta was highly capable and was every bit as personable and affable as she was bright. While Dad sold and delivered, Loretta took care of the details. It was the perfect combination. She was everything Dad was not. Dad was a hard worker, but without Loretta, I'm sure he would not have enjoyed such fabulous success in the oil business.

With the sale of the oil company, Loretta was no longer in the picture. Dad was heading into the skating business and entrusting the important details to his son-in-law, Barry.

Roller Junction had its grand opening in the fall of 1981. It was a beautiful, ultra-modern monstrosity of a skating rink. Glitzy and glamorous, it had mirror balls and flashing starburst lights. The epoxy skating floor was harvest gold, and an eclectic mural with scenes of Americana highlighted the walls. There was a snack bar with comfortable seating and an arcade with pinball machines and video games.

Mom worked the snack bar. I was the DJ and janitor. Susan was the business manager and worked the admission gate. Dad and Barry worked in the skate rental area and were floaters taking care of whatever needed attention. In addition, Roller Junction employed ten or so part-time snack bar workers, several skate guards, and a big, burly security officer. Everyone wore the official company uniform consisting of black pants and a short-sleeved, pale blue shirt with the Roller Junction logo neatly screen-printed on the pocket.

There was a lot of publicity and buzz surrounding Roller Junction. The local newspaper called it "Clair Lauver's bold, new endeavor."

I enjoyed my job as the DJ. You'd think that being functionally illiterate would make DJ-ing a tough task, but for me it turned out to be the easiest job in the world. Just by the very nature of being an eighteen-year-old, I listened to the radio all the time. I knew every song in the Top 40 and discovered I had a good ear for mixing music as well as a natural sense of how to transition from one mood to the next — like how to move into a slow couples' skate or what song would get everybody out on the floor.

All our music came on 45-rpm records. I quickly figured out which song was on which record simply by listening to it and memorizing the graphics and pictures on the label. Then, I separated the records into slow, medium, and fast by putting a little round red, yellow, or green sticker on each one. I also memorized what the Harrisburg radio DJs said about new songs and repeated that in talking up the music.

Behind the big smoked-glass windows of the DJ booth, I became a bit of a mysterious character and a teen heartthrob by default. I think you could have stuck the ugliest guy ever in the DJ booth, and the girls would have gone crazy over him simply because he was the DJ.

Girls often walked up to me and exclaimed, "I love your voice." I'd say "thanks," but didn't understand what all the fuss was. Maybe Mrs. Parsons liked my voice back in the first grade, but now, at eighteen, it just sounded plain and Pennsylvania Dutchy to me — nothing special as far as I was concerned. Although, I imagined being the DJ at the skating rink was sort of close to Mrs. Parsons' dream of me being a broadcaster.

I liked girls — a lot — and all the attention from them was good for my ego but a little bit overwhelming. I might have had a fair amount of self-assurance in other areas of my life, but when it came to girls, I was terribly shy and backward.

Even though I'd had a few girlfriends throughout high school, deep down inside I still carried around the same insecurities I had in the first grade when I met Debbie. And I worried that even if a girl did want to date me, she might just like me for a little while, then squash my heart. Maybe one of my biggest insecurities was that, if a girl gets too close, she might figure out I have a problem with reading and writing, then dump me for sure.

Suffice it to say, my romantic acumen was not terribly keen, and girlfriends from the skating rink came and went quickly.

Business went gangbusters the first year, and people stood in line to get in. The skating rink was crowded all the time, yet there still wasn't enough money to cover the out-of-control overhead.

After the first year, the novelty of skating started to wane. Roller Junction struggled for air, and every month Dad had to supplement the rink's income with his oil company payout just to make ends meet.

Despite my being just the janitor and DJ, Dad made me a partner in the business too. After incorporating he gave each of us (Carl, Susan, and me) a sixteen percent share of the stock while retaining a controlling fifty-two percent himself. Barry had assumed that he and Dad would be fifty-fifty partners because the skating rink was his idea, but he never communicated those thoughts to Dad. He was furious when he learned that Carl and I were included in the stock split. Instead of directing his anger toward Dad or toward himself for not effectively communicating his assumptions — or even Carl, who was never around to help — he directed his anger at me. As far as he was concerned, I was just some eighteen-year-old punk who muscled in on his action and had done nothing to deserve any of the stock that, in his eyes, was worth a bundle. To make matters worse, because I was single, I owned sixteen percent of the stock by myself, making me the second largest stockholder. Barry and Susan, as a married couple, were sharing their sixteen percent cut of the stock, as were my brother, Carl, and his wife. Of course, the stock had no value because of the lack of profits and high debt.

I knew the skating rink, with its big mortgage, killer overhead, and lack of a sustainable customer base was in a death spiral, but I continued to try to keep my mouth shut and work hard. It quickly became clear to me that I would have to formulate an exit strategy to keep money in my pockets. No matter how I looked at it, it seemed like I'd be forced to try to revive my scrap metal business when the skating rink went belly-up, and I'd be taking my chances without health insurance.

For Barry, Roller Junction wasn't his main job. He had a well-paying, full-time job with Pennsylvania Power and Light. Dad worked a day job, too. He was now a full-time salesman for the company that bought his oil business.

Even though I was sure the skating rink would eventually fail, I took my job seriously and did my best. I was always on time for work, people liked the music I played, I got along well with all the other employees, and I did a fine job cleaning the toilets. In fact, as the janitor, I took great pride in the overall appearance and cleanliness of the facility. And for all my hard work, my take-home pay was about a hundred bucks a week, a bargain for my contribution as far as I was concerned.

Regardless of my hard work at the skating rink, Barry had a long list of complaints about me and often angrily voiced them to my father. *If he wants to complain about something legitimate,* I thought, *he should call attention to all the snack bar profits I eat and drink.* Yet, to my great surprise, it never came up.

Chiefly among his complaints was his allegation that I did a poor job running the machine that scrubbed the skating floor, but I did it exactly the way Barry instructed me to.

He constantly complained to Dad, "The skating floor isn't being properly cleaned!"

Scrubbing the skating rink floor took about four hours, once a week, and was a pretty straightforward job. First, I went around and around in a large oval pattern walking behind the big orange machine as the scrubbing wheels scrubbed the floor with abrasive pads and liquid detergent. There was a built-in squeegee and a vacuum that sucked up the residue. Then, I repeated the process two more times with plain water to rinse the floor clean of any soap residue.

Barry and Dad were at their day jobs while I scrubbed the floor, and often Barry accused me of not doing the job at all.

After a year or so of bitter complaining about my poor performance as a floor scrubber, Barry was finally successful at convincing Dad that I was "worthless." Dad had reached the breaking point and felt only one thing would straighten me out.

In an uncharacteristic rage after receiving yet another heated phone call from Barry about the poorly cleaned skating rink floor, Dad informed me we were going for a ride.

"Where are we going, Dad?"

"Don't ask questions, just get in the car!"

I figured Dad just wanted to talk. He seethed with anger, clenched his teeth, and gripped the wheel tightly as he drove in complete silence. After about twenty minutes, we arrived in the parking lot of the United States Army Recruiter's office in Lewistown. I was sure at this point that Dad had lost his mind.

"Come on, we're going inside," Dad said in a gruff, angry voice.

"I'm not going in there!" I told him.

"You'll go in, or I'll drag you in!"

"Fine, Dad, I'll go in and watch you make a fool of yourself."

We walked through the door, and Dad told a snappy, well-groomed Army recruiter, "He's nineteen years old. Sign him up, Lieutenant!"

I politely informed the recruiter, "I will not be enlisting in the United States Army at this time."

The recruiter tried his best to sell me on the idea to no avail. Dad was incredulous when the recruiter finally gave up and told him, "Being a father does not afford you the right to enlist your son in the Army."

We got in Dad's car and headed back to the skating rink. Dad didn't say a word but looked a bit embarrassed. It was very quiet in the car for about ten minutes, and then Dad broke out into laughter at how foolish his notion had been. I couldn't help but laugh, too, even though I was really, really pissed off at him. Soon, Dad broke out in song, and I joined in.

"You're in the Army now. You can't get out no how. So dig that ditch you son of a bitch, you're in the Army now!" We both laughed and sang it a few more times.

We drove to the skating rink. It was closed when we arrived, and the place was empty. He said, "Show me how you scrub the skating rink floor." During the demonstration he concluded that there was possibly something defective with the scrubbing machine itself.

He went to the office and called the salesman who'd sold us the floor scrubber. He left a message with the answering service to set an appointment to come to the skating rink and examine the scrubber. Several days later at that meeting, the salesman who had originally delivered and assembled the scrubber told us that someone had "reversed several of the small hoses inside the machine." In other words, according to the salesman, the floor scrubber had been sabotaged.

I'll never forget the look on Dad's face. It was the only time in my entire life that I heard him use the "f-word." Dad apologized to me profusely, and I wasn't sure if he was apologizing for starting a family feud, using the "f-word," my brother-in-law's accusations that I was a "bad floor scrubber," trying to sign me up for the Army, or for all the above.

I felt that there was another explanation for the floor-scrubber situation. Sabotage wasn't Barry's style. I saw for myself that the salesman was telling the truth — the hoses inside the machine were indeed crossed, causing the machine to malfunction. I couldn't imagine that Barry was the responsible party. When Barry was angry, he couldn't hold it in. He had a very direct, in-your-face type of style.

"I think the machine was screwed up from the beginning," I told Dad. "I think the salesman made a mistake putting it together. Barry may be a jerk, but he's not a go-behind-your-back, sneaky sort of jerk." Even as much as I disliked him at the time, I couldn't help but appreciate his directness.

Regardless of my thoughts, Dad was sure that Barry was the culprit. He struggled with how to handle the situation. He didn't confront him with his belief that he had sabotaged the floor-scrubbing machine. Instead, he started to observe the dynamic between Barry and me with a different mindset.

As the business continued to implode, the relationship between Barry and me — and within the whole family, for that matter — grew more tumultuous. Barry lost his temper often and blamed me for the decline of the skating rink. I tried to stay out of his way but sometimes reminded him with a smart-ass tone, "I scrub the toilets and spin records — you're crazy if you think this mess is my fault."

I didn't really care if he ranted and raved and his blood pressure went through the roof, but my sister had to live with him. Even though I enjoyed pushing his buttons sometimes, I was always careful to temper it with concern for my sister's well-being. But sometimes, I just couldn't help winding him up a little.

Slowly but surely the customer base wore out. The small Juniata County population had tired of Roller Junction. Not wanting to cause any more family discord, I kept my thoughts to myself but believed that our best chance to salvage the situation was to try to sell the building to a buyer who would use it as a factory or something like a furniture store. I also thought we could possibly revive the skating business, at least for the time being, if we tapped the market in Perry County to the southeast. Perry County had a much larger population with a better income base. There was a four-lane highway connecting it to Juniata, and there was no skating rink in that area. It was a twenty-five-minute drive, but I thought that, with the right marketing and advertising, we could persuade would-be skaters to make the trip.

A family meeting was called at Mom and Dad's house to talk about ending the feud and saving the skating rink. I finally spoke up with my thoughts and ideas. Dad was impressed, but Barry wasn't. He sprang to his feet, put on his coat, declared in a loud voice, "Nelson is an asshole and should be fired!" and stormed out of the house. With that, it was obvious the objective of the meeting had failed.

The real problem was that the ship was sinking. Instead of bailing water and repairing the holes, instead of trying to find solutions to our problems, we were at each other's throats. What made it even sadder is that during this time, Dad was starting to have health problems. His personality was showing subtle changes. When Dad had refused to at least listen to my suggestion of halting the construction of the skating rink, I thought he was just being stubborn. However, after the trip to see the Army recruiter, the thought crossed my mind that something might be wrong with him. Shortly after the meeting at Mom and Dad's house, Dad was diagnosed with a brain tumor.

He was scheduled for surgery, and his doctors felt confident they could remove the small benign tumor that was placing pressure on his pituitary gland. Dad continued to go about his day-to-day routine and, while on occasion had slight lapses in clarity, for the most part he was still good old Dad.

One evening at the skating rink, Dad asked me, "Could you get a shovel and dig a ditch?" A torrential thunderstorm had left the employee parking lot flooded. A well-dug ditch would create an outlet for the backed-up water and allow it to drain away nicely.

I was digging the ditch when Barry came out of the building and got in his car to run an errand. I was aware of his presence but focused on the task at hand. As usual, I tried to ignore him to avoid any trouble. Everyone was growing weary of the feud.

He drove away, but about ninety seconds later returned with screeching tires.

He jumped out of his car and came running toward me in a blind fury. He was upset that I failed to acknowledge him when he was leaving in his car.

He grabbed me by my jacket and screamed in my face. "WHY WOULDN'T YOU LOOK AT ME WHEN I WAS LEAVING? I'M GOING TO KNOCK YOUR GODDAMNED TEETH OUT!"

I had a firm grasp with both hands on the handle of the shovel that was now standing upright between us. *All I have to do is ram this shovel handle straight up, and it'll break his jawbone in a million pieces.*

He continued to scream and I pushed downward on the shovel handle with everything I had, trying to resist my urge to drive it in under his chin.

As he hollered with spit flying in my face, I could no longer hear what he was saying. All I could think about was the blood that poured from Mr. Summer's face when I'd punched him several years earlier.

I knew if I rocketed the shovel handle under Barry's jaw it would knock him to the ground. I was afraid, especially with a shovel in my hands, that once I started I wouldn't be able to stop.

I could see Dad running toward us out of the corner of my eye.

Dad pulled Barry away as Barry screamed, "CLAIR, HE WOULDN'T LOOK AT ME AS I WAS DRIVING AWAY! HE WOULDN'T LOOK AT ME, CLAIR! HE WOULDN'T LOOK AT ME!"

Barry jumped back in his car and sped off into the night.

He had snapped. This time it was more than just a temper tantrum. He was in a full mental meltdown. He had failed to live up to his own expectations. His dream of being a businessman had become a nightmare, and the anger and disappointment that boiled inside him finally came to the surface like an erupting volcano.

After pausing for a moment and watching him drive away, I resumed my ditch-digging chore. Dad gathered his thoughts and came over to talk to me as I placed my overabundance of adrenaline into the digging of the ditch.

"I'm very proud of you, Nelson, for not using the shovel on Barry; a lot of people would have. You showed great restraint."

I didn't say anything.

I went home that evening with a sense of relief and doom all at the same time. I thought, *I'm relieved that I didn't hurt Barry but mortified that I wanted to.*

I lay in bed that night unable to sleep as I tried to evaluate my life.

Does my personality drive people over the brink of insanity, or does my personality simply invite the wrath of the insane? Either way, I just want it to stop! Is the craziness in my life ever going to go away? I thought this nonsense would end when high school was over. Maybe it will never end. Maybe Juniata County is just one big nuthouse, and we're all twirling around inside it like a barrel of freaking monkeys!

The next morning Dad called me and said, "I want to have lunch with you today. Meet me at the skating rink at 11:30, and we'll drive up to the Green Gables Restaurant in Lewistown."

"Okay, I'll be there."

At lunch, Dad said, "Barry has to go — I don't want him around anymore. He's just too much of a hothead. We can't have this kind of violence and carrying-on in our family. I'll have a talk with him."

I felt bad for Barry and wondered how I could have handled the situation differently. All the skating rink was to me was a minimum wage job. But for Barry, the skating rink was his big dream, his chance to be the successful businessman he had always wanted to be. It all came crashing down around him. He took it very hard.

I have no idea what the conversation was between Dad and Barry; all I know is Barry never came back to the skating rink.

All civility left the family. Gatherings like Easter, Thanksgiving, and Christmas ceased to exist. Even though the relationship between Barry and me had disintegrated, I still adored my sister. However, I felt that having contact with her would only make the situation worse.

So here we were, the Lauvers. Dad had a brain tumor; my sister and her husband were no longer involved in the family business; my brother, Carl, was continuing on a self-destructive path as a drug user; Mom was occupied with Dad's health needs. The only person left standing to run the business was the functionally illiterate son who scrubs the toilets for $3.35 an hour.

On the advice of Dad's attorney, he called in all the skating rink stock that he had given his three children and made a deal with the bank to take the building and land out of the corporation and put it in his personal name. He re-issued 100 percent of the worthless stock to me and asked me to take over the business as the owner and pay him a monthly rent for the building.

I was scared to death but thought, *Why not, what do I have to lose?* It wasn't like IBM was knocking on my door to recruit me as V.P. of operations. I was functionally illiterate, and my prospects outside of buying and selling scrap metal didn't look good. The doomed skating rink was the only thing I had going for me.

To compound the problems of the skating business, liability insurance for skating rinks was quickly becoming cost-prohibitive to obtain.

Along with the boom of roller skating in the late 1970s and early 1980s came a slew of lawsuits by people who had been injured in skating accidents.

In addition to turning all the stock over to me, moving the real estate out of the corporation was another means of making sure the corporation had as little value as possible in case of a lawsuit.

My first act as the new twenty-year-old president and lone stockholder of Roller Junction Inc. was to go through my daily routine, which included cleaning the toilets. Right after that, I hired a bookkeeper/secretary. I needed someone to take care of anything that had to do with reading and writing.

I had watched my family fail in their attempts to prosper at the skating rink. I felt the biggest problem, outside the fact that the facility was overbuilt and lacked a sufficient market, was simply our inexperience. The Lauvers knew nothing about the skating business and had made almost every mistake possible in the operation of the rink.

Every other roller-skating rink operator I'd ever talked to had touted a consultant from Columbus, Ohio, named Skip Cloverman as a guru in the roller-skating business. His picture was always in the roller-rink trade publications. *Skip Cloverman says you oughta do this, Skip Cloverman says you oughta do that.* Everyone agreed that Skip Cloverman was the smartest guy in the room.

I was smart enough to know that I wasn't smart enough to turn around a floundering skating rink. So, I hired Skip Cloverman.

Utilizing Skip's business acumen, he and I were able to create a model for day-to-day operations. Once the plan was in place, Skip worked with each of the managers to train them on their responsibilities. Whether or not Skip realized it, by being the one to train the managers, he was helping to protect my secret.

Skip spent about six days a month at Roller Junction. The rest of the time, we stayed in regular contact over the phone.

I made sure the model was executed correctly in our day-to-day operations and floated through the business watching everything like a hawk.

At night, after the skating rink closed and there was no one to interrupt me, was when I really enjoyed my work. That's when I'd walk though the rink and go over everything with a fine-toothed comb. I'd test the equipment and make sure the facility was in good repair. Being unable to write a list, I made my rounds with a microcassette tape recorder in my hand, leaving instructions for the day manager for anything that needed to be taken care of.

When the manager walked in the next morning she would find a little cassette tape on her desk with various instructions and friendly re-minders that she could handle directly or delegate to other employees. It could be anything from "the soda machine needs to be cleaned," to "don't forget the video game vendor is coming today," to "the wheel-washer water needs to be changed," or "I see we're running low on soda cups," etc.

The skating rink began running like a well-oiled machine. Although it seemed as if my lack of literacy skills were undercover, one isolated incident unnerved me.

The skate rental shop was a favorite hangout for employees dur-ing break time or after they had punched out for the evening. In the back of the shop was a skate repair area. It had a big, sturdy L-shaped workbench and cream-colored cabinets overhead filled with tools and spare parts. One day while hanging out near the workbench, talking with Sarah, a skate guard, we both noticed that someone had used a pencil to scratch some graffiti on the cabinet door. She squinted and leaned in for a better look as she read aloud, "Nelson Lauver is the national poster child for illiteracy."

"What does that mean?" she said, laughing.

I laughed, too, and said, "I don't know, I guess someone is trying to be funny." Although laughing was the last thing I felt like doing. I was mortified. I felt exposed, violated, angry, and ashamed. I thought I'd been doing a good job at hiding my secret, but obviously somebody figured it out. And that somebody had to have been a part-time teenage employee. If that person could figure it out, who else knew? Maybe I wasn't as adept at hiding my literacy problems as I thought?

First thing the next morning, I bought paint in the same color as the cabinets and painted over the graffiti until it was completely hidden. It gave me a temporary measure of relief but ultimately added to the angst inside of me.

The good news was we were beginning to raise revenues at the skating rink. With Skip's advice and execution skills, we targeted the untapped market in Perry County — and it worked!

I was still stuck with a great deal of the corporation's unpaid bills from before I took over and struggled to slowly get them paid off.

I'd love to tell you that the skating rink became a huge success. Describing the business as achieving a small modicum of success would be a more factual statement.

Business was slowly turning the corner. But I knew in my gut that, even with the geographically expanded market area, there still weren't enough warm bodies in the pool of potential customers to sustain the massively overbuilt facility for the long haul.

I felt that if I tapped this new customer base to its maximum and ran an exciting and entertaining skating rink, perhaps I could, with the guidance of Skip, work the market for four to eight years before wearing it out — if I didn't get sued by an injured skater first.

Being the new owner of the skating business left a funny feeling in the pit of my stomach where Barry was concerned. I wasn't sure if I felt guilty and sad or ruthless and victorious.

But I wondered how Barry felt. Did he think I was plotting this takeover all along? Is that why he disliked me so much?

Two years prior, I'd graduated dead last in my high school class. Now, in the middle of this family business war, the word "last" had taken on an entirely new meaning. Now, whether by accident, doggedness, or a little bit of both, I was somehow the last man standing. 🌿

Chapter 16

The Exit

I N 1990, I WAS TWENTY-SEVEN YEARS OLD, and my best friend was a guy I had lunch with almost every day: Clair Lauver. Of course, I called him "Dad." He was retired now from his sales job with the oil company that had bought him out, and he had survived two surgeries to remove a brain tumor. Wherever I was at 11 a.m., on any given weekday, Dad showed up with the same question, "Where're we having lunch today, Nelson?" I'd smile and say, "Wherever you want to, Dad."

I loved Dad more than any other person on earth, but when it came to money and business matters, I could hardly protect him from himself. Since first having the brain tumor and subsequent surgeries, I could see subtle differences in Dad. Everyone else said he seemed great. He did seem great, but he was different. While maybe the general public couldn't see it, I could. His clarity and judgment were not what they had once been.

After his retirement, Dad invested in a local construction business that was having financial trouble. Dad had hoped to be part of a turn-around, but it was not going well. Dad involved me in the initial talks, and at first, I thought it might be a good investment for him. But, the more I learned about the company and the people involved, I came to realize it was a bad idea. They had a poor business reputation and no bank around would even consider giving them a loan. But it was Dad's nature was to help people. He thought everyone was as good as their word, and when the owners of the company promised they would pay Dad back, he believed them.

I pleaded with him not to get involved, but he insisted.

"Nelson, I'm committed to helping this company, and I can't back out now." To quote Yogi Berra, it was déjà vu all over again.

I was still renting the skating rink building from Dad and operating Roller Junction. I had been successful at increasing revenue and providing myself with a modest salary by opening new markets. However, those markets, as I had predicted, were merely suitable to keep the huge facility at break-even. Break-even in itself was worth celebrating, considering where the business had been. Liability insurance for the skating rink was still financially out of reach. If someone were to be seriously injured in a skating accident, I could possibly spend the rest of my life trying to pay off a personal injury court award. It had been almost seven years since I had taken over the skating rink, and I felt I had dodged the legal bullets long enough. I wanted out and was working on an exit strategy.

Considering my lack of literacy skills, filling out a job application was out of the question. I needed to start another business. It had to be something simple and straightforward that didn't require a lot of paperwork, reading, or writing.

I had desperately been searching for another way to support myself. I tested a few small business ideas, looking for something — anything — that would sustain me post-roller-rink. Through a trial-and-error approach, I explored things like buying and reselling classic cars and hawking balloons and novelties at carnivals and parades. I took out an ad in the paper for cleaning out basements, attics, garages, and vacant industrial buildings. I purchased soft drink vending machines and placed them throughout Central Pennsylvania to try to make a profit. I had gone out in search of scrap metal again, only to learn that the area had been picked clean by people trying to make ends meet during the last recession. The list goes on. Some of the business ideas I tested made a little bit of money, while others failed miserably, but I was determined to keep pushing. I knew that if I kept trying, eventually I would find something that worked.

One day while driving along Route 35 I started thinking, *What can I do for a living that will keep food on the table, pay the rent on my little apartment, and keep my telephone and electricity connected?* Just as I was mulling the thought, I looked down from the road into the parking lot of a local truck stop. The parking lot was nearly empty, and I couldn't help but notice the parking lot lines were in need of a fresh coat of paint. As I continued to drive, I noticed every parking lot I passed had faded, worn-out lines. I had never before given any thought as to who paints parking lot lines.

I spent the next couple days driving all over Central Pennsylvania looking at parking lots and realized there was an obvious need for a parking lot line painter in the area. Parking lots with dull, worn-out lines, or no lines at all, were overwhelmingly abundant.

THAT WAS IT! There was a need, and I could satisfy it. I was going to keep money in my pockets by painting parking lot lines. I knew it would work.

The timing of my new venture couldn't have been more perfect. The construction company Dad had become involved with was quickly going down the tubes. Dad had taken out a second mortgage on the skating rink property as collateral for a loan to invest in the construction company, and the skating rink was going to have to be sold to pay off the loan. I was sad and relieved all at the same time. It was a financially devastating blow to Dad, but to be rid of the behemoth skating rink was like a ton of bricks being lifted from my chest.

Painting parking lot lines was a far cry from the dreams I once had for my life, but it paid the bills and kept me from joining the ranks of the homeless.

I already had a pickup truck, so my total investment to get started in the line-painting business was about $2,000. I purchased a state-of-the-art, self-pressurized, walk-behind, paint-striping machine, hired a bookkeeper to help me with the accounting and billing, and started painting like gangbusters!

I knocked on doors all over Central Pennsylvania, sticking out my hand and smiling while I asked, "May I give you a price on repainting your parking lot lines?" Nobody ever turned down a free quote. Meeting people and making deals was fun and reminiscent of those days, years ago, when I drove around making deals on scrap metal.

The work itself was hard, if for no other reason than it was blistering hot on the sun-baked blacktop — but I was just happy to have work.

As time went on, I even bought a second-hand bucket truck so I could hoist myself up in the air to paint metal light poles in parking lots. It turned into a nice little business. Although it wasn't necessarily what I wanted to do with my life, I could see myself painting lines and light poles forever if I had to.

After all those years of being a failure at school, the family fighting, and the headaches with the skating rink, I just wanted to live a normal life. I welcomed the mundane routine that came with being a parking lot line painter. I had a nice circle of acquaintances and even a few ladies in my life from time to time.

I managed to get into a routine that was comfortable for me. I enjoyed going out to dinner with people and had ordering (without being able to read the menu) down to a science. Sometimes, I ordered one of the specials announced by the server, or I'd get the same thing someone else at the table ordered. Sometimes, if I was stuck, I'd just ask the server for a suggestion and made a choice based on that.

I had strategies to get around almost any situation that came up on a day-to-day basis. Excuses like, "I'm sorry I don't have my glasses with me," remained an easy out. I continued to use my listening and memorizing skills to the best of my ability. I usually did business in cash and paid my utility bills at the bank in person. When it was necessary to have a check written, I had my bookkeeper take care of it. I always used directory assistance to get phone numbers and addresses, and when driving, never hesitated to ask for directions if necessary. For the most part, I knew the roads in Central Pennsylvania well, and with its rivers and mountains acting as landmarks, it was easy to navigate. I didn't venture outside of Central Pennsylvania without someone with me who could read a map.

Although reading a book was out of the question, I still craved knowledge and was a huge history buff. I watched local and world news as well as countless documentaries on TV. I also secretly watched Sesame Street, to try to glean a few nuggets that might help me. At what I would guess to be about a second-grade reading level, I could read and write just enough to get into trouble.

I had quite a bit of line painting business up in the town of State College and frequently drove past a building on South Atherton Street.

There was a sign in the yard with several words on it, but one word I could make out appeared to be "Shelter." One weekend, I was cleaning out my closet and thought it would be a good idea to donate some of my old clothing to that shelter. I stopped at the building Monday afternoon with a large box of clothing in my arms. I clumsily made it through the front door and walked up to a pleasant-looking woman seated behind a desk.

"I'd like to donate this clothing," I said.

She looked at me quizzically and asked, "Why are you bringing it here?"

I said, "Aren't you a shelter for the homeless?"

"No sir, we're the Shetler Insurance Agency."

Red-faced, embarrassed, and humiliated, I turned around and walked out the door. I put the box on the back of my truck and drove home to the little rented house that I had recently moved to in Lewistown.

Lewistown was a twenty-five-minute drive from where I grew up in McAlisterville, close enough to easily visit back and forth with my parents. Although my sister, Susan, and her husband, Barry, lived close by as well, I had seen very little of them over the past few years. When I did see them, it was awkward at best. I was sure that there were still bad feelings.

I didn't see my brother, Carl, very often either. But on occasion, the doorbell rang, and as I glanced through the sheer curtains covering the glass front door, I'd see Carl's distinctive silhouette standing on my front porch — tall, thin, wearing a baseball cap with a curled brim, and dangling a cigarette from his mouth.

When Carl appeared at my door, it was a safe bet he wanted

something from me — something unreasonable. Despite this, he generally stacked the deck against himself from the get-go by ignoring my request that he leave his cigarette outside.

Sometimes, he'd want to borrow money or use my phone to make some long-distance calls. Sometimes, he'd just want me to go to a bar with him because he didn't want to go alone. Whatever it was, if I didn't oblige, he'd be angry with me, and he was angry with me a lot.

One particular summer evening, I'd invited some friends over to my place for dinner — a girl I had been casually dating and another couple who lived a few doors down. It was a Friday night, the end of another long, hot week on the blacktop, and I'd picked up some porterhouse steaks, local sweet corn, and cold beer. I'd just brought the steaks in from the grill, and we were about to sit down to eat when the doorbell rang. I looked toward the front door and saw the unmistakable silhouette of Carl; a feeling of dread washed over me.

I knew he could see me, too, so ignoring the doorbell was not an option. He would just keep ringing it. *Oh boy, this is all I need right now; this isn't going to be good.* I told everyone to go ahead and start eating as I resolutely walked to the front door. I was hoping that whatever Carl wanted, he would stay outside and leave quickly without causing a scene. As I opened the front door, he barged right in. He was in a panic.

"Nelson, I need your gun!" he demanded.

"What? No!" I said in a hoarse whisper as I motioned toward my company in the dining room, hoping he would get the hint and lower his voice.

I was pretty sure he was high, and for the sake of my guests and my personal embarrassment, I wanted to get him out of the house as quickly as possible. I put my hand on his shoulder as I herded him out to the front porch and closed the door behind us.

Carl and his wife had split up a year or two earlier, and he was now dating Roxanne, an older, married woman he'd met in a bar a few months back. Apparently, Roxanne's husband found out about the affair and was furious.

"You don't understand, little brother," Carl said. "Roxanne's husband says he's gonna kill me."

"Look, Carl, I'm not giving you my gun, but here's some advice: One, stop screwing the guy's wife, and two, get out of the area until the guy calms down."

"No way," he said. "I love Roxanne, and I'm moving her into my apartment with me."

No matter what, I wasn't going to give Carl my gun. That gun would be a lightning rod for trouble, and I knew someone would get hurt or, even worse, killed.

Trying another tack, Carl said, "Look, Nelson, I'm not actually going to use it on the guy. I just want him to see that I have it. It will frighten him, and he'll leave us alone."

"No, Carl!"

I wasn't giving in, and I could see Carl was becoming exasperated. Suddenly he went for the door. He stormed back into the house, past my guests in the dining room, and bounded up the stairs taking three steps at a time with his long, gangly legs. I was right on his heels. He surmised correctly that my revolver would be in my bedroom and began frantically going through all my dresser drawers.

I was already embarrassed in front of my company, but the last thing I needed was for my crazed brother to get his hands on my gun and start waving it around.

I picked up the phone on my bedside table and said, "Carl, you have to leave now, or I'm calling the cops!"

That statement sunk in. He stopped looking for the gun and decided to throw a little guilt my way instead.

"Hey, when was the last time you saw your sister?" Carl asked in a loud accusatory tone.

"She loves you, ya know, regardless of what her husband thinks of you."

"I haven't seen her in quite some time, Carl. I'd like to see her, but that has nothing to do with you barging into my home while I have dinner guests and insisting I give you a gun. Now get the hell out before I call the cops."

"Okay fine, I'll leave, but if Roxanne's husband kills me, it's going to be on your conscience, little brother, for the rest of your life."

He went down the stairs but before leaving introduced himself to my guests. He mockingly said to them, "Hi, I'm Nelson's brother, Carl. I bet you didn't even know Nelson had a brother, did you?"

To which my startled guests shook their heads no. That only angered Carl more.

He stormed out the front door, slamming it behind him, got in a rusty old pickup truck and sped away.

The episode lasted no more than five minutes but seemed like an eternity. I apologized as I sat down at the dinner table and answered everyone's questions about what had just happened. They seemed understanding and took turns trying to ease my embarrassment by relating their own crazy family stories. I appreciated it but couldn't get the fiasco, and my concern about Carl's well-being, out of my mind. The evening ended early.

My relationship with Carl had been strained for a long time because of his drug abuse. He could be such a great guy but was so unpredictable.

I went to bed that night thinking, *Why do I still have that damn gun?*

It was a shiny, stainless-steel, Saturday Night Special, 38-caliber revolver with walnut grips. I'd bought it back in the days when I regularly carried the evening's receipts from the skating rink to the night depository at the First National Bank. I constantly debated with myself: *Should I take the money to the after-hours depository tonight, or should I just lock it in the safe and deposit it tomorrow in the daytime?*

Every evening after closing, I'd lock all the doors and go out to one corner of the skating rink floor. There on the floor, I could spread out the ample collection of small bills around me. Ones and fives made up the majority of the cash, followed by tens then twenties and the occasional fifty and one-hundred-dollar bill.

The bank had strict policies on the way deposits were to be prepared. All heads on the bills were to be turned the same way. Ones were to be bundled in packs of fifty, fives in packs of $250, and so on. I took pride in preparing the bank deposits in a very meticulous fashion. I may have been functionally illiterate, but I had no trouble counting money.

After the counting, I placed the money in a lockable canvas zipper bag. I placed that bag in a large satchel, set the burglar alarm, locked the door behind me, and walked to my car with my hand underneath my coat on the handle of the gun. There was never a time that I made a night deposit without butterflies in my stomach.

I didn't like carrying the gun but saw it as a necessary evil. In a place like Juniata County, a couple thousand dollars would be a tempting haul for any crook, whether it be a desperate, down-on-his-luck family man or a seasoned criminal.

I tried to vary my route to the bank, but knew it would be only a matter of time until someone tried to rob me. I had often rehearsed in my mind the potential robbery scenarios and how best to handle them. But, when the actual time came, all the preparation and calculated logic in the world took a backseat to my survival instincts.

One Friday evening after midnight, as I walked out of the skating rink with my deposit, I saw a car stop on the road in front of the building, about fifty yards away. Two men got out. One of them stayed with the car while the other came rushing toward me, wielding a bat and screaming, "Give me the money!" I instinctively drew the weapon from under my coat and leveled it at the bandit thirty yards away.

He stopped for a moment, then started toward me again with his bat. *Oh God, I don't want to kill this guy.* I moved the gun several degrees off to the side and fired a warning shot. He stopped for about ten seconds. He must have been weighing how badly he needed the money and whether or not I seemed like the type of person who would actually shoot him.

He started toward me again, this time at a slower pace, but with the bat now hoisted above his head for the death blow. His eyes were wild and his face was beet red. In the subfreezing night air, steam shot from his nostrils like an angry bull.

He moved to where we were now only ten yards apart.

"Jesus Christ man," I hollered. "Don't you understand, I'm going to have to kill you!"

He stopped again, with only five yards between us now. The hammer was cocked, my hands trembled, my sweaty finger was on the trigger, and my heart thumped in my chest. I was sure someone was going to die, and I was determined, as frightened as I was, to stand my ground. I refused to surrender my hard-won life to the business end of a baseball bat.

I reasoned with him one last time, "Walk away!"

He paused for a moment, locking his eyes with mine while seeming to search for an indication of how serious I was, then he lowered the bat in dejection, turned around, and sprinted down over the bank to the waiting getaway car. The tires squealed and the car quickly disappeared out of sight.

I went back in the building, sat at my desk, and opened my desk drawer. I pulled out a bottle of Canadian Club and took a big slug. I pressed the speed dial for the police. A state trooper I knew well appeared shortly.

"He was coming at you with a bat! Why the hell didn't you shoot him, you dumbass?" the trooper wanted to know.

"I would have if he would have taken another step," I said.

"Jesus Christ, Nelson, you could have done the world a great service. Next time, the son-of-a-bitch will kill someone."

I made up my mind there wouldn't be a next time for me. I began locking the money in the safe at night. I figured any criminal who wanted it could have it if they could get through the wailing burglar alarm that was transmitted to the police barracks up in Lewistown. I figured there was a fifty-fifty chance the cops could get there by the time the burglars cut through the safe with a torch. And, if the cops didn't make it in time, so what, it was better to stand the loss of a couple thousand dollars than be placed in a kill-or-be-killed situation.

They never caught the guys, and I never made a night deposit again — opting instead for daytime visits to the bank.

After I got out of the skating rink business and moved up the road to Lewistown, I still had the gun, and Carl knew it. I had a love-hate relationship with it. I loved it because it had saved my life. On the other hand, the gun's barrel was too short to be used for sporting purposes. Its sole function in design was for the taking of a human life. I hated that thought.

I lay awake that night, thinking about Carl and how desperately he wanted that gun. I thought about all the possible outcomes of the gun in Carl's hands, and none of them were good. The next morning, I took the weapon to a friend who was an avid collector and sold it to him. After all, a parking lot line painter doesn't need a handgun. ✒

Chapter 17

The Professor

SUMMERTIME WAS THE BUSIEST TIME of all for line painting. After a while, I got so used to the scorching heat on the blacktop that I didn't need air conditioning to sleep even on the warmest summer nights.

One evening after a long, hot day, I came home to a message on my answering machine from a car dealer who wanted his parking lot lines painted.

The next day, I went to look at the job and gave the dealer a price. He worked me over on the numbers so badly in an attempt to get a better deal that I finally said, "No, I can't do it for that," and politely ended the negotiations.

After thinking about it for a few days, I called the dealership back and said I would do the job for the money offered. It was a big job, and I hated to turn it down even though there wasn't a lot of profit in it.

I showed up early that Saturday morning and started painting lines. About an hour into the job, an older gentleman walked toward me from across the parking lot. I assumed he must want me to paint lines for him. The best advertising in the world was to simply be seen painting lines. At least half of my jobs came to me that way.

I turned off my paint machine only to learn parking lot lines were the last thing on his mind.

He was looking for a nearby greenhouse and needed directions.

"Well, that's simple to get to," I told him. I rattled off the directions as only a local could, then pulled the start-cord on my paint sprayer and got back to work. He went back to his car only to return several minutes later with a tablet and pen.

Seemingly confused by my country-boy directions, he asked if I would write them down.

I turned my paint machine off for a second time. I was becoming aggravated by the thought that time is money, and if this paint machine isn't running, I'm not paying my bills.

I repeated the directions to the greenhouse as he forced the tablet and pen on me.

I tried to draw a map and now, in a slightly confrontational voice, gave him verbal directions for the third time.

It was obvious that if I simply wrote down the directions I could get rid of this guy and get back to making money. My struggle with writing was painfully apparent to both of us.

He persisted, "Could you just write down the directions?"

Finally, he took the pen and the tablet back and asked, "You can't read and write, can you?"

I paused for a moment, taking a deep breath to help quell my embarrassment, and then stated, "You are correct, Sir, I am functionally illiterate."

"Have you ever heard of dyslexia?" he asked.

"Sir, I've never heard the term you just spit out, but I can tell you that as a boy my father had me evaluated by some of the best medical minds. They couldn't figure out what was wrong with me, and I'm doubtful that, at this point in my life, anyone can help me."

"I disagree wholeheartedly," he said. "If you are indeed dyslexic, as I suspect you may be, there is great hope for you. Let's sit down over here on the tailgate of your truck for a few minutes and talk."

The conversation lasted an hour and a half.

For the first time in my life, I opened up. I opened up to this stranger, who had a comfortable grandfatherly quality to him. I told him all about my school years, when my reading and writing difficulties began, how I covered it up, and the unfortunate results. I opened up and told him about my fears of being the dumb kid and how I just wanted to be normal.

He listened intently and told me that, while my history was a bit extreme, "Your story is not unusual. Many people have struggled through school with an undiagnosed learning disability."

He went on to tell me that dyslexia has nothing to do with one's level of intelligence and rattled off a list of people throughout history who were thought to have dyslexia, like Nelson Rockefeller, FDR, and Albert Einstein. He told me about some celebrities and even a personal story about a good friend of his with dyslexia.

"Dyslexia is simply a disconnect, a processing issue inside the brain, that makes reading and writing difficult. It has absolutely nothing to do with your IQ," he said.

Having a name for this problem made me feel hopeful, but at the same time, I was completely overwhelmed with all the information coming at me. *If this is what my problem is, how, at my age, do I possibly begin to get a handle on it?*

I had always had the desire to grow and be more, but growth had been a very painful experience that took me well out of my comfort zone. At least, for the time being I had put my thoughts of personal growth on the back burner. I had settled into my current life as a line painter and was finally feeling comfortable. This new information changed everything, and I was anxious as to what might lie ahead.

What if he's wrong? What if I can't be helped? Then I will have exposed my limitations to others and will feel even worse.

But this stranger showed a genuine caring and understanding for my situation that no one ever had. He was bright, articulate and very reassuring. Cautious optimism was growing inside me.

"So," I asked, "Where does a person start?"

He suggested I start by contacting the Pennsylvania State Office of Vocational Rehabilitation (OVR) to get an evaluation from the experts there.

I thanked him for his time, and we said our goodbyes.

I returned to the parking lot and continued working. I thought about how thankful I was that I had changed my mind and decided to take on this low-profit painting job and how thankful I was that the older gentleman came along to ask for directions.

I called my mom that evening and told her that I'd met a gentleman who thought I might have something called dyslexia. Mom said that just a few days earlier she had caught a news snippet about dyslexia. She encouraged me to follow through.

I decided to take the stranger's advice and put aside my pride (or shame, depending upon how one looks at it) and take the first step.

My initial meeting with an OVR caseworker took place at the

Office of Employment Security in Lewistown. I felt a little embarrassed going to my first OVR session. Even though the gentleman in the parking lot had been very adamant that dyslexia had nothing to do with intelligence or lack thereof, I was still concerned that others wouldn't see it quite that way and would view me as being dumb.

My caseworker set up an appointment for an evaluation with a doctor in State College who specialized in learning disabilities.

As suspected, I was diagnosed with dyslexia. Although the doctor determined my above-average strength in auditory processing (listening skills) would be helpful in my rehabilitation, her official report noted great weakness in visual memory and stated, "Because of his age and the severity of the involvement, extensive intervention will be needed."

Her recommendation was that OVR set up an appointment on my behalf with the Penn State Diagnostic Reading/Learning Disability Program for further evaluation and to determine a course of vocational rehabilitation.

Although I wasn't surprised with the diagnosis, I was frightened by how serious the problem seemed to be. *How could it be this bad?* The reality of my situation felt overwhelming, and I fought to keep myself moving forward rather than retreating back to the comfort that came with the thought that I could simply paint lines forever. I had been looking forward to changing my life, but I didn't think it would be this hard. I was hoping for a magic pill, and this evaluation starkly stated that was not an option.

I knew it was time to take responsibility for my life, accept the past, and start preparing for the success of my future.

About three weeks later, I reported to the Penn State Reading Lab for my scheduled appointment. As I took a deep breath and walked through the heavy glass doors, I was greeted by a receptionist who led me to the evaluation area where I met three pleasant female graduate students who would be collectively evaluating me.

Judging from the small size of the furniture, I noted that I was probably one of the few adults whom they had worked with. I couldn't help but laugh as I sat my six-foot-two frame on a little, red, plastic molded chair more appropriate for an elementary school kid. From the moment I entered the room, I felt like I was being analyzed. However, I liked the graduate students, and they immediately put me at ease.

I spent the next four hours answering their questions and going through all sorts of evaluative tests of my auditory and visual memory, as well as sequencing abilities. By the end of the session, I could tell one graduate student stood out from the rest and seemed extremely interested and attentive. They told me they would score my evaluation and, when complete, would call to set up another meeting.

At the follow-up meeting, each graduate student explained a portion of the results. I appreciated their concern for my feelings as they did their best to play up my positive areas, like auditory processing and auditory memory, while carefully sugar-coating some of my serious problems in the area of visual processing and visual memory.

The bottom line was that they believed it would be nearly impossible for me to make any significant progress in learning to read and write on my own. My best bet, they said, would be to hire a tutor to work with me one-on-one. On the drive home that day I thought, *How the hell do I go about finding and hiring a tutor?* With all the information flying around, I hadn't thought to ask the question.

I returned home that evening to a message on my answering machine from one of the graduate students, Cheryl. I called her back and she offered her services as my private tutor at no charge for as long as I needed. She said she was willing to put in the time if I was serious about learning. I immediately took her up on her offer. The problem was solved!

I began visiting Cheryl's apartment in State College two to three evenings a week for ninety-minute tutoring sessions. I was amazed at how dedicated she was, and so well prepared with a fresh new lesson plan at each session.

Contrary to popular belief, dyslexia is generally not seeing words and letters backwards or upside down. In my case, at least, dyslexia is more of a confused mass of letters and words on a page. The best way I can describe it is like somebody placing a piece of window screen over the text and then moving it around while I try to read through it. With Cheryl's help, I was quickly learning to understand how the dyslexia affected me. We soon discovered that larger, double-spaced print made a tremendous difference for me.

She also suggested we try placing various colored sheets of cellophane over the text. It worked! Yellow cellophane filters helped calm the chaos and anxiety in my brain.

Another extremely helpful tool in my new quest to learn to read and write was an inexpensive set of phonetic audio teaching tapes I bought at a yard sale for five dollars. The tapes were homemade and rather amateurish. They sounded as if they were recorded around a kitchen table by a husband and wife with a guitar and a great deal of knowledge on sounding out letters and words.

Within six weeks of working with Cheryl, I had made great progress. I was starting to get the basics down pat. My visual confusion was becoming more manageable. I was getting through multi-syllable words and sometimes even to the end of a sentence. I was excited and motivated to keep going. I had no fear or desire to turn back now.

I still saw Dad almost every day at lunch. He and I talked about a lot of things, but we didn't discuss my tutoring. He and Mom knew that I had gone through evaluations with OVR, and I had shared the diagnosis with them. Thankfully, my sister Susan and I were starting to mend our relationship, and I shared the evaluations with her as well.

When I initially talked with my parents about the evaluation results, I could see how upset they were. They blamed themselves and apologized for not pushing harder to find help for me when I was a kid. I decided to keep the details of my reading and writing difficulties from them. I told them I was getting help but didn't tell them how extensive the process was. I just didn't want to make them feel any worse.

After line painting all day, I spent almost every evening studying. On the nights Cheryl didn't tutor me, she always assigned homework, and I always made sure my homework was complete. I wanted to honor her hard work and never disappoint her.

Cheryl was extremely encouraging to me, and in turn she was encouraged by my progress over the ensuing months. She was excited that she had the ability to teach me, and I was excited that I was learning. We were a team. We became fast friends and very comfortable with each other. I didn't feel like she judged me or thought that I was stupid. For the first time, I wasn't afraid of making mistakes or asking questions.

At the same time I was working with Cheryl, OVR paid for me to go to counseling to get my head on straight. Amazingly, I learned that dyslexia had not necessarily been my greatest impediment to learning to read and write. Anger, guilt, fear, and blame held me back as much as the learning disability itself. It took many sessions with many well-trained clinicians to get past that. I worked on trying to understand the choices I'd made and how those choices held me back. The most valuable thing I learned that moved my life forward in a quantum leap was the fact that blaming others was getting me nowhere.

Yes, I had been done wrong. And yes, my education could have been handled differently. But that was in the past, and if I were going to be honest with myself, I had to accept my part in what happened. I was the one who made the choice to be the bad kid. I was the one who refused to participate in class for fear of being embarrassed. I was the one who turned away from well-meaning educators who tried to reach out to me. I pushed buttons, agitated authority, and stirred the pot as a means of hiding the fact that I was functionally illiterate.

As my tutoring sessions with Cheryl continued, the excitement of our success fed into itself. Soon, we were having drinks together to celebrate, then dinner, and then a romantic relationship developed. I really enjoyed her company, but I guess I saw the relationship differently than she did. I soon learned she was much more serious about where this was going romantically than I was.

Cheryl told me about her family and background, and it was obvious that they were extremely well off. I just couldn't imagine that I would be someone she would want to spend time with over the long haul. When she laid it on the line as to the way she saw the relationship, it was different than the way I saw it. Part of me really wanted a loving and caring relationship, but I don't think I was capable of that sort of connection at that time. Even if I was crazy about her, I would have been emotionally inadequate. Our relationship ended, and Cheryl was terribly hurt. I still feel bad about it.

My ability to write was more challenged than my ability to read. I knew the words I wanted to write, but getting them out of my brain, down my arm, and through a pencil was an extremely difficult process. Everything I tried to write still resembled the chicken scratch that Mrs. Clark transcribed from my paper to the blackboard in third grade.

Thankfully, there was help for me on that front, too. A vocational rehabilitation specialist recommended I try using a word processor to see if typing would prove easier than writing. I started to hunt and peck the keys and only got up to fourteen words per minute with lots of errors. For me, that was a huge improvement compared to writing by hand. Thank God for spell check.

So, I began to practice, practice, practice. I plunked away at the keys.

I started by trying to look at a book and type what I saw. I soon realized the dyslexia made that extraordinarily difficult. Instead, I decided I would type from my memory. I'd been a storyteller-in-training my entire life, and it just seemed natural that, if I were going to type something, it should be the great stories that filled my head — the stories of my family, friends, heroes from history, and the colorful tales from Juniata County.

Just like the cash register at the gas station and the calculator I carried everywhere, the word processor proved invaluable.

Eighteen months after starting my rehabilitation, I was now ready to read my first book. I selected Booker T. Washington's autobiography, *Up from Slavery*. Although it was the first book I ever read, in my mind it remains the most powerful one. Booker T. Washington's story is perseverance at its finest, and the inspiration born of his struggle and ultimate success remains with me.

For years after meeting the gentleman in the parking lot, I struggled to remember his name. I was so overwhelmed by all the information he gave me that day, that after we shook hands and parted company, I couldn't recall his name.

He gave me a business card that day, but not being able to read it, I didn't pay much attention to it and quickly stuck it in my pocket. Fortunately, I did remember what the card looked like. It was tan and had two brown, oddly-placed vertical lines running down the side. Fifteen years later, while going through some items in a storage bin, I found the card.

A quick Google search revealed that Dr. George M. Guthrie, Ph.D., professor of psychology at Penn State University, passed away in 2003.

I tried to reach his widow at an address I found online, but to no avail.

When I share the story of meeting Dr. Guthrie, people often ask why I opened up and talked to this stranger. Why did I share with him what I had worked so hard to hide my entire life?

Part of the reason was simply his manner and the way he asked me — there was no denying it. Moreover, Dr. Guthrie had care and concern in his voice, and although I didn't think there was anyone who could help me, I sensed that he might be able to offer some sort of insight.

There was another reason, though. I had recently made a new friend — a fellow entrepreneur — and greatly admired his business savvy. He asked where I had gone to college, and because I was so embarrassed by the truth, I lied and told him I was a graduate of nearby Penn State. I had worked so hard to hide my illiteracy over the years, but now to come out and tell a blatant lie was shameful. I was consumed with guilt from that lie and couldn't stop thinking that it was time to get to the bottom of my literacy issues.

I've often wondered if Dr. Guthrie already knew of my problems with literacy. Had I met him somewhere before? Did we, perhaps, have a mutual friend who also recognized my difficulty? Did Dr. Guthrie make the forty-mile trip from State College with a determination to find me and help me? Why didn't he go into the dealership where it was comfortable and air-conditioned to ask for directions? Why did he walk past three or four salesmen on the lot, way out to where I was painting lines, and single me out to ask for directions? I was obviously busy running a piece of noisy equipment. Why bother me when there were many others who could help? Why didn't he simply write the directions down as I dictated them instead of brazenly forcing the tablet on me? Why?

Because of Dr. Guthrie, I learned to read and write. I changed my life. I wish I could have thanked him personally. ✤

Chapter 18

All Hell Broke Loose

PRING 1994: I WOULD SOON BE THIRTY-ONE and was no longer
functionally illiterate. My reading had improved dramatically but
not without eighteen months of determined practice.

It was time to make a decision about my future. The goal of my
rehabilitation was to help me reach my full potential in a career that
I was well-suited for. One career counselor suggested a future as a
commercial real estate agent. Another thought I would do well in business management. Often on my drives to see my caseworker I thought
about the same two careers I had dreamed of since the time I was a boy.
Mrs. Parsons had planted the seeds a long time ago, and as elusive as
those dreams had become over the years, I always felt a little glimmer
of hope that maybe someday things would be different.

Early on in my rehabilitation, my counselor told me that college
was certainly an option to explore and gave me the contact information for Penn State's Office of Disability Services. I set up a meeting
with the department director who specialized in opening the doors of
the university to students with learning disabilities. Believe it or not,
she said that with the assistance of disabilities services, I could go to
college and then on to law school if I desired — and there were even

programs to help me with the costs. The thought of practicing law was exciting for me … but all those books!

All this great news during my meeting was, however, dampened by the unsettling smell of the floor wax at the university. It smelled exactly like the floor wax used at East Juniata. Suddenly, my mind was back in high school, and my stomach was in knots.

I was confident I could overcome that irrational fear and was excited at the thought of achieving a childhood dream, but I had another choice to explore, too: broadcasting. As I weighed the options in my mind, the notion of expressing my thoughts and ideas over the airwaves as a broadcaster appealed to me more and more.

I sat down with the caseworker.

"I'd like to be a broadcaster," I told him.

"Wow, we've never had anyone make that request. I'm not sure where to begin."

I had been kicking that around in my head for a while. I told him I thought the best place to start would be to visit a professional recording studio to make an audition tape of my voice. He agreed.

Within a couple of weeks, I recorded my first voice audition tape at a studio in Lancaster, about two hours away. Among the generic radio commercials on the tape was one of my stories that I had typed on the word processor as part of my rehabilitation practice. The story was about my Uncle Roy and how during WWII he was forced to parachute out of his aircraft after it had been hit by enemy fire. Not only did he survive the incident, but with the help of the French underground he spent ninety days on the run, riding a bicycle and disguised as a peasant woman. He eluded German troops and was finally triumphant at making his way back into Allied territory.

The studio owner thought it was rather odd to place a story like this on a demo and tried to talk me out of it. But being different was exactly what I wanted. I didn't want my demo to sound just like every other radio guy's demo. I wanted to be unique. I wanted to be noticed.

I decided to throw myself completely into my new career. I sold all of my line-painting equipment, except for my pickup truck, and hit the road throughout Central Pennsylvania in my blue Chevy S10 splattered with yellow traffic paint.

I traveled around shaking hands, smiling, and talking with everyone from ad agencies looking for voices for radio and TV commercials to documentary filmmakers who hired narrators. Slowly, I was developing a studio schedule as a freelance voice-over artist. As it turned out, that story on my demo became the hook that made people sit up, pay attention, and ultimately hire me. Producers loved the fact that I was just a real guy who could tell a good story.

I purposely stayed away from radio stations in my job search as I had learned the pay was low. Voice-over work was far more lucrative. Surprisingly, narration work wasn't that hard to come by. At that time there was a demand in the market, and it seemed that I had what they were looking for. It wasn't huge money, but it got much better as time went on.

In my search for work, someone told me that Accu-Weather — one of the world's largest privately-owned weather forecasting services — was hiring voices. Emboldened by my recent successes, I decided to do a cold call visit to Accu-Weather.

I actually got to meet with the director of broadcasting. He seemed reluctant to take me seriously because of my lack of "newsroom experience" as he put it, but I finally convinced him to take a listen to my audition tape. By the time I left, I had a part-time job. Accu-Weather produced and sold local weather reports to hundreds of radio and TV newsrooms throughout the United States and Canada. I, along with a handful of other broadcasters, provided the voice. Ironically, here I was, the kid who had been petrified to read in front of twenty-five of my fellow students, now reading the weather broadcast to millions of listeners.

Occasionally, as I sat in my broadcast booth at Accu-Weather, watching the clock and waiting for my queue to go on the air in Duluth, somewhere in Texas, or perhaps in a sleepy little town in Kansas, I was haunted by my school years.

My public school experience was long over and done with. It was water under the bridge. I couldn't go back and change anything. But I wondered about the kids who were now trying to navigate the same system. *What about the kids who may, at this very moment, be going through what I went through?* East Juniata still had the same principal, and most of the same teachers were still there — even the bad ones.

In my mind, while I had accepted culpability for my role in receiving a botched education, Morgan and the others weren't off the hook if they were still operating with the same methods.

I tossed and turned in bed at night as I thought about the kid who could be Morgan's prisoner in the vault come morning. I laid awake thinking about the kids who were now dealing with Fairfax, Summers, and Clay.

Can I truly be considered rehabilitated if I simply go on with my life with no thought for those who may be struggling now?

It was doubtful that Principal Morgan would have mellowed or gotten a handle on those few thug teachers. But perhaps what troubled me most was that Mr. Brookfield, the sadistic remedial math teacher, had left teaching and was now an elected member of the board of education.

How could anything possibly be different if Brookfield, of all people, is on the school board?

My life was turning into a constant debate with myself.

This isn't your problem, Nelson, I told myself. *If there are kids at East Juniata facing these difficulties, they have parents who should step up and help them.*

It really isn't my place to get involved in other people's lives. People need to solve their own problems.

Why in God's name would I get involved in such matters now? It's been over a dozen years since I got out of school. My life is great now! Shouldn't I just leave all that behind me? If I buck the system, there will be backlash. I stand a good chance of being socially ostracized.

Then again, maybe just like in my case, the kids aren't talking to their parents about the troubles they're having at school. Obviously someone had stepped up to help me at one point. Isn't it time I use my voice and step up to help someone else?

The debate went on in my head for months. I finally came to the conclusion that, at the very least, I needed to approach the superintendent of schools and ask a few questions regarding the current policies on identifying students with learning disabilities, punishment practices, and most concerning of all, the use of the vault.

The superintendent, Dr. Leonard Kirk, had been at the helm of the Juniata County School District for almost thirty years. Most considered him a hero, some considered him a villain.

Those who saw him as a hero revered him for his ability to keep property taxes the lowest in the state. He did that by running the school district on a shoestring budget. Out of 501 school districts in the state of Pennsylvania, Juniata County had the lowest-paid teachers, and was within the bottom few districts in per-pupil spending. Over the years, the district had tucked away millions of dollars of surplus cash.

Those who saw him as a villain cried foul, saying that the meager budget denied aid to students with special learning needs. And with such low teacher pay, Juniata County had difficulty attracting the best teachers. All the while, Dr. Kirk received an exorbitant salary for a school district as small as Juniata County. Some people were suspicious of his fancy Cadillacs, his luxurious home, his appointment to the board of directors of a local bank, and his overall opulent lifestyle, which included dining out of town in fine restaurants.

While some citizens questioned Dr. Kirk's motives, few ever confronted him face-to-face. Those who tried found him hard to reach. He spent his days insulated in a small twelve-by-twelve office, guarded by a secretary. People outside of Dr. Kirk's inner circle were seldom invited behind his closed door.

In the small fishbowl of Juniata County, most agreed Dr. Kirk was the power broker of all power brokers. In the mid-1990s he was a tall, handsome, well-dressed man in his early sixties. He was admired by many for his fabulous business mind and yet reviled by others who believed he possessed a cold and ruthless heart.

I contacted various special education advocacy groups throughout the state to inquire how the Juniata County School District measured up when it came to providing services to children with learning disabilities. I wasn't surprised when I learned that the school district was seriously deficient and out of compliance with state law.

Unfortunately, the Commonwealth of Pennsylvania Department of Education was sadly understaffed in the area of enforcement. They were a watchdog without teeth. Dr. Kirk was savvy enough to take advantage of that lax enforcement, saving lots of money and ultimately denying countless children the education guaranteed them by the state constitution.

I thought long and hard about how to reach out to Dr. Kirk. I knew I'd never get an appointment to see him and figured getting him on the phone was next to impossible. I decided to send a letter.

I used my word processor and wrote briefly of my own story and detailed the punishments I had received while attending East Juniata. I expressed my concern for current students who may be in need of special services to help them with learning challenges such as dyslexia. I inquired about current forms of punishment being employed, and more specifically, asked if students were still being confined in the school's fireproof vault.

Dr. Kirk didn't answer my letter, so I wrote to him again. Still no answer.

I placed several calls to his office, but was politely told by his secretary, "the doctor is unavailable to speak at this time."

Maybe I should just forget about it. Who am I to take on the most powerful man in Juniata County?

I decided I would try making one more phone call to Dr. Kirk. If I didn't get a response, I'd just leave well enough alone. *I'll let people fight their own battles.* Of course, Dr. Kirk refused my call.

After a few more restless nights, I knew what I needed to do, and I knew what it meant for me personally. If I went forward, everybody would know what I had been ashamed of for so long — the fact that

I had been functionally illiterate. Everyone in my community would finally know that I was the "dumb kid."

Regardless of how embarrassing that admission would be, it could have never compared with the guilt of turning my back on kids like me.

If I don't stand up and become the voice of kids who don't have voices of their own, I'm no better than Kirk, Morgan, Fairfax, Brookfield, Summers, and Clay.

I knew there would be serious backlash. I knew that calling Dr. Kirk and the Juniata County School District on the carpet would anger local taxpayers who idolized the superintendent. Dr. Kirk, as far as most locals were concerned, was the patron saint of dirt-cheap property taxes.

As I strategized my next move, I was well aware that once the genie was out of the bottle it could never be put back.

I sat on the sofa in my living room and stared at a list of phone numbers in front of me. Finally, I mustered the courage, picked up the phone, and started placing calls to various local and regional news organizations. I told them my personal story and expressed my concern that there may still be students in Juniata County with special learning needs who are not receiving help. I further expressed my concern regarding heavy-handed punishments and the use of the vault.

All hell broke loose. Members of the press showed up in Juniata County with pens and pads, microphones, news vans, satellite dishes, TV cameras, and all those things that go with the sensationalism of a breaking news story.

Within an hour of the first news van rolling up to the School Administrative Building, a knock came at my door. It was a private courier with a sealed envelope. My name was typed neatly on the front. Inside, on Juniata County School District stationery, was a personal letter from Dr. Kirk requesting a meeting to discuss my concerns at a time and place of my choosing.

I called Dr. Kirk's office to make an appointment, and was immediately put through to the superintendent himself.

I met Dr. Kirk and Principal Morgan two days later at Dr. Kirk's office in the district's administration building. Both men were furious that I had the audacity to contact the press regarding my concerns, and they immediately began unloading on me.

An infuriated Principal Morgan quoted a Bible proverb, explaining that, if you have a problem with another man, the Bible says you are supposed to approach that man directly to discuss it. The verbal lashing continued as Principal Morgan railed, "You're nothing but an ungrateful punk! I'm the one who made sure you got a diploma and this is how you treat me?"

Finally, Dr. Kirk spoke up and demanded, "What exactly do you want, Nelson?"

I told him that I simply wanted answers. I wanted answers to questions like: What steps are you taking to identify students with special learning needs? Do you still use the vault to lock up kids? Are students still pounded into submission? Are children with learning problems still paddled as "remediation" for their learning difficulties? What steps are you taking to become compliant with the special education laws?

Dr. Kirk sat at his desk, red-faced and fuming. In a controlled, rage-filled voice, he stated, "There has never been any child abuse in Juniata County Schools, and we are compliant with the law!"

I was ready for this fight and was not going to be intimidated. I told Dr. Kirk that he'd obviously had his head in the sand for a very long time.

"You should try getting out of your office and actually visiting some of the schools in your kingdom," I said.

Principal Morgan sat back in his chair, aghast.

"Nelson, you have to call off the press," he said. "A lady TV reporter barged into my office yesterday asking questions about the vault!"

I chuckled and said, "I'm flattered, Principal Morgan, by your notion that I have some sort of button that turns the free press on and off. Yes, I made the phone calls to the media — but your actions invited them to come. I tried to reach out to the school district to start a dialogue. My good-faith effort was ignored. You're on your own now. I can't help you with the press."

"This will not go well for you, Lauver," the superintendent told me.

"I'm not afraid, Dr. Kirk. I can't imagine that, even with all your power, there is anything you can do to me that's worse than what I've already survived."

It was obvious that Principal Morgan and Dr. Kirk had no interest in discussing my concern for students. They only cared about the reporters and how to get rid of them.

At least they're scared, I thought as I left Dr. Kirk's office. Morgan seemed so frightened that I felt he was probably too paranoid to ever lock up a student in the vault again for fear a reporter might get wind of it.

I left the two men in the superintendent's office frantically wondering how to dodge the media. The ever-brilliant Dr. Kirk proved quite adept at avoiding the press, but Principal Morgan wasn't as skillful. At a local school board meeting, he hurried for a backdoor as a TV crew chased him down a hall asking if he had ever locked children in the vault. "No comment, no comment," he said as he dashed out of the building to his waiting car.

The press shared my concerns with the public, and for a time, there was outrage. Though, as I expected, much of the outrage was pointed toward me for airing the school district's dirty laundry.

I received letters, phone calls, and voicemails from angry citizens who felt I had no right to "meddle" in such matters.

At the same time, my phone rang off the hook with calls from parents who were concerned about the overzealous punishments their children had received at school. My fears were confirmed over and over by parents who spoke of the lack of help for their children with learning problems. However, few were willing to stand up and fight, for fear of retaliation.

One man told me, "My boss worships Dr. Kirk. If I cause trouble, I'll lose my job." Another person told me, "Principal Morgan could make it really rough for my kids if I go public." People were clearly afraid.

Eventually reporters lost interest and moved on to the next sensational story, but a small group of parents and community leaders started to organize and question the practices of the Juniata County School District. For the most part, their questions were ignored. Then Juniata County changed forever.

In a relatively short period of time, four separate suicides by teenage boys from East Juniata High School rocked our community to its core. Each of the boys was having trouble at school. Finally, the good and decent people of Juniata County found their voices, stood up, and started asking questions about the state of education in the county.

This time, there were too many voices to be ignored.

The family of one of the boys who'd committed suicide filed suit against the school district in the United States District Court for the Middle District of Pennsylvania. The lawsuit stated that the young man frequently visited the principal's office pleading for academic and emotional help. The suit asserted that the sixteen-year-old boy had clearly been denied the services guaranteed to him under state and federal law. The young man finally reached his breaking point. Feeling there was no hope for him, he used a gun to take his life in the living room of his family's home. Attorneys for the school district bristled as they vowed to fight the "baseless lawsuit."

It was obvious after countless legal depositions from many former students — including me — as well as faculty and administrators that East Juniata High School had been an unpleasant and often brutal place for children with learning problems. The depositions made it clear that, if you were a kid in need of special help, Juniata County, Pennsylvania, was the last place you wanted to attend school.

Principal Morgan was also deposed under oath. In his testimony he finally admitted that he had, indeed, used the school's fireproof vault as an isolation chamber over the years to punish many students.

Shortly after Principal Morgan's shocking admission, the case was settled out of court for an undisclosed sum of money.

Morgan left East Juniata High School after being principal for thirty years. He took a position with a Christian school in a neighboring county. Dr. Kirk retired a wealthy man. The newly-empowered people of Juniata County voted in a new board of education that worked diligently to bring our schools into compliance with state and federal laws regarding special education. 🌿

Chapter 19

Out of My Comfort Zone

IT WASN'T A SPECIAL OCCASION. Dad just decided to throw a little late summer get-together for family and friends. The location: a rustic, white clapboard cabin nestled on the Shade Mountain behind McAlisterville. The cabin, and its grand front porch had been a gathering place for the Lauvers for as long as I could remember. It was always a relaxing respite with its cool breezes and the glorious sounds of the rushing waters of Lost Creek forever within earshot.

Dad invited Mr. Yeisley, the gentleman who had lived next door when I was growing up in the stone house. Mr. Yeisley's wife had died from Hodgkin's disease at about the time I was getting out of high school. He seemed lost for a few years and then met another lady on the golf course and remarried. He sold his house and moved in with his new wife, about a dozen miles away from McAlisterville.

I hadn't seen him in years, but the time had created no distance between us. Mr. Yeisley and I sat on a big porch swing and talked and laughed, picking up where we'd left off some ten years earlier. I was now thirty-two, and he was seventy-seven.

"How have you been, Mr. Yeisley?"

"For goodness sakes, Nelson, why don't you call me Frank?"

"Old habits die hard, and if it's all the same to you, out of respect, I'd like to continue calling you Mr. Yeisley."

"Okay," he said as he smiled. "I'm sure your father told you that I'm dying."

"Yes, he did, and I was very sad to learn that."

"It won't be long now. I have no regrets, it's been a very good life."

We enjoyed an iced tea and talked for an hour before dinner was ready. He had many questions about my work as a voice-over artist in the Philadelphia and Harrisburg markets.

"I understand New York City is the voice-over capital of the world," he said.

"You're right, Mr. Yeisley, it is."

"Are you getting any work out of New York?"

"No, I haven't ventured into New York yet."

"So, Nelson, what you're telling me is that you're satisfied to just catch the little fish that live in the shallow waters right off the side of the dock?"

I smiled as I remembered Mr. Yeisley's "big fish in the deep water" metaphor from when I was a kid fishing off the dock at Tingley Lake. I may have been thirty-two years old, but I wasn't too old to receive counsel from a wise sage.

"The big fish live in the deep water, Nelson. Go to New York."

That evening was the last time I saw my old friend. A few days after the gathering on the mountain, he headed for his winter place in Florida, where he died several months later.

I could see two monstrous skyscrapers from miles out as my train sped forward. I was unfamiliar with them and couldn't believe how big they were and how they towered over the skyline of an approaching New York City. I had boarded in Harrisburg and stopped over at 30th Street Station in Philadelphia to connect with the train for New York.

Always curious, I turned to the friendly looking, heavy-set middle-aged lady sitting across the aisle from me. I asked, "Excuse me, Ma'am, what are those big buildings?" She smiled and said in a kindly tour guide sort of way, "Those are the Twin Towers of the World Trade Center."

"Oh," I said. I'd heard of the World Trade Center, but not the term Twin Towers. It was obvious that I'd just announced to everyone within earshot that I was not from around here — a total newbie to the Big Apple.

Since I'd started doing voice-overs, I had taken the train to Philadelphia many times for voice jobs. Although the city of brotherly love seemed big and intimidating, getting around town was never a problem. I just hailed a taxi and gave the driver the address of where I wanted to go — easy.

But as a country boy who'd grown up in a small town where the highest building was two stories plus a steeple, nothing could have prepared me for the fearful anticipation of visiting New York City for the first time.

Based on Mr. Yeisley's advice, I cast my bait into the deep water by sending audition tapes to fifteen talent agencies in New York City.

Just three days prior to this train ride, I'd received a phone call from a prestigious talent firm that liked my demo. The agent went on about how much she loved my voice and compared my work to someone I had never heard of before and still can't remember.

"Can you come into the city and meet with me?" she wanted to know.

"Absolutely," I said.

As I hung up the phone, I immediately sat down on a nearby kitchen chair to try to gain perspective. *OH MY GOD, NEW YORK CITY! I'm really going to do this!*

Obviously, I knew little about New York City — except, of course, for the criminal mayhem I had witnessed on TV cop shows. All those police dramas I'd watched over the years led me to think of New York as a place of slums riddled with murder, drug deals, stabbings, shootings, muggings, gangs, and Mafia shakedowns.

Before I left, a few regulars I hung around with at Brownie's Tavern told me, "Don't make eye contact with anyone on the street, and stay out of the subways!" They all agreed that you couldn't pay them enough money to go into that "sin-infested den of thieves," but they wished me the best of luck anyhow.

As my train pulled into New York's Penn Station, I cautiously made my way through the corridors to street level, confident that I was ready for whatever came at me. I wore rubber-soled shoes for better traction, in case I was caught in some sort of struggle. I had placed my wallet in my front pants pocket so as to outsmart the pickpockets who I felt surely lurked near every street corner. In my other front pocket was a large, cumbersome pocket knife that weighed my pants down. It was terribly uncomfortable but necessary, I thought, just in case I was cornered by a couple of gang members.

Coming out of the train station, I was relieved to see two police officers standing near the entrance to Madison Square Garden. Curious, I walked up to them and asked if it was safe to ride the subway.

"'Course it is," the one officer said, with a thick New York accent. "Dere's cops all over da place downnair!"

I had picked up a New York City map a few days earlier at the Lewiston AAA office to guide me through the streets to my meeting with the talent agent. Despite the reassurance I'd just received from the police officers, I chose not to descend into the "dangerous" subway. The warnings from the Juniata County locals were still fresh in my mind.

I slung the strap of my shoulder bag crisscross on my chest, just like my drinking buddies told me, and started walking with determination, vowing to myself that I would fight off any thug who tried to get the better of me. And, as coached by my friends, I refused to show any fear.

I walked for a good thirty minutes and finally arrived at the corner of Park Avenue South and 19th Street. My meeting with the talent agent was at 3 p.m. on the tenth floor — I was two hours early.

A few doors up, I spied a nice-looking bank building that appeared to have an area in front where I could hang out on the street unobtrusively. I strolled over and found an out-of-the-way alcove to stand, and thought, *I won't move from this spot*, for fear of getting lost or killed. I held on to the strap of my shoulder bag and was painfully aware of the pocket knife that, after the brisk walk down Park Avenue, felt like a hundred-pound weight in my front pocket.

As I stood there passing the time, I observed everything around me. The people of Manhattan were different, but not THAT different. They were of every race, color, size, and shape. I quickly realized they all seemed to have one thing in common — they walked with a purpose. They were all going somewhere, and they seemed very determined to get there in a speedy fashion.

To my sheer amazement, absolutely nobody seemed interested in stealing my shoulder bag or wallet. No one seemed to even notice me, let alone express any desire to stab, shoot, or harass me.

I quickly concluded that all the New York City criminal hype I'd witnessed on television had been overstated for the benefit of producing commercials to persuade country bumpkins like me to buy Tide, Corn Flakes, and Chevrolets. Laughing to myself, I reconsidered all the "safety" advice given to me by the folks back home as I realized that many of them had probably never even ventured out of Central Pennsylvania. I waited in front of the bank building until 2:55 p.m. Then, I tossed the cumbersome pocket knife into a garbage can on the street and proceeded to my meeting.

The elevator opened on the tenth floor directly in front of the receptionist who seemed very indifferent to my arrival. I announced myself and was told to take a seat in the waiting area. Within minutes, I was greeted by the lovely talent agent I'd spoken to on the phone just three days earlier. As she escorted me to her office, she told me again how impressed she was with my voice. We sat at her desk, and she told me of the boundless opportunity available to someone with my "talent" who was willing to apply himself.

As we were talking, her phone rang. It just so happened to be that big name voice-over artist to whom she'd compared me.

He was calling from London. I gathered from the conversation that he wouldn't be able to get back to the U.S. for another three days because of production delays, and that he would have to call off their regular Friday afternoon meeting.

I thought to myself, *Holy Shit ... London! It took all I had to get to freaking New York City! What if she wants me to go to London!*

I sat in her office trying to exude all the confidence I could muster and hide the fact that New York City was all very new to me and that I felt terribly intimidated.

Stepping out of my comfort zone would be a regular feat as I worked to expand my career in broadcasting and voice-overs. Defying fear and self-doubt was a constant. It wasn't enough just to be good, or even great, at my craft — dogged persistence was key.

It took two-and-a-half years of nonstop sales and marketing to get to the point where I was established enough to earn a comfortable living (although I never made it to London). Consistent marketing and calling back every lead as soon as humanly possible were as much a part of my day as the actual voice-over work. I always had my eye out for new leads at ad agencies, talent agencies, video-production companies and jingle houses. I kept all my contacts on index cards in recipe boxes and would send out three-hundred to four-hundred audition tapes at a time.

I loved being behind the microphone doing voice-over work. I realized my narration style was best when I was simply me — comfortable and conversational. Regardless of whether the commercial might be heard by tens of thousands of people, I always practiced the read while imagining that I was sitting in someone's living room having a conversation with them. For a thirty- or sixty-second spot, I'd spend the time to practice until I felt I had it down, then attempt to nail it in one take. Similarly, if narrating a book or video, I'd work in paragraphs or scenes, practicing the conversational quality and inflection of each word, then record and move on. All would then be masterfully edited together by a sound engineer.

Believe it or not, I think dyslexia made me better at my craft specifically because of the strong auditory memory I developed. I had no problem remembering the inflections and tonal qualities between practice and the final take. Dyslexia did mean I had to do one thing a bit differently: that was blowing up the typeface on the script to eighteen point and double spacing it, which helped to clear the visual clutter that was so much a part of the disability.

Travel for the most part was pretty barebones in New York and Philadelphia. Although I was beginning to make an okay living, profits could quickly be eaten up by the high cost of lodging in the cities. So, rather than stay at the expensive hotels, I opted for hostels. The price was right. In New York City, for twenty-two dollars a night I slept in a dormitory-style room with two sets of bunk beds and shared my quarters with up to three other people. For seventeen dollars a night, I shared a much larger room that could sleep up to twenty. In Philadelphia, eleven dollars a night was a fantastic deal, but that meant sleeping in a room with beds for up to forty travelers. Not exactly the comfort and style I had hoped for, but it was a great value. For dinner, I always looked for a good deal as well, and that was usually Chinese. Ordering was sort of like not being able to read and write all over again — I'd just point at the pictures.

While I loved what I was doing, there was a lot of loneliness that came with the job. I was on the move so much, never staying in one place very long, so I didn't have any real friends on the road. At one point, I felt so overwhelmed by loneliness I went to the library and found a self-help book on how to overcome it. I thought it would be embarrassing to take it up to the counter and check it out, so I stuck it inside my coat and walked out with it. I read the book and then returned it a week later in the nighttime book drop.

That little book packed a big wallop in that it made me realize one thing loud and clear — my loneliness stemmed from the fact that I trusted nobody. Although I had many acquaintances back home, and usually a girl in my life to some degree, I kept everyone at arm's length. It had become my defense mechanism. I realized that it was going to be a long, lonely life unless I could figure out how to trust. I also knew that it wouldn't be an easy fix.

My unconventional method of book "borrowing" was limited to that one occasion. The rest of the time, I made great use of my library card, checking out (and returning) many books.

Now that I was able to read, the world was open to me and my insatiable curiosity. I began researching biographies of great American achievers to try to figure out what drove them. What were their habits? What made them successful? I wanted to take that information, plug it into my brain, and see if it worked for me.

After reading and researching, I'd go to my word processor and slowly plunk out a story about them. By now, I had amassed quite a number of short stories.

I had been encouraged by the results of my writing. Not only did recording some of them on my demo tapes make me stand out in the voice-over world, but the people who heard them commented on how much they enjoyed listening.

Over the last few years so many things had gone right for me: from meeting Professor Guthrie, to Cheryl's help as a tutor, to the incredible investment that the State Office of Vocational Rehabilitation made in me, to everyone who gave me a chance as a voice-over artist. I began thinking that I needed to give back, and my stories seemed like the perfect vehicle.

I selected nineteen of my stories and recorded them in a studio in

Lewistown owned by John Xanthopoulos, better known as Johnny X (for obvious reasons). Johnny, a skilled musician, also scored the stories with original music. I ordered 1,000 tapes and 1,000 CDs and began selling them locally with the profits earmarked for literacy organizations.

The local press picked up on it, and then the Associated Press news wire. Soon, people across the country were reading the story about the twenty-nine-year-old parking lot line painter who had been functionally illiterate but learned to read and write and had now produced an audio book.

In no time, local civic groups were calling me to come to their meetings and give a talk. Maybe I got a meal or a few bucks out of it, but mostly I was doing it for free.

Standing up and talking in front of a group proved to be nerve-wracking. In those days, I was too nervous to even crack a joke. I'd just talk for a half hour or so about learning disabilities and then share my own story. Every time I spoke to a group, I always vowed it would be my last. I thought, *I should be focusing on making money, I have bills to pay*. Then, someone would call me again to speak to a local group, and I'd end up saying yes.

One day, out of the blue, I received a call from a woman in Kansas with a request that would take me as far out of my comfort zone as I had ever gone.

She'd somehow learned of my story and tracked me down. She introduced herself as the sales manager for a large insurance agency. Initially, I assumed she was calling to hire me to do a voice-over for her company, but that wasn't what she wanted. She said, "Nelson, I know your story, and I've concluded that you must be an extremely tenacious guy who knows a thing or two about overcoming obstacles. I'm in charge of a group of insurance salespeople who are having a lousy year and need some motivation. If you come to Kansas and tell the story of how your life started, the challenges you faced, and where you are today, I think my people will be inspired."

I was speechless. Finally, I said, in a very friendly tone as I laughed, "Ma'am, with all due respect, you must have bumped your head. I am flattered with the offer, but I'm simply not qualified to stand up before an audience and give a motivational talk."

"I beg to differ," she said. "You are the perfect candidate. I could hire any one of a thousand motivational speakers to come and talk to my people, but I'm looking for a real person with a real story of determination and grit. I know you're the person for the job."

I again declined her offer and thanked her for her kind words. Then, she uttered an almost magical phrase that changed my life forever. The power a few simple words can have over a person is amazing.

"Nelson, I'll pay you $3,500 plus expenses," she said.

A month later, I appeared before the insurance salespeople. I was nervous at first, but as time went on I loosened up and began to really enjoy myself. At the end of the talk, the group gave me a standing ovation. I was energized!

I flew out of Wichita, Kansas that night, feeling confident and thinking I just might want to pursue more public speaking. I did a bit of research and learned about a gentleman who ran a speakers bureau in Hollywood that specialized in speakers with a disability. I called him. He was friendly, but I wasn't sure if he would take a chance on me. He had never met me and had no idea whether or not I had good stage presence.

About six weeks later, he called me back. He wanted to send me to Minnesota to speak at a community college. The college didn't have a very big budget, and I don't think he had anyone else on his roster who would go for the small amount of money offered, so he decided to take a chance on me.

It was a solid engagement, and the audience liked me. Soon, the speakers bureau began sending me out more often. I told my personal story to live audiences all over the country. Just a few at first, and then more and more as time went on. I was speaking at corporate conventions, colleges, universities, governmental agencies, and teacher conferences.

I could hardly believe it when NASA booked me for a keynote address at the Kennedy Space Center. But, of the thousand-plus speaking engagements I've had since that very first in Kansas, there is one that will always stand out as the most personally rewarding. On October 24, 2003, I was invited to my old high school, East Juniata, to give a talk to a small classroom of about twenty students who were facing the challenges of having a learning disability.

It started with a voicemail from a young teacher named Miss Conrad. She asked me if I would be willing to come in and give a talk to her class of special education students. As I listened, I sat down at my desk, flabbergasted, thinking that this well-meaning young lady had certainly not consulted the principal of the school. Principal Morgan was no longer there, but I was sure that even the new principal would bristle a bit at the thought of having Nelson Lauver return to East Juniata.

I immediately called her back.

I said, "Miss Conrad, are you sure about this? Years ago I was responsible for unleashing the press on the Juniata School District and its lack of services for children with special learning needs. I can't imagine your principal would welcome me at the school."

To my shock and surprise, she said, "I've already talked to the principal, and he thinks it's a fabulous idea."

I nearly fell off my chair.

"Let me know when you want me, and I'll be there," I said.

On the morning of the twenty-fourth, I arrived at the school, signed in at the office, exchanged pleasantries with the new principal, and proceeded to walk through those familiar halls to the designated classroom.

Miss Conrad was a delight. She was tremendously dedicated to every one of the twenty kids in her class. And she wasn't alone. When Miss Conrad decided to take the position, she confided in her grandmother that she knew it was going to be a tough job. Her grandmother told her, "If you take this job, I'll come in every day and help you as a volunteer." Her grandmother was equally dedicated to each child's success. It was clear the students loved this committed team of teacher and grandmother. I was very touched by their dedication; as far as I was concerned, the Conrad ladies were nothing less than heroes.

Before I talked to the class, Miss Conrad gave me a little background. She told me that, although special education is changing, and they are starting to get the tools they need, the school district has a long way to go. She told me she was working every day at bolstering the confidence of her students. Unfortunately though, the kids were still having a hard time with self-esteem — many of them were convinced they were the "dumb kids."

"They feel like other kids make fun of them, which unfortunately is the case," she told me.

I greeted the class of ninth and tenth-graders and began to share my story. I didn't sugarcoat it, I gave them all the details, even about remedial math. I told them what it was like for me, twenty-some years ago, sitting in the same seats they were now sitting in.

I talked to them about their future and the fact that their destiny is completely up to them. If they had a dream or a goal, they should hold on to it and never allow anyone to take it away. They should never think they can't achieve it.

They had so many questions. The hour went by in a flash.

Before leaving, I stopped at the office to sign out and shake the principal's hand. I thanked him for allowing me to come to the school and talk to the kids.

Driving home, I was elated. I knew there was still a lot of room for improvement, but it was obvious that special education in the school district had come a long way if for no other reason than they were hiring teachers like Miss Conrad.

I knew that I had helped to bring about the change I had witnessed. But most of all, I realized that the time I put in as a student at East Juniata had not been in vain. It made me strong and helped me find my voice. For the first time since graduation, I saw my diploma as having honest value. 🌿

Chapter 20

So Long, Old Friend

M OM STEPPED OUT OF THE PASSENGER SIDE of Dad's car and, with a little help from Dad and me, got herself standing and well-stabilized with her crutches. She had been in a serious auto-related accident some months earlier and was now on the mend.

We stood in the driveway of a beautiful log home perched atop a pristine wooded hillside in Juniata County.

"I just can't believe how beautiful it is," she exclaimed. I couldn't believe it either. The home was magnificent with a rustic wraparound porch, vaulted ceilings, a gorgeous stone fireplace, hardwood floors, and stunning craftsmanship throughout.

The thing that was most impressive about this showstopper of a home was that it was my brother's home. Carl had remarried and used his mechanical talents to find a great job in the highway construction industry. Together, he and his new wife set a goal to build their dream home. The goal was a large part of Carl's motivation to get clean. I was impressed but moreover, I was proud of Carl.

Carl and his wife worked tirelessly to build their new home. No detail was overlooked. They spent every weekend sawing, pounding, and leveling. Dad helped, too, spending many days from sunup to sundown at Carl's side.

The end result was one of the finest homes I had ever seen. Soon after they moved in, there was another reason to celebrate. Carl's wife gave birth to a beautiful baby boy.

At about the same time, however, Dad began experiencing vision problems and severe migraine headaches. These symptoms were not unfamiliar to him, and he immediately scheduled an appointment at Geisinger Medical Center in Danville. Sure enough, Dad's problems were being caused by another brain tumor. This time the doctors at Geisinger said the tumor was inoperable and most likely malignant.

Mom was slowly healing from her accident, and now Dad was also struggling with serious health problems.

Mom's recovery had been quite remarkable and was a testament to her strong-willed nature. Her injuries were so severe that her doctors had given her a verbal list of things she would never do again, which included walking and driving. She got out of her wheelchair and, one by one, crossed everything off the list. She was eventually able to walk for short distances without the aid of her crutches. She said she had to because "I have to take care of my sick husband."

The ravages of cancer were spreading quickly throughout Dad's body. Soon, he was no longer able to drive and even needed help to move around the house. As if Mom's accident and Dad's illness weren't enough, Carl was starting to have health problems too, in the form of relentless muscle twitches. He went to the family doctor who suggested an appointment with a neurologist.

Mom, Carl's wife, and my sister, Susan, accompanied Carl to the appointment while I sat with Dad.

When Mom returned home, she walked into the living room, sat down on a chair, and laid her crutches beside her on the floor without saying a word. Her face was flushed, and she appeared overwhelmed and exasperated.

Dad and I sat there anxiously, waiting for her to say something, anything.

"Well, what did the doctor say about Carl?" I asked.

She hesitated for a moment and then said in a very calm voice, "It's ALS, Lou Gehrig's Disease. The doctor told Carl he has three to five years to live."

I watched Dad's face. He gritted his teeth as he shook his head and said, "That's not fair, damn it, that's not fair."

It was April 1999 and Carl was thirty-eight years old. I would be thirty-six in another two months. I sat quietly on the sofa in Mom and Dad's living room, trying to process the news. I had become so proud of Carl over the past few years. Everything had finally begun going so well for him and now this horrible news. *Carl must be devastated*, I thought.

There has to be some other explanation, I said to myself. First Mom's accident that will leave her physically challenged for the rest of her life, then Dad's terminal cancer diagnosis, and now Carl is going to die too? Dad's right, it isn't fair. My stomach was turning somersaults, my head was spinning, and I could hardly breathe. Nothing in all my life ever compared to the feelings I was experiencing. I was in shock and disbelief. I felt like I was going to cry, but the tears wouldn't come. My mouth was dry; I couldn't swallow. I was sweating profusely and could feel myself shaking.

"How did Carl take the news?" I asked Mom.

"Not well, not well at all. He cried."

I wondered, *What is happening to my family? This is so wrong! Why can't I just wake up from this bad dream, and we can all get in the car and ride to the Cocolamus Dam to listen to the bullfrogs or wait for the train to come around the bend, then count the cars and blink the lights at the man in the caboose?*

Over the next several months, Dad's health deteriorated rapidly. The powerful pain medication played tricks on his mind. I stayed with him as much as I could, waiting for those brief moments when he would find clarity and we could talk.

ALS was wreaking havoc on Carl. He was no longer able to work. It was quickly having an effect on his speech, and his muscles were withering away at an alarming rate. By fall, Carl was having difficulty walking.

In late September, I found one of those moments of clarity with Dad, and we talked. I knew it wouldn't be long until he was gone. I held his hand in mine.

"Dad, I'm scheduled to speak at a university in Minnesota in three days," I said. "But I'm sure they will understand if you need me to stay here with you."

"What the hell are you talking about? You have an important job to do in Minnesota, and I expect your ass will be on that plane. You get on that stage and give those people some Nelson Lauver motivation!"

"I will, Dad, I will."

It was the last conversation we ever had. By the time I got back from Minnesota, he had slipped into a coma. I stayed by his bedside for days talking to him, telling him, "It's okay, you can go over to the other side if you're ready, Dad. We'll be fine. I'll make sure Mom is well taken care of. You have no worries left here."

Finally, on the morning of October 8, 1999, he started with the *death rattle*.

I had heard people talk about the death rattle but had never heard it for myself. It's an awful sound — a combination of labored breathing and fluid "rattling" in the dying person's lungs.

I continued to talk to him. "It's okay, Dad, you can go. Don't worry about us. This is your time. You lived a fabulous life, and we are all very proud of you."

My sister, Susan, her husband, Barry, and my brother, Carl, came to Mom and Dad's house that evening. Over the years, we had all had our problems with one another. But, at this very moment, we were a strong family. Our past differences were now trivial and childish. We quickly became a team with a single purpose: being there for Dad as he struggled to let go of this world and grab onto the next.

Carl knelt down on the floor beside Dad's bed and held his hand as he said a little prayer. Each of us laid a hand on Dad. As Carl struggled to clearly form his words, made difficult by ALS, Dad found the last little bit of strength he had left. He forced himself into consciousness and opened his eyes. His eyes moved around the edge of the bed as he took a moment to look at each of us one last time, and then the rattling stopped. Clair Lauver was seventy-three. 🌿

Chapter 21

Hope Drove the Car

IT HAD NOW BEEN NEARLY EIGHT YEARS since I'd started practicing with the word processor — and I was up to a whopping twenty words per minute. I had a nice little collection of short stories about friends, family, interesting people I'd met along the way, and heroes from history. I had created a second CD with my stories, this time for profit, and was selling it on consignment in stores around Central Pennsylvania with a nice amount of success. I was encouraged by the positive local response to my stories.

And then ... I had an idea!

What if I continued writing stories? And what if I got behind the microphone, recorded all my stories, scored them with music and offered them to radio stations as a four-minute daily radio feature? *Wow, this is going to be a huge hit! Everybody loves a story!*

I searched the Internet for every major syndication company in the United States, looking for someone to distribute my fledgling radio feature to stations across the country. I called each and every one of them and said, "Hi, my name is Nelson Lauver. I'm calling from Juniata County, Pennsylvania, and I have an idea for a radio feature that you might be interested in."

That's about as far as I got before they said, "No, thank you," and abruptly hung up the phone. I quickly learned that jaded syndicators get dozens of calls weekly from people who have a new radio feature that they think is the best thing ever. Often they won't even listen to an enthusiastic person with a new idea, and with that mistake, syndicators miss out on some great opportunities.

From the moment I got the idea to put my stories on the radio, it was as if I had been charged with a million volts of electricity. I was driven, and nothing could dampen my spirits. I was so excited with the notion of radio listeners across the country driving down the road smiling, or laughing, or crying, or thinking, or relating to, or just enjoying one of my stories.

As each syndicator hung up on me and dismissed the idea that I dubbed "The American Storyteller Radio Journal," I grew angry and frustrated. *Why can't they see the potential?* I wondered. But with each hang up, I became more determined than ever to succeed. At no point did I ever consider giving up.

In my search for a syndicator to distribute The American Storyteller Radio Journal, I ran across a fellow in Washington, D.C. who was slightly nicer than the rest. When I say that, I guess it's sort of like saying Mussolini was nicer than Hitler. Maybe a better way to describe this fellow is to say he wasn't quite as mean as the others because although he spoke with me, he was far from encouraging.

He told me he was sure, based on his "vast inside knowledge of the radio industry" and his years of experience, that my idea would fail for lack of a listening audience. I asked him what he thought about my chance for success if I tried going it alone without a syndicator, distributing the radio feature by myself, directly to radio stations. His voice took on a belittling tone, as if to say he was done wasting his time speaking to someone who had such a ridiculous notion.

He told me that, if, in my attempts to test-market my own radio feature, I were to get more than three stations to come onboard, I should call him back and schedule a time to come to Washington, D.C., where he would kiss my ass on the White House lawn. His slick tone and callous manner really started to irk me. He was convinced I would fail. That's when the phone conversation became more heated ... and that's when he told me, "Go fly a kite and don't ever call back again." Then he hung up on me.

Within several weeks, I started marketing The American Storyteller Radio Journal to radio station owners and managers across the country. Instead of twisting arms to find three stations, as the self-proclaimed expert in Washington predicted, my first round of marketing yielded forty-two radio stations. I picked up stations in Alabama, Alaska, Illinois, Indiana, Kansas, Kentucky, Louisiana, Maryland, Michigan, Minnesota, Missouri, Montana, New York, North Carolina, North Dakota, Ohio, Oklahoma, Oregon, Pennsylvania, South Carolina, South Dakota, Tennessee, Texas, Virginia, Washington, West Virginia, Wisconsin, and Wyoming!

I quickly discovered radio station owners weren't that much different from the farmers and saw-millers I'd made deals with on scrap metal as a kid. Nor were they much different from the car dealers, grocery store managers, and restaurateurs to whom I sold parking lot stripes — or the producers and advertising agencies for whom I provided voice-over services. Radio station owners were, for the most part, friendly, hardworking, everyday small-business people just like me. It was just as easy to pick up the phone and talk to a radio station owner as it was anyone else. There was no secret formula, simply, a friendly chat: here's what I have, here are the benefits for you, and I'd be delighted to be of service.

As the four-minute feature began running in earnest across the nation, I started to hear from radio stations and listeners too — they loved the stories!

About a year later, the same man who told me to "go fly a kite" and insisted I never call him again called ME. This time he had a different tone. He told me the "higher-ups" at his company would now be interested in forming a "business relationship" with me and my radio feature.

He asked if I could mail him some information regarding how many stations I was now running on, what market each station was in, and the time of day the feature aired on each radio station. I told him, "I am so delighted to hear from you that I'll go one better and overnight a package to you."

"Oh, that would be great!" he said.

The next morning, he opened a FedEx package with nothing inside but a kite. I never heard from him again.

I'm kind of ashamed of myself for sending the kite, but it sure did feel good.

In the end, I'm thankful that he and all the other syndicators turned me down, because I figured out how to do it on my own. I trusted my gut, believed in myself, and never gave up.

With the national broadcast of The American Storyteller Radio Journal, I came to a realization. I was no longer the rookie "storyteller in-training," who sat in Shirley's Restaurant or hid under my dad's desk listening to the "big talk," and taking in every word from the masters: George, Doc, Dad, and Peanut. They unwittingly groomed me, and I had now graduated to become a full-fledged storyteller in my own right. Although none of them lived to see it, I'm thankful that I now have the opportunity to share them with my listeners and readers across America and the world.

The success of The American Storyteller Radio Journal created even more public-speaking opportunities for me, which I have now found to be one of the greatest passions of my life. Connecting with a live audience, making them laugh — but mostly making them think — is what I now feel I was born to do. When I look back, for as difficult and unpleasant as my earlier life was, it was those experiences that prepared me to relate to other people and their struggles. I wouldn't go back and change a thing even if I could. I believe that what Oliver Wendell Holmes Sr. said is true, "Trouble makes us one with every human being in the world."

From the stage, I use stories to encourage people to recognize the vastness of their potential, harness their inner drive, inspire them to advocate for themselves and their dreams, and find the tenacity and courage to push self-doubt out of their way. It's all about a well-told story that leaves the listener asking, "Why not me?" and, "Who says I can't achieve great things?"

When we use facts, figures, formulas, and theories to teach, we hope to open people's minds. When we teach through storytelling, we open people's hearts as well — that's where truly great learning and enlightenment take place. A great story draws people in, they feel it, it takes them there, and they see themselves as the characters in the story.

Throughout the year, I speak to a wide range of audiences from corporations, associations, and government agencies, to colleges, disability awareness groups, and community service organizations. August has become one of my busiest months as a speaker. August is the month that teachers prepare to return to the classroom, and it's my job as a keynoter to send them back with renewed motivation for the start of the school year.

On August 28, 2008, I took the stage in Ripon, Wisconsin. I was speaking to several hundred teachers. They were a tough crowd. Their attendance was mandatory, and it was clear they didn't want to be there. The weather outside was beautiful. It was the end of the day, and the last thing they wanted was to stay in their seats for another hour listening to the closing keynoter.

I started off with a funny story and they laughed. Within fifteen minutes they'd softened up, and we were connecting. I liked them, and they liked me. They stopped yawning and sat up straight in their seats. Their eyes followed me as I moved across the stage. I opened my heart and shared my personal story of what it feels like to be a kid with a learning disability.

They gave me a standing ovation, and I knew that, come the first day of school, they would be looking at "problem kids" in a whole new way. After I closed, the superintendent of the school wanted to know if anyone had any questions for me.

A pretty woman in her forties raised her hand.

"Tell us about your wife!"

I assumed the lady had noticed I was wearing a wedding band. My heart immediately came up in my throat. I got goose bumps and could feel my eyes getting moist. I miss my wife when I'm on the road, and to talk on stage about her and all she means to me can be a bit of an emotional challenge, but I quickly regained my composure and a big grin appeared across my face.

It was obvious to the crowd that the question threw me a bit. It made them laugh, and I took a deep breath and said, "My wife is the coolest person on earth." They laughed louder and clapped as they realized they had me on the spot.

I'd met Jane years earlier, in the spring of 2003, on a blind date. We spoke on the phone several times prior to the date, and she invited me to her house, two-and-a-half hours away, for dinner.

On the long drive to her home, the little voice of self-doubt inside my head tested me. That ugly voice had me pondering why I was setting myself up for disappointment. *Since high school, your life has been a revolving door of brief relationships*, the little voice said. *Even if dinner with this young lady does turn out to be more than one date, it will surely, just like all the others, end in disappointment for one or both of you. So why are you putting yourself through this again?*

Deep in my heart I knew the answer to that question. It was hope that drove the car two-and-a-half hours east on Interstate 80. Hope that someday, even if I had to try a thousand times, I would find the one thing I wanted more than anything else, the one thing that, up until that point in my life, appeared to be an elusive joy reserved for a lucky few.

Even though I'd been working on myself since I "borrowed" that book from the library, a big part of me still didn't trust enough to give or receive love. But, if I were to be true to myself and all the progress I had made, I needed to push that little voice of doubt out of my mind and find the courage to knock on her front door.

Jane opened the door with one hand while holding back a very enthusiastic seventy-five-pound, mixed-breed rescued dog named Lola with the other. Jane was stunningly beautiful. A tall, statuesque brunette with dazzling green eyes and a movie star smile.

She was thirty-seven, and I was thirty-nine. It had been almost ten years since I had made up my mind to change my life.

There was a second date and a third and many more.

Jane was my big test, the test to see if the rehabilitation of Nelson Lauver was complete. I cared for her immensely, but I was afraid to show her. I fought to hide my vulnerability.

Jane had her life together. My fear was that she would not accept me because of my past, regardless of how hard I had worked at bettering myself. She grew up as an honor student, went to college and graduated magna cum laude. She had a job in the advertising world of New York City.

From time to time, the little voice would rear its ugly head and test me. "Nelson," the voice said, "You didn't really graduate from high school. They gave you a diploma to get rid of you. You will always be a country boy. You can never escape the fact that you were the dumb kid. Jane was the intelligent, pretty girl in the class and can have any guy she wants."

If I were to completely open up with Jane and surrender my heart unconditionally, if I could admit that I was falling in love with her, it would not only be a great victory over the little voice of self-doubt, it would be proof of my growth as a human being. It would be the culmination of a dream. My ultimate goals in life were to be happy and successful. I knew neither would be one hundred percent realized until I found and opened my heart to my soulmate.

Regardless of how much I wanted to surrender, the little voice continually reminded me that this bright, pretty woman could pluck my heart from my chest, throw it on the ground, and to quote John Denver in a country song, "mash that sucker flat."

Jane could clearly see my lack of trust. At times, it was a playful challenge for her, but at other times it was a maddening frustration. Through it all, she was getting to know me as well, if not better, than I knew myself. Chip, chip, chip ... like a patient sculptor with a piece of marble, Jane chipped away at me until finally, after two years of chipping, she won. But of course, the real winner was me!

Jane and I moved in together. The ugly little voice was defeated.

On occasion, when her busy schedule permitted, Jane traveled with me to speaking engagements. In the spring of 2006, while sitting in a plane on the tarmac of the Mexico City Airport waiting to take off, Jane made a declaration.

We had arrived in Mexico City four or five days earlier and were chauffeured a couple of hours south to the beautiful colonial city of Puebla. I spoke in an enclosed soccer stadium, sharing my story with a crowd of 8,000 Mexican citizens. It was a great engagement, and the city of Puebla was a relaxing place to spend a few days.

On stage, I had a translator for those who did not speak English, but on the streets of Puebla I had to depend on Jane and her three years of high school Spanish to translate. We stayed in an old mission that had been tastefully converted into a small and delightful hotel with beautiful rooms, antique décor, and a wonderfully attentive staff.

We were a long way from home, and our minds were clear and relaxed.

After our stay, we returned to the Mexico City Airport and boarded our plane for home. The pilot taxied to the runway and informed the plane filled with passengers headed for the U.S. that we were number nine for takeoff.

As we sat there waiting, Jane turned to me and said, "Nelson, I'm going to leave my job in New York City."

"What? You love your job!" I replied. "You make great money and have fabulous benefits! You can't leave!"

She was adamant.

She'd graduated from college with a degree in marketing and had been a stellar performer in her position in New York. Nevertheless, she had made up her mind it was time to move on. She had turned forty a few months earlier and was ready for a career change. She said she wanted a job that was more fulfilling and impacted people's lives.

"I want to work with you as your business manager," she told me.

"Really?" I sat back in my seat, astounded by her statement.

For me, Jane's decision was, and remains, the single greatest compliment of my life. The fact that someone as well-educated and talented as Jane would desire to become part of this "thing" I'd created from nothing but persistence still boggles my mind. The fact that Jane believed in me enough to hook her wagon to my dream and make it her own is a compliment for which I am simply at a loss to adequately express my gratitude.

Soon after Jane left her job and took over the day-to-day operations of the business, we decided to get married. We knew we didn't want a huge wedding, just something small and intimate for maybe twenty or so close friends and family. And for a ring, Jane knew exactly what she wanted, which meant that — after searching twenty-five jewelry stores — we still couldn't find it. We finally stumbled upon a local jewelry craftsman and explained the ever-so-simple yet elusive ring. He went into NYC's diamond district, bought some loose stones, brought them back into his shop, called us in. In no time, we had the perfect design.

The ring was ready in time for Valentine's Day, and I got down on one knee and presented it to Jane that evening, along with a gigantic, decorated heart-shaped box filled with chocolates — a tradition we'd started with our first Valentine's Day together. Each year, we fill that same box with candy and write the year inside the lid. It's a big box, but we hope someday to run out of space to inscribe the year.

Our thoughts on the small intimate wedding began to unravel as the list kept growing because if you invite this person, you HAVE to invite that person. Somehow, it just didn't seem like fun anymore. So, we both agreed on a new plan.

We applied for our marriage license, called the local justice of the peace, and set a date about a week out, April 4. We didn't tell a soul.

On that day, as we happily walked into the court building, we practically bumped into two police officers who were escorting two freshly arraigned, handcuffed gentlemen in orange jumpsuits from the very courtroom where we were to be married. It was a nice touch.

We brought along another couple to be our witnesses, and fifteen minutes later it was official. We disappeared for a few days and then made the dreaded round of phone calls explaining to annoyed friends and family why we hadn't told anybody sooner.

We settled into our new life in the Cherry Valley with Lola and our latest canine kid, Lacey, another adorable rescue. Mornings quickly became our favorite time together. That's when we all gather in the kitchen with coffee for us and Milk-Bones for the "kids" as we scratch puppy ears, review the latest news, and plan our day.

So yes, Jane is not only my best friend, my wife, soulmate, and business partner — as far as I'm concerned, she is the coolest person on earth.

Jane's office is right across the hall from my writer's den, and yet

I often find her sitting at the desk in my den staring at me as I sit in a plush, burgundy leather recliner (a memento from my dad) pecking away at a laptop, and telling a story. She waits for me to finish so I can read to her.

My desk is actually a large rectangular antique oak table that Dad found somewhere in his travels. It's three-and-a-half-feet wide and six-feet long. When Dad first dragged it home all those years ago, it was used as a dining room table and comfortably seated eight people. Some years later, Dad found another dining room table more to his liking, and I quickly laid claim to the old oak table.

After I emerge from the semi-conscious state, far away in the world of writing, I read to Jane.

She is sitting at my desk at this very moment, with her chin in her hands, looking at me with that big, devilish smile and waiting for me to finish writing so I can read to her.

She has no idea yet that I'm writing about her and am about to tell *her* story.

Jane's mother and father divorced when she was a girl of eleven. Jane and her mom moved in with her mom's sister, Aunt Leonore, a delightful and demure lady, who owned a home in the small town of Northampton, in eastern Pennsylvania.

Aunt Leonore was the intelligent, sophisticated secretary to the president of the famous Lehigh-Portland Cement Company. She had never married and found volunteering with the local United Way, library, and her church to be great social outlets. Together, Aunt Leonore, Jane's mom, and Jane embarked on a new life as a non-traditional family.

Meanwhile, Jane's father was sinking deeper and deeper into the abyss of alcoholism and compulsive gambling. In his earlier years,

Jack, as everyone knew him, had been a dashing and gregarious young Italian-American gentleman. He was well-dressed and well-spoken. Jane's mother insisted she would only marry him if he gave up his lucrative day job as a "bookie." He agreed.

He had been a good-looking party boy, but after getting married found the only legitimate, marketable skill he possessed was on the other side of the party, behind the bar as the bartender. Name the drink and Jack could shake, stir, mix, or pour it. For Jack the bartender, pay didn't come in the form of a regular check but as cash tips. Unfortunately, because of his addictions and compulsions, the cash often failed to translate into regular household income. Instead, it was disbursed rather quickly for alcohol and gambling.

Jane's mom was optimistic that Jack could turn himself around. At times he tried with great determination but would inevitably fall off the wagon.

Eventually, hope faded. After Jack went months without working, the family applied for welfare and food stamps. For the sake of Jane, her mother knew what she had to do. To get off welfare, she took a job as a teacher's aide and eventually filed for divorce.

For the next several years after the breakup, Jack spiraled out of control. Years of drinking, smoking, and the non-stop party life had caught up with him. His hair was as white as snow, and his frail body was wracked from decades of abuse. He died at age fifty-one in a hospital in Allentown. Jane was fifteen at the time and describes the loss of her father as "painful, yet a relief," because she knew his suffering had ended.

By the time Jane was preparing to graduate from high school, her mom had been working almost a decade as a teacher's aide, helping in the classroom to guide and shape the lives of developmentally disabled children. Jane's life away from her father had taken on a grounding stability. Jane, her mom, and Aunt Leonore had become a true family. They took vacations to the seashore, were active in the community, and of course, Jane was a good student.

From the time she was a young girl, there had never been any question in Jane's mind that she wanted to go to college. Over the years, her mother had been saving a little each week from her small paycheck. A few dollars a week had grown substantially, and with a bit of scholarship money, college was paid for lock, stock, and barrel.

Jane graduated from Kutztown University, magna cum laude, with a degree in marketing. Among my many heroes are Jane's mom and Aunt Leonore. While they didn't know it at the time, their good work on behalf of Jane was also an investment in the future of a troubled kid they had never met, some 150 miles to the west, in the tiny village of McAlisterville.

Of all my heroes, the biggest one is the person who encouraged me to write this book — the person who is sitting at my desk with her chin in her hands, smiling with great anticipation, patiently waiting to hear the ending. I love her with all my heart.

Epilogue

VIOLENCE AND THE VAULT — When this book was nearly complete, my editor gave the manuscript to a fellow editor to read. One of the comments from that guest reader was that she was suspicious that the violence I described in the schoolhouse had been embellished — "embellished" in this case is a very kind way of asking if I was lying. I talked with my editor about how to convince readers that the violence was real and did indeed take place.

After our conversation, I sat in a quiet room of my home for several hours pondering that very subject. Finally it dawned on me that it is not necessarily a bad thing to have a reader question the extent of the violence. Thank goodness this guest reader questioned it! Thank goodness what I experienced was so distant from what she, and perhaps you, experienced as a school kid.

While I recognize that some people know what it is like to suffer abuse from individuals in trusted positions, I also realize that most people never have and cannot fathom that experience — and for that I am very thankful. Of all the abuse I detailed in the book, what is sure to raise the most doubt among readers is probably "THE VAULT." If you are suspicious of its existence and use as an isolation chamber, you are not alone. For many years, there has been great debate among citizens in Juniata County about whether the vault at East Juniata High School actually existed. Locals who quizzed Principal Morgan or Superintendant Kirk had a difficult time getting a straight answer.

In a Federal Court deposition on June 7, 2000, Principal Morgan finally admitted to not only the existence of the vault, but to the fact that he used it to isolate children. Principal Morgan's deposition came three weeks after the deposition of his assistant principal, the Rev. Terry Smith, which had left him no choice but to acknowledge the vault and its diabolical use.

I don't think Reverend Smith was anxious to testify about the vault, but given the penalty for committing perjury in federal court, he opted instead to tell the truth. The truth couldn't have been more revealing. Smith's testimony corroborated my statements and those of numerous other students, who for years had been accused of fabricating the story of the vault.

The following are highlights from the Assistant Principal Rev. Terry Smith's deposition in U.S. Federal Court — Civil Case — C.A. NO. 1: CV 99 — 0650, Estate of Jason Lee Schlegel, Plaintiff — Vs. — The Juniata County School District, Defendant.

Cross-Examining Attorney hereafter referred to as "ATTORNEY."

Assistant Principal Rev. Terry Smith hereafter referred to as "SMITH."

Highlighted testimony starts here:

ATTORNEY: Have you ever isolated students from other students in separate rooms as a form of punishment?

SMITH· In separate rooms meaning ...?

ATTORNEY: Well, have you ever put a student in a room by himself or herself as a form of punishment?

SMITH: Yes, I would say that that had happened.

ATTORNEY: And where in the school would that have happened?

SMITH: Might have been my office. There were times when I might have assigned a student not necessarily by themselves but to another teacher, usually a master teacher who could supervise them.

ATTORNEY: Was there a ... a vault or a room that could be locked in the principal's office or in the suite around the principal's office?

SMITH: There was a vault at one time.

ATTORNEY: And when ... when you say at one time, when was that?

SMITH: I'm trying to think what year it was broken into. Somebody took a torch and cut into it. After that, a complete renovation had to be done; and I don't remember what year ... the vault door was removed and another door was ... was put in place there. For some time, it ... it wasn't of ... of a vault because the entire mechanism had been destroyed. I don't recall what year that was that the vault was broken into.

ATTORNEY: Were students ever placed in the vault to your knowledge?

SMITH: Yes.

ATTORNEY: And during what period were they placed in the vault?

SMITH: Meaning ...?

ATTORNEY: What period of time?

SMITH: Years?

ATTORNEY: Yeah, or years.

SMITH: It would have been in the '70s.

ATTORNEY: And who would make the decision to place them in the vault?

SMITH: Generally the principal.

ATTORNEY: Why don't you tell me what the practice was that you were aware of for placing students in the vault.

SMITH: To my knowledge, when a student was placed in the vault, it was in a desk. There was a desk in there.
Note from the author: Building plans show the vault dimensions as being seven feet by ten feet.

ATTORNEY: What was in the vault? You indicated there was a desk there. What else was there?

SMITH: There was a safe inside the vault.

ATTORNEY: Anything else?

SMITH: Not much else. Not much was kept in it.

ATTORNEY: What kind of ventilation did the vault have?

SMITH: I don't know.

ATTORNEY: How often did you use the vault for punishment?

SMITH: I didn't use the vault. I've used my office.

ATTORNEY: Why didn't you use the vault?

SMITH: I had my office available; and I'd ... you know, if ... like I said, generally I was not in the office that much because I was teaching and had my office available.

ATTORNEY: Would you lock your office when you left a student in there?

SMITH: No, generally left the door open.

ATTORNEY: You indicated that there was a locked door on the vault and that that was replaced after it had been torched. Somebody had torched into it?

SMITH: Uh-huh.

ATTORNEY: I assume that that door had been locked if it had been torched into. Is that a correct assumption?

SMITH: The secretary would generally lock it before she left for the evening.

ATTORNEY: Was it locked with a key or was that a combination?

SMITH: I think that was a combination on that one; but I never dealt with the ... about the only thing that was kept in there like I say was the ... the safe and locker keys. The locker key cabinet was set on ... on top of the safe.

ATTORNEY: Can anybody walking by the vault close the door?

SMITH: I would think you probably could.

ATTORNEY: Was there a written policy concerning the use of the vault for students?

SMITH: Not that I'm aware of.

ATTORNEY: How long a period could a student be placed in the vault?

SMITH: I ... I don't know. I don't recall how ... how long that would have been.

ATTORNEY: Did anyone aside from the principal have the authority to put someone in the vault?

SMITH: I don't think anyone else would.

ATTORNEY: Did you think it was all right to put students in the vault?

SMITH: That was the principal's decision. That's not my —

ATTORNEY: You had no opinion on it at all?

SMITH: That was not my decision. When I viewed what was ... the students who were placed in the vault at times, I believe ... and this is purely, you know, my speculation ... I believe it was generally students that ... who had very serious problems and had not behaved in another placement perhaps. And you'd have to ask ... you'd have to ask the principal about that directly.

ATTORNEY: Were students placed in the vault who had emotional problems?

SMITH: Not ... I think discipline was the ... the ... the question, not ... not emotional. I don't know that ... and again, I don't recall, and again, emotional, are you talking about people who are labeled emotionally ... emotionally disturbed, or you just mean somebody who is distraught?

ATTORNEY: Well, let's start with were there any students who were labeled emotionally disturbed who were placed in the vault?

SMITH: Not that I am aware of.

ATTORNEY: How about students who were displaying emotional issues?

SMITH: I think in ... in general if it was an emotional issue ... it was because they had a ... discipline problem, not ... not they were having an emotional problem and they were placed in the vault.

End of highlighted testimony.

THE AFTERMATH OF EIGHTH-GRADE REMEDIAL MATH — While the pop I felt in my neck during the beating by Mr. Brookfield in remedial math class for dropping my books was thankfully not a broken neck, the injury did result in nerve damage that, over the years, has become progressively worse. Four times a year, I receive a series of seven to nine injections in my neck to control muscle spasms and quell a slight tremor from the nerve damage. The treatment is going well.

⌒

PAUL YEATER — One of my fellow classmates from the remedial math class still resides in McAlisterville. He is now a professional truck driver. In the spring of 2000, he gave courageous testimony in a federal court deposition regarding the abusiveness of Mr. Brookfield's remedial math class.

Paul has shared with me a first-hand account of how his elderly grandfather heroically confronted Principal Morgan on behalf of the children in remedial math.

"My grandfather went to the school and raised hell!" Paul told me. It is an inspiring story in itself. I never met Paul's late grandfather but wish I could have. I would have enjoyed thanking him personally.

⌒

MR. BROOKFIELD — Mr. Brookfield stepped down from his position as a school board director. He resides on a farm just outside the small town of Port Royal, Juniata County, and continues to be active as a minister.

⌒

PRINCIPAL MORGAN — Principal Morgan is retired. He still resides in Juniata County, where he continues to be active in his church as a lay minister.

⌒

GAIL THOMAS AND MR. FAIRFAX — Gail Thomas divorced Mr. Fairfax after sixteen years. On March 12, 2002, in a case unrelated to Gail Thomas, Mr. Fairfax was charged with lewd and obscene behavior and stalking. The female victim was another former East Juniata student. He pled to a lesser charge, paid a fine in Juniata County Court, and avoided jail time. Mr. Fairfax is currently retired from teaching.

⁓

DAD AND DYSLEXIA — We never talked about it much, but after I was diagnosed with dyslexia, my dad realized that he too was mildly dyslexic. After Dad's death, Mom confided in me that Dad had a great deal of trouble writing. For as bright as he was, he had a difficult time connecting the dots between his own problem and mine.

⁓

MOM — She is doing well and now lives in a small apartment with an affectionate little black cat that she loves dearly. She is as feisty as ever. Whatever you do, don't piss her off!

⁓

MY BROTHER CARL — Carl was diagnosed with Lou Gehrig's disease in the spring of 1999. At the time he was diagnosed, doctors speculated that he would live three to five years. As of March 2010, Carl is still alive. Several years after his diagnosis, he made the decision to have a feeding tube inserted in his stomach, and he uses a ventilator to aid him in breathing. Carl currently is cared for in a medical facility in western Pennsylvania. Doctors have said that with the use of the feeding tube and ventilator he could live for many years.

⁓

Susan and Barry — Susan is still the charming girl she's always been. She and Barry are retired and very active in their community

MAYBE YOU WEREN'T MENTIONED IN THE BOOK — I set out with the idea of sharing many more aspects of my life than I was able to. I never thought this book would take so long to write or have as many pages as it does. I touched briefly on several romantic relationships, but of course there were more. I would like to apologize to everyone who played a significant role in my life who may not have been mentioned. Of course, maybe some of you are breathing a sigh of relief over that fact.

THE FUTURE OF THE AMERICAN STORYTELLER RADIO JOURNAL — Due to the fact that I can't walk and chew gum at the same time, I placed The American Storyteller on hiatus while I wrote this book. I also encouraged radio stations to place it on hiatus as well. Some chose to continue airing reruns. Now that I am finished with this book I am going back to The American Storyteller. My focus may be a bit different after giving it a two year rest. I might make the stories shorter or longer or maybe different in some other regard. I really love (adore, am addicted to, can't get enough of) Public Radio and may look for a home there.

A NOTE TO TEACHERS: In this book I detail my unpleasant experiences with several teachers. When I talk about that aspect, I'm always concerned that people might think I dislike teachers. That is the furthest thing from the truth.

My personal feelings about teachers: 1) The teaching profession is the most important profession in history; 2) In general, I believe the good teachers of America are underpaid; 3) I love teachers!

A FEW MORE WORDS ABOUT LITERACY AND DYSLEXIA: Illiteracy is a monster with its hands around the throat of America. It adversely affects individuals, families, communities, and the country as a whole.

According to recent statistics, approximately 1 in 7 Americans is functionally illiterate. Chances are high that you know someone who struggles with reading and writing.

A functionally illiterate person cannot read and write well enough to manage the demands of daily living and many employment tasks. They generally read at or below the fourth or fifth grade level.

Unfortunately, you cannot help an adult with reading and writing difficulties unless they want to be helped. You can't force or shame your father, cousin, friend, or next-door neighbor to get help. However, you can try to open a compassionate and caring dialogue.

On the other hand, if you are a trusted confidant of someone who desires help, you are in a very important position. As a person in a position of trust, you can research tutoring resources in your area and advise your friend or loved-one about what is available. And of course, you yourself can become a resource as a literacy tutor or advocate. Visit proliteracy.org for some helpful information.

In this memoir, I hope to illustrate that illiteracy does not have a specific "face." It is not limited to a specific demographic or minority. It is still frighteningly easy for kids to slip through the cracks.

I'm not a clinical expert on dyslexia, but from my experience I believe, like many conditions, one simply learns to manage the challenges that come with being dyslexic. In the broadest sense, being dyslexic refers to a person who has difficulty processing and producing written language. Dyslexia and IQ are not related. Many dyslexics are of above average intelligence. Interestingly, a disproportionate number of entrepreneurs are dyslexic. Some estimates put the number as high as thirty-five percent.

Since dyslexia is an "invisible disability," it is often difficult to assess and requires testing.

If your child is having difficulties, you have the right to have your child tested in school. Please don't delay or think that perhaps your child will grow out of it.   Early assessment is very important. Again, learning disabilities are not a reflection of intelligence they are simply learning differences.   And with learning differences can come many gifts. A great resource on dyslexia is the International Dyslexia Association: interdys.org.

When it comes to kids learning to read and write, the teacher in front of the classroom is key, but moms and dads are the most powerful advocates any kid can have. Find your voice, become a partner in your child's education.

Most of all, keep in mind that no child wants to fail. Often, a perceived behavior problem is a decoy for another issue. Please don't give up.

Helping a child reach his or her highest and best is the most valuable gift you can give.

About the Cover:

T HE COVER IMAGE IS from my third grade
school picture. The upside down concept
was the idea of our highly talented designer,
Peri Gabriel. What the cover represents, I hope
very clearly, is a life turned upside down by an
undiagnosed learning disability.

For more about Nelson, his latest appearance
and speaking information — or to listen to some
great audio stories — visit his website:

www.theamericanstoryteller.com

Look forward to hearing from you!